DEVELOPING NEW PRODUCTS AND REPOSITIONING MATURE BRANDS

RONALD SERIES ON MARKETING MANAGEMENT

Series Editor: FREDERICK E. WEBSTER, Jr.
The Amos Tuck School
of Business Administration
Dartmouth College

GEORGE S. DOMINGUEZ, *Marketing in a Regulated Environment*
ROBERT D. ROSS, *The Management of Public Relations: Analysis and Planning External Relations*
VICTOR WADEMAN, *Risk-Free Advertising: How to Come Close to It*
FRANK H. MOSSMAN, W. J. E. CRISSY, and PAUL M. ISCHER, *Financial Dimensions in Marketing Management*
JACOB JACOBY and ROBERT W. CHESTNUT, *Brand Loyalty: Measurement and Management*
WILLIAM E. COX, Jr., *Industrial Marketing Research*
FREDERICK E. WEBSTER, Jr., *Industrial Marketing Strategy*
CLARK LAMBERT, *Field Sales Performance Appraisal*
JEAN-MARIE CHOFFRAY and GARY LILIEN, *Market Planning for New Industrial Products*
EUGENE J. CAFARELLI, *Developing New Products and Repositioning Mature Brands: A Risk-Reduction System that Produces Investment Alternatives*

DEVELOPING NEW PRODUCTS AND REPOSITIONING MATURE BRANDS

A RISK-REDUCTION SYSTEM THAT PRODUCES INVESTMENT ALTERNATIVES

EUGENE J. CAFARELLI
Center for Concept Development

A RONALD PRESS PUBLICATION

JOHN WILEY & SONS, New York • Chichester • Brisbane • Toronto

Library of Congress Cataloging in Publication Data:

Cafarelli, Eugene J   1938-
  Developing New Products and Repositioning Mature Brands

  (Ronald series on marketing management)
  "A Ronald Press publication."
  Bibliography: p.
  Includes index.
  1. Product management.   2. New products.   I. Title.

HF5415.15.C24   658.5'75   80-13112
ISBN 0-471-04634-5

Printed in the United States of America

10 9 8 7 6 5 4 3 2 1

Series Editor's Foreword

Marketing management is among the most dynamic of the business functions. On the one hand it reflects the everchanging marketplace and the constant evolution of customer preferences and buying habits, and of competition. On the other hand, it grows continually in sophistication and complexity as developments in management science are applied to the work of the marketing manager. If he or she is to be a true management professional, the marketing person must stay informed about these developments.

The Ronald Series on Marketing Management has been developed to serve this need. The books in the series have been written for managers. They combine a concern for management application with an appreciation for the relevance of developments in such areas of management science as behavioral science, financial analysis, and mathematical modeling, as well as the insights gained from analyzing successful experience in the marketplace. The Ronald Series on Marketing Management is thus intended to communicate the state-of-the-art in marketing to managers.

Virtually all areas of marketing management will be explored in the series. Books now available or being planned cover advertising management, industrial marketing research, brand loyalty, sales management, product policy and planning, public relations, overall marketing strategy, and financial aspects of marketing management. It is hoped that the series will have some effect in raising the standards of applied marketing management.

Hanover, New Hampshire
June 1977

FREDERICK E. WEBSTER, JR.

Preface

In preparing this manuscript, I attempted to address myself to the needs of two different groups. On one hand, I tried to view new product development from the standpoint of general management. For this reason, the thread that weaves its way through the entire book is that new product development is nothing more than a step-by-step risk-reduction process that leads to investment decisions. These investment decisions must be in the same form as any other investment decisions available to the management of the firm and must fit within the firm's overall strategic plan. One chapter is devoted to this latter issue.

On the other hand, the book is also meant to appeal to the practitioner. A system that I have used successfully is described. Each step is explained by its specific objectives and the specific research or creativity tools that are appropriate at that step. A liberal use of examples and a case study will complete the reader's understanding. I have been active in new product development for over ten years and most of the examples and the case study, although disguised, represent actual experiences and, I hope, will be of benefit to the reader.

Of equal importance, however, is that this book represents my attempts (most often with the unstinting help of many generous colleagues) to make the process of new product development less risky. Some of the results of this research and experimentation that are explained are: the preparation of concepts for use with consumers; the construction of a Baysian statistical system to view concepts as potential business propositions; the use of creativity tools in the generation of new product concepts; and a research system that allows concepts to be translated into the language of the research and development department and the advertising agency. It is my opinion that these techniques make an inherently risky process a little less so.

This book assumes that the reader has been introduced to the basics of marketing management, managerial economics, and the business disciplines, in addition to having a slight familiarity with the research tools of the social sciences. I do not assume, however, that the reader is an expert in any of these areas and, where an issue goes beyond the basics, I attempt to provide sufficient information. As such, this book might prove useful as a supplementary reading text in courses in marketing management. Instructors using this text in that manner should be advised, however, to provide additional case study materials—particularly those that require student interpretation and analysis.

EUGENE J. CAFARELLI

New York, New York
August 1980

Acknowledgments

I wish to dedicate this book to my father, whose intelligence, discipline, and elemental fairness have been a model to me during my entire lifetime, and to Marilyn and Edward for their understanding and support during the many hours spent writing away from home.

I also express my appreciation to Melvin Roboff, Thomas Johnson, Frederic Nitschelm, James Quest, and Richard Stockton, who gave of their time and intellect to help me formulate my thinking about this subject, and to Nesta and Janet for their administrative assistance.

E.J.C.

Contents

xi

DEVELOPING NEW PRODUCTS AND REPOSITIONING MATURE BRANDS

1 Introduction

It is generally conceded among professional marketers that in the last two decades there has been an explosion of new product activity. In fact for many industries there are periodicals devoted solely to new products. A good example is the following excerpt from a publication that covers the new product activity in the food, toiletries and over-the-counter drug industries.[1]

The December, 1979, issue of *New Products News* reports the introduction of 85 new products including different flavors, colors or varieties. The comparable totals, by month, for previous years are as follows:

	Average 1964–1973	1974	1975	1976	1977	1978	1979
January	57.3	59	86	76	81	78	79
February	59.0	52	80	79	96	81	90
March	68.8	62	77	86	86	107	88
April	71.8	81	89	95	102	122	101
May	65.7	83	80	110	112	125	123
June	63.5	84	83	95	116	102	101
July	58.1	80	92	75	95	104	92
August	56.3	77	76	98	115	111	93
September	67.2	84	91	102	112	91	104
October	71.0	83	93	100	97	96	96
November	72.0	102	81	109	113	93	112
December	60.4	84	95	103	93	87	85
Total	771.1	931	1,023	1,128	1,218	1,197	1,164
			(+10%)	(+10%)	(+8%)	(−2%)	(−3%)

[1]*DFS New Product News,* December, 1979. There are many services available that compile this data, but it's my opinion that this particular publication is one of the most thorough.

1

The total number of flavors, colors, or product varieties reported in the
1964–1979 period were as follows:

Year	Number		Year	Number
1964	1224		1972	1509
1965	1080		1973	1389
1966	1334		1974	1751
1967	1514		1975	1885
1968	1339		1976	2179
1969	1431		1977	2628
1970	1374		1978	2635
1971	1332		1979	2581

16-years total   27,185

If we combine new products and include product line extensions, the
number has more than doubled in the period 1964–1979.

By removing the product line extensions and concentrating on new
products, a fairly consistent trend for the last four years emerges. Generally it is upward. I think you will find similar data in most industries
(particularly those with intense competition and heavy market segmentation), although it is usually conceded that the food, toiletry, and drug
industries are particularly aggressive in new product development.

All this is amazing if you consider that the very same people who
would agree to the statement "the last two decades have seen an explosion of new product activity," will also agree with the statement that
"less than one percent of all new product ideas on which companies
actually spend time or money achieve success." Like the earlier statement, it's one of those things we all accept, even though we do not have
hard data to support it.

.... THEN WHY BOTHER WITH NEW PRODUCT DEVELOP-
MENT? ISN'T IT TOO RISKY?

I think that there are three reasons why firms engage in new product
work:

1 Properly done, new product development can constitute a reasonable *investment opportunity* for a firm. In a single sentence, this is
the thread that will be woven through this book.

2 Product life cycles seem to be growing shorter. This means that we reach a period of *declining unit profitability* more quickly. To compensate for deteriorating profits, we either have to introduce new products continually so that our "profit mix" is bolstered by the *high unit profits* of products in the early stage of their growth cycle, or we need to reposition our existing brands when the need arises.

3 Many new products are introduced for *defensive reasons*. This can be as simple as attempting to defend one's market share in a specific category. A more complex defense would be an attempt to reduce the amount of market available to our competition by segmenting it one more time, thereby putting a competitor in the position of having a sales volume potential too small to have real economies of manufacturing and marketing.

Whatever the reason for wanting to develop and market new products, the purpose of this book is to help you do it with as little financial risk as possible and to enhance the financial rewards for taking that risk.

Before I go any further, I want to define what I mean by a new product and repositioning products.

By a new product, I mean a product/service that is significantly different from anything a company currently offers (and one normally requiring a separate treatment in terms of marketing, packaging, advertising, financial control, etc.). This usually includes product line extensions (and they fit easily into the system that we will be talking about later). This definition does not include, however, product improvements, which usually require only a modest introductory effort.

A repositioned product is a product that is an evolutionary step beyond a current product. Although sometimes the physical product (the design, formulation, etc.) is changed, invariably the *communications* that the consumer receives about the product are changed so that it is viewed in a new light. This may mean that it will be (a) used by a new group of consumers, (b) used in a different way by the current group of consumers, (c) used in the same way by current (and new) consumers but used with greater satisfaction because now it does more for them; or some combination of these. When a product is repositioned, the brand name and basic *physical product* usually remain more or less the same. Things like packaging design and advertising (what is being said—not necessarily how it's being said) are changed.

THE DISCIPLINES USED FOR DEVELOPMENT OF NEW PRODUCTS OR REPOSITIONING CURRENT PRODUCTS ARE BASICALLY THE SAME AND THE SYSTEM WE WILL TALK ABOUT IN THIS BOOK WILL HANDLE BOTH.

To simplify matters, from this point on, we will deal only with new product development and then at the end of the book show how the system (which by then will have evolved) is applied to the repositioning of a mature product.

. . . . WHAT THIS BOOK IS ALL ABOUT.

This book is a step-by-step approach to the development of new products. At the end of the process we will have a new product developed to the point at which we can confidently think of it as an investment alternative for the firm. Our system will utilize reasonably sophisticated marketing tools. These tools will be described, and their uses demonstrated—but we will not get into their intracacies. That's the work of specialists, and their help can be gained from other sources.

THE PHILOSOPHICAL BASIS OF THE SYSTEM

The system is based on a couple of ideas that I would like to explain at this point, because it will help in understanding what we're doing as the system evolves.

1 The system starts with a *consumer orientation.* Most key judgments about the ultimate product to be marketed will either be made directly by consumers or be heavily influenced by what they say to us. Consumers will design the product to fill a need. They will tell us the kind of product they want, how it will perform, what it will look like, what we will say in the advertising; AND WE WILL HAVE THIS DATA IN SUCH DETAIL THAT THERE WILL BE LITTLE DOUBT IN OUR MIND THAT WE ARE ON THE RIGHT TRACK. At the very end, we will check to make sure (a) that our advertising is communicating the ideal product described to us by the consumer throughout the research and (b) that our actual product matches this ideal.

2 The system works to develop a clearly defined position and suggests design-formulation parameters for the product.

The word positioning has been around marketing for almost 10 years and, unfortunately, can be used in more than one sense. A good definition that fits our point of view appeared a couple of years ago in the *Journal of Advertising Research:*

> The product is a bundle of objective and subjective attributes. Objective attributes of an automobile would include power steering, automatic transmission, engine size, color, and price. Subjective attributes are intangible and would include styling, luxury, prestige or ownership, etc. Clearly, (new product) marketing is involved with both the objective (product) features and the subjective (consumer perception) features.[2]

Thus, the positioning of the product is a fairly complex thing (similar to those Chinese ring puzzles that we had as children containing a number of pieces that all fit together in a smooth geometric shape).

Some of these features are physical attributes that lead to an end benefit. Others are communication attributes (values) that lead us to try the product in the first place and offer support for the end benefit of the product, and may be an end benefit in themselves. This system is aimed at identifying these key communication values (and a numerical relationship among them) and also the end benefit of the process. These allow us to prepare the Positioning Blueprint which starts the development of the advertising. By using it we can be certain that our advertising is communicating the proper end benefit, and supporting it with the right "communication attributes" (in the correct proportion). This system also performs the same function for product development by providing a Product Blueprint.

3 Another piece of our philosophy is that, in the earlier stages of the new product development process, we should *think of a product as a concept—rather than as a physical thing.* Consumers are able to evaluate a prospective product in the concept stage. They do so every day and that's why they choose to try one new detergent as against another, purchase one brand of stereo equipment versus another, and so forth.

NEW PRODUCT IDEAS CAN BE EVALUATED IN CONCEPT
FORM AND THIS ALLOWS US TO EVALUATE THEM IN LARGE

---

[2]*How Advertising Can Position a Brand,* by Robert E. Smith and Robert F. Lusch, Vol. 16, No. 1, February 1976. This article is a clear explanation of positioning and I recommend anyone who would like to pursue it to obtain a copy of the article.

NUMBERS, TO SELECT THOSE THAT SEEM MOST DESIR-
ABLE, AND TO ELIMINATE THE OTHERS EARLY.

It also allows us to do this relatively cheaply by avoiding costly product research and development until a concept is shown to be viable.
Therefore, I restate that you must avoid thinking about new products
in terms of their physical form early on in the process. It's too expensive. And relatively minor issues, such as graphic design problems and
the like, merely muddy the whole process.

4 A key premise behind this book is that new product development is
basically a process of *developing investment opportunities.* As a part of
that, it is necessary to look on a new product idea (or piece of technology that does not have a customer idea for it but still represents a new
product) as a *new business opportunity.* Once you are able to view it as
a business opportunity with all the attendant sales-profit data and investment data, you are better able to judge the worth of the investment.
Therefore, the thrust of the book is to review product development as a
developer of business opportunities and thus investment opportunities.

5 Next, I hope you'll accept the idea that a step-by-step approach to
new product development is really a *step-by-step risk-reduction process.* It is not possible to say that as we move from step to step we
reduce the risk each time by a set percentage. We just aren't that precise
—yet. What I do think you'll see, however, is that we will move from
the "one-chance-in-a-hundred" to something a lot more reasonable,
even before we enter the test marketing stage. This increases the degree
of certainty even more. So, through a step-by-step process, we are
trying to produce an investment alternative that has about the same
amount of uncertainty associated with it as any other investment alternative a chief executive officer may face.

6 Basically, our system leans toward a combination of qualitative and
quantitative techniques. Experience has shown that qualitative research, however helpful in areas like understanding consumer percep-
tion, is not enough. We need to understand the magnitude of the consumer's desire to try a new product. We need to understand, in some
numerical way, the relationship between the various facets of the positioning of a product—not merely that there's more than one facet. I
think you'll find this book is not a slave to numbers. However, we will
be attempting to generate the kinds of quantitative data that will allow
us to discuss our work in investment terms.

7 What is needed is a controlled, disciplined approach. NEW PROD-

UCT DEVELOPMENT SHOULD NOT BE APPROACHED ON AN AD HOC BASIS. YOU SHOULD HAVE YOUR STEP-BY-STEP PLAN IN MIND WHEN YOU START THE PROCESS, NOT DEVELOP IT AS YOU GO ALONG.

You will find that this system has enough flexibility to handle those special situations. Personally, I find speed and flexibility are very important marketing tools (and very underrated). However, they take place within a disciplined format and do not replace it.

I think that's as much philosophy as this book requires. Let's move on to an explanation of the system itself.

SYSTEM OVERVIEW

As we have mentioned, we will use a system approach in this book. A diagram of this system can be found in Figure 1-1. Although it may look imposing because of all the steps and lines, do not be put off. It follows a logical sequence. In fact, a number of the steps are really only check points that can be taken care of in a couple of hours, or a day at most (although I have always allocated a week for these—thus allowing ample time to discuss the business implications of the most recent steps and the next steps with your management).

AS YOU LOOK THROUGH THE SYSTEM, PLEASE REMEMBER TWO THINGS. FIRST, WE ARE TRYING TO DEVELOP BUSINESSES THAT CAN BECOME INVESTMENT OPPORTUNITIES, AND THAT'S THE REASON FOR THE EMPHASIS ON DEFINING THE CORRECT POSITIONING OF THE PRODUCT. SECOND, TO ACHIEVE THIS, WE TAKE A SERIES OF STEPS THAT ALLOW YOU TO COME FULL CIRCLE—THAT IS, REFINING THE END BENEFIT AND SUPPORTING ATTRIBUTES WHICH THEN ALLOW US TO DEVELOP ADVERTISING (THE POSITIONING BLUEPRINT), A PHYSICAL PRODUCT (THE PRODUCT BLUEPRINT) THAT MATCHES THESE, AND THE FINAL PERFORMANCE TESTING TO MAKE SURE THAT WE ARE NOT ONLY COMMUNICATING THE RIGHT END BENEFIT AND VALUES, BUT ALSO SATISFYING THEM WITH THE ACTUAL PRODUCT.

A BRIEF EXPLANATION OF THE STEPS

A.   GUIDELINES AND OBJECTIVES

Suffice it to say, you need both a set of guidelines and very specific objectives (by time period) for your new product development program. If you don't have them, you take the chance of either spending a lot of time and money on projects that are unacceptable to the firm, or losing time because, at every step, on every project, you will be forced to explain why it's a good idea, and why it meets the firm's objectives. It will be stressed in Chapter 2 that the guidelines and objectives not only be cleared by top management, but also be disseminated to and agreed upon by all departments and parties concerned. You've got to get together as early as possible because new product development is a team effort. That's the reason why you need to agree from the very beginning on your guidelines and objectives.

B.   CONCEPT GENERATION

As part of your new product development program, you will need to acquire a large number of new product concepts—let's call them your concept portfolio. A large number is very important. You should avoid dealing with one good idea until the latter stages of the program. Chances are one idea will not come to fruition. There are just too many problems. Consumer research may prove it is not such a good idea after all. R&D and Manufacturing may not be able to design and produce a product that matches the concept, or your top management may decide that the product, or the risk associated with it, is unacceptable to the firm. So let me state Rule #1 of concept generation: always work, in the early stages, with a large number of ideas and handle them in convenient groups. That way, you are able to pick the best and are not put in a position of seeking something good in your good idea. You will always have another product concept ready if your current product becomes impossible to pursue. There is a definite relationship between quantity and ultimate quality in new product development, and we will discuss this topic in Chapter 4. In Chapter 4 we will also examine the techniques for developing a large number of ideas and note that these techniques can be used for the development of concepts matching a given technology or, on the other hand, aimed at satisfying known consumer needs (with the appropriate technology) to be selected later.

C. BUSINESS ANALYSIS

The next step in the system is the business analysis. Remember, the WHOLE OBJECTIVE OF NEW PRODUCT DEVELOPMENT IS TO DEVELOP A BUSINESS. In the business analysis system covered in Chapter 5, we apply a system of analysis to each concept. This system combines hard data (such as known market size for certain products, the sales trends of this market, etc.) and what we'll call soft data, or our best estimates of other key factors (for example, how aggressive and how powerful is the competition). This system allows us to sort our concepts by viewing them as potential business propositions. It will allow us to estimate future efforts before we spend any market research dollars. We will go back to the system after each step and apply it, quickly, again to make sure that we are indeed developing a business that is worthwhile. I cannot emphasize too often that no matter what we are doing in new product development, whether we are dealing with social scientists as they refine the concept, or with R&D personnel as we refine the physical product, we must always keep in mind that *our ultimate goal is to develop business, not products.*

D. THE CONCEPT REFINEMENT SYSTEM—QUALITATIVE REFINEMENT

The refinement process begins with focus group interviews involving members of the target market or segment. The number of focus sessions depends on a number of factors: for example, the complexity of the market structure, and so on. In the most simple case, three focus groups should suffice for up to six concepts. Each group consists of about 12 participants, and is moderated by a trained, professional moderator. This first step of our concept refinement system has several objectives:

1 First, it allows us to identify the new product concepts that have some general consumer interest. These are concepts that we probably

will want to take to some subsequent step. Also, it allows us to identify those concepts that are clinkers. It's a good idea to wash them out at this stage.

2 Second, in any focus group, a large number of concepts will neither immensely interest nor be rejected by the consumer. These fall into a gray area where they either (a) appeal to a narrow band of people or, (b) more likely, have some interesting aspects, but as currently stated do not represent an interesting idea. These can usually be re-introduced in later focus groups *after they have been strengthened by using the results of the initial focus groups.*

3 Perhaps the most important thing to be learned from the focus groups is the consumer's understanding of the product concepts; the attributes, and the competitive environment within which they would exist. In research language this is sometimes called the perceptual framework and really means little more than the attributes of products that exist in a category, the language used to describe these attributes, and the relative importance of these attributes. On occasion, when you have perceptual framework with a large number of items (attributes and attitudes), it may be necessary to engage in a statistical step that allows you to cluster these around key factors. Usually, the number of factors is not that large and it is not necessary to go through this statistical step.

Ideally, at the end of this step, you will have isolated a few new product concepts (or positionings for a mature product that you wish to reposition) that appear to be interesting to the consumer, and, importantly, the list of attributes for these concepts (either individually if the concepts are somewhat different from one another, or for the group as a whole).

E.   QUANTIFICATION AND THE BLUEPRINTS

Once the concepts have been polished by qualitative research, we need to ascertain the nature and magnitude of the business proposition we are facing. This step has the objective of providing us with the following data:

1 An estimate of each concept's sales potential (trial, usage . . .).
2 Demographic (target) refinement (including psychographics).

3 The Positioning Blueprint (for use in creating advertising, packaging, and naming the product).
> End benefit
> Communications attributes[3]

4 The Product Blueprint (for use by R&D).
> End benefit
> Product attributes[3]

The sales volume figure is important because it will be a key factor in your equation of just how desirable a business this new product concept really is. Previously, at the business analysis stage, you looked at this new product concept from the standpoint of being a business. However, missing from the inspection was a good sales volume estimate. After this step, you have that piece of data and can utilize it in the next step to check the desirability of this business.

The blueprints are the most important output of this system. The Positioning Blueprint is the base for all consumer communications (advertising, packaging, product name, point-of-sale material, etc.). The Product Blueprint is the communication with the R&D/Manufacturing Group which tells them (a) what the new product looks like, (b) who will use it, (c) what the end benefit of this product is, (d) what the product attributes are that support this end benefit, and (e) the necessary data such as packaging, shipping container, and so forth. Figures 1-2 and 1-3 are examples of blueprints. In Chapter 6 we will go through the refinement system, and you will see the logic of the various steps.

The research methodology of quantification may take a variety of forms. In the case of a concept that exists with a commonly familiar frame of reference (e.g., travel services), a nationally representative mail panel might be used. When personal usage is indicated, in-home or in-plant interviews may be called for. Telephone and shopping area intercepts are also useful for other types of products.

In each case, however, a general procedure is followed. This involves exposing the respondent to a verbal and/or visual statement of the concept, followed by some assessment of the concept's positives

---

[3]These attributes are shown in their relative weights—to allow for the proper trade-offs.

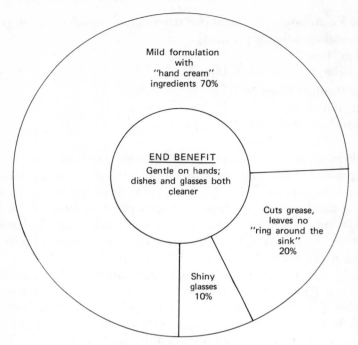

Figure 1-2 Positioning Blueprint

and negatives. This is followed by a presentation of the selected perceptual factors with a rating of their significance. Finally, a measurement is taken of trial intention and anticipated frequency of use (or use-up rate). Quantification normally involves 200 to 1000 target consumers with costs relative to the sampling technique to be used and the number of concepts being tested.

At the end of this step, you are in the position of being able to select the business(es) you want to develop.

F. BUSINESS ANALYSIS CHECK

We are now ready to re-evaluate each concept utilizing the data from the previous steps. You should use the same business analysis system that you utilized in the Business Analysis step (C). However, you now have two additional and very important pieces of data. First, you have a rough sales potential projection for each concept. This will allow you to refine your business analysis for each concept by adding in an im-

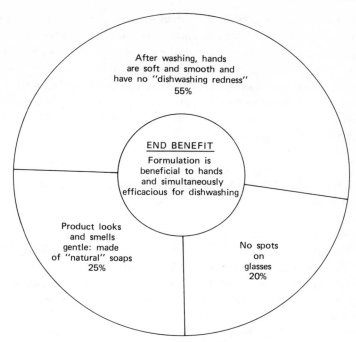

After washing, hands
are soft and smooth and
have no "dishwashing redness"
55%

END BENEFIT
Formulation is
beneficial to hands
and simultaneously
efficacious for dishwashing

Product looks
and smells
gentle: made
of "natural" soaps
25%

No spots
on
glasses
20%

Figure 1-3   Product Blueprint

portant factor which you were forced to estimate (or skip) previously. The second important thing is that, with the positioning and product blueprints, you are now able to see much more clearly how the final product should appear, what must be built into it, and what you want to say about it. Although the product is still premature (since you have not preformed any R&D), this may change your idea about the necessary investment for the products.

Adding these two into your business analysis will now allow you to form concepts based on a profitability/investment basis. It is from this list that you should select the concept(s) that will actually be developed into products and advertising.

G.   DEVELOPING AND TESTING OF PRODUCTS

At this stage, you are able to submit the Product Blueprint to the R&D/ Manufacturing Group. This blueprint will not only tell them what is is that you're aiming to market, but also allow them to judge the desirability of various trade-offs in the development process, because it will show the relative weights of the various product attributes that are part of the product. During the development process a great deal of testing with the actual consumer should be done. It is necessary that these tests always be done in conjunction with the concept. After all, you are not trying to develop the perfect product—you are trying to develop an appropriate product that matches the concept for which you already have a good deal of test data.

H.   DEVELOPMENT AND TESTING OF ADVERTISING AND PACKAGING

While the research and development is going on (assuming that no large changes will be made in the product concept by R&D), you should be developing and testing its consumer communications. In most cases, most of this will be done by the advertising and the package. Since we will be dealing with this area in a subsequent chapter, it will be necessary to note only a few points here.

First, the end benefit and supporting product attributes from the Quantification step (E) that form the Positioning Blueprint must be used to prepare the creative objectives for the advertising and the objectives for the name of the product, if you intend to have something other than a descriptive name or a company name (for example, Xerox).

Second, I see little value in name tests, but quite a bit of value in packaging tests. However, there isn't much room for personal opinion with testing advertising. It must be tested. Ideally several alternatives should be tested.

Third, when developing the advertising, it is necessary that you aim to prepare advertising that plays back (a) the end benefits and (b) the supporting attributes *in the correct proportions,* as you found them, in the Quantification stage (E). When you have found advertising that does this, YOU HAVE COMPLETED THE COMMUNICATIONS HALF OF THE CIRCLE (represented in Figure 1-4)—PREVIOUSLY YOU FOUND OUT EXACTLY WHAT YOU WOULD HAVE TO SAY ABOUT THE PRODUCT BECAUSE THE CONSUMER TOLD YOU THEY WANTED IT. NOW YOU HAVE CREATED ADVERTISING THAT REPEATS TO THE CONSUMER EXACTLY WHAT THEY TOLD YOU THEY WANTED TO HEAR.

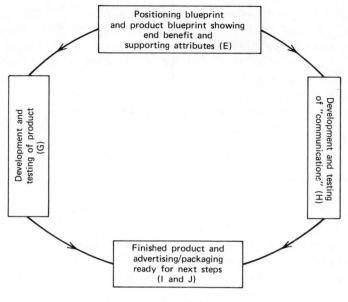

Figure 1-4

I. BUSINESS ANALYSIS CHECK

This is probably the last step you can make before spending money in the marketplace. At this point, you should utilize your latest trial and repeat-frequency data from product and advertising testing to prepare a tight financial plan. Also, using your business analysis system, you should make a last check of the other variables to make certain that no large changes have occurred since you first sent this concept (now a product) through the system.

J. MARKET TEST

You are now at the point where you probably will want to obtain market data on the actual behavior of your product compared with competition before you engage in full-scale marketing. I say probably because with some product categories, for example, fashion consumer goods and many industrial products, this is not usually done. Obviously, there is expense, and the loss-of-confidentiality issue, and these are enough to dissuade a lot of people. Sophisticated test marketing models can, as a rule, overcome the problem, but for some product categories buying models seem inappropriate or untested and, therefore, do not represent a solution.

Unless you want to take the plunge without any further testing, you must now expose the entire marketing plan to the consumer and the marketplace in some form. Basically, you have two choices. First, a traditional test market—which could be a geographical location (or a certain group of your customers). Or, you can use a mathematical model that simulates conditions in your industry. We'll discuss these in Chapter 10.

The method you choose should yield the following:

1 Very tight financial data. This means trial and repeat/frequency data that can be converted into sales volumes, and P&L statements.

2 If you use an actual market, it should give you a great deal of data in the following areas: (a) advertising weight and its relationship to consumer awareness and trial; (b) marketing strategy and programs (such as couponing, cents-off display material) and further, trade strategy and programs (allowances, display materials, in-store sales promotion material, etc.). This step represents the last chance for obtaining the kind of data that make for an intelligent investment decision and should be approached from that standpoint.

K&L. *BUSINESS PLAN PREPARATIONS AND FULL SCALE MARKETING*

At this point, you are ready to convert what you have learned into a full investment decision. A final business plan and its execution in the marketplace should reflect what you've learned in the test marketing stage. If you have used an actual test market or test situation (with a group of potential customers), you'll have some fairly tight financial information. Should you not be able to do this, for whatever reason, it is still necessary to make a financial marketing plan based on your best judgment. Only after you have done this, will you be able to properly view a business you've developed.

After the system is established, we will begin to examine each piece more thoroughly. This will be accomplished by examining the relevant issues in a chapter devoted to that specific piece, and then, through an on-going case, seeing how that part of the system might be applied in a real-life situation.

2 Organizing for Success

Before we unfold the system for new product development, there are a number of organizational considerations that need to be discussed. These set the stage for the successful development of new products by defining the new product development program's charter and role in the firm. These are:

1 The role of the chief executive officer in new product development.
2 Organizing for the development of new products.
3 Defining corporate assets of the new product developer.
4 Setting the guidelines and objectives for the new product development program.

At the end of this chapter, we will begin the case study that will be used to illustrate the philosophy of each chapter.

THE ROLE OF THE CHIEF EXECUTIVE OFFICER IN NEW PRODUCT DEVELOPMENT

Make no mistake about it, the Chief Executive Officer of the company, either implicitly or explicitly, always sets the tone for the new product development program of a company. By tone I'm referring both to objectives, long-range goals, level of acceptable risk, and the like, and to subjective values such as commitment. The same way the chief executive officer affects these parameters in other areas of the firm's endeavors.

This is as it should be. However, the difficulty here is that in many firms this is done implicitly rather than explicitly. And this is always a

17

costly mistake. After all, in all but the most disorganized firms, we would expect a chief executive to have a reasonably tight answer to the following questions:

▶ What are our sales goals for the year? Are we planning any new marketing programs for the year? If so, what are the objectives? Are there any changes necessary in our marketing department to reflect changes that we see in the marketplace?

▶ What are the trends in our fixed and variable manufacturing costs? How do they compare to our objectives for the year?

▶ Is our manufacturing organized for maximum efficiency? What kind of facilities will we be needing for next year? What kind of people should we be looking for?

It is possible to go on with questions like this, but I think you are beginning to see the pattern. It is basically this. New product development is just another activity of the firm. Just like manufacturing or marketing, it requires thought and explicit direction by the Chief Executive Officer, or it will continue to limp along, setting its own objectives (often not quite compatible with those of the firm), and often turning out products that, when they are ready to be marketed, may not be relevant to the firm.

To avoid this, the chief executive needs to do the following:

1 Make available to the new products development department the long-range plan of the firm.

2 Properly organize the new products development department to fit his organization.

3 Arrive at agreed-to guidelines and objectives for the entire new product development program with the executive responsible for this program, and then to fund it adequately, based on the agreed-to objectives.

4 Monitor without becoming involved in the day-to-day procedures the activity of the new product development program.

Let me explain these a little further.

The Long-Range Plan of the Firm

To make any kind of investment decision correctly, the firm should have a long-range plan. From past experience, the ones that I thought were most useful were divided into three sections. The first section contained the plans for the coming year; the second section contained the plans for the years two through five, and the third section contained the plans for the remaining years. With this kind of format, it is always possible to view how the decisions at the moment are relevant to what the firm has to accomplish immediately, or immediately thereafter. And more important, it is possible to plan all your activities accordingly.

If your firm does not have a 10-year plan, I would suggest that you prepare a brief one before you proceed to spend money on new product development. If you don't want to go through the rigors of preparing a full-blown plan, then, at the very least, you should ask yourself the following kinds of questions with the objective of obtaining a fairly clear positioning for your company in your mind over the next ten years.

▶ What will my industry look like in five or in ten years—in terms of number of firms, overall growth rate?[1]

▶ How do we want our firm to fit into the industry? Do we want to be the industry leader? Do we want to be more diversified than the average firm?

▶ What will our size be—in sales and assets?

▶ What kind of physical facilities do we expect to own? Technologies? Channels of distribution?

▶ What kind of people do we expect to have—particularly those whose behavior affects the guidance of the firm?

▶ What kind of markets do we expect to serve in terms of consumers and geography?

This is an abbreviated list, of course. However, if you, as the C.E.O., have some fairly clear feelings about these questions, you're able to provide considerable guidance to the person who will be responsible for the new product development program. On the other hand, if you're the person who will be responsible for this program, and you are not provided with this kind of information, then it is advisable to rough it out on your own and, with considerable humility, submit it along with your specific program objectives to the executive responsi-

[1]You should actually do this for every industry your firm competes in.

ble. After all, he should have a perspective of the business situation that is like yours if you are going to develop a successful program.

ORGANIZING FOR NEW PRODUCT DEVELOPMENT

When we talk about organizing the new product effort in a firm, there are usually two areas for consideration. First, what kind of organization should it be? Second, to whom in the firm should this organization report?

The answer to these questions depends as much on the management style of the firm as it does on the kind of firm it is, and the objectives for its new product development program. The following shows some alternatives with some of the advantages and disadvantages and should allow you to make a reasonable choice for your firm. I want to stress that this is a more important area than initially meets the eye. I've had a number of experiences in which the firm's new product program suffered an organizational problem. What made this hard to understand was that, generally, these firms would be considered well-managed firms. I have to assume that the problem really was that the Chief Executive Officer never organized the new product program correctly. Usually the effort was free floating with a lack of common goal, structure and so forth. Invariably there were personality or departmental conflicts, and departmental or personal objectives conflicted with overall corporate objectives; inefficiency was one result. The other was failure. The type of organization and reporting system of the new product development program is the most important decision a Chief Executive will make with respect to the entire effort.

Types of Organization

Basically, there are three kinds of organization that can be used in the new products development area:

The New Products Person

In small firms, and in some large firms where the new products development function is viewed as unimportant, the new products function is usually the responsibility of one person. He is responsible for all facets of the program (finance, marketing, R&D, production planning, dealing with outside groups, etc). He does this by calling on the expertise of various members of the firm. Ideally, this person should have at least the following qualifications:

▶ A knowledge of the industry's marketing practices and an appreciation of consumer data in formulating new product development programs;

▶ An appreciation of the technology of the industry;

▶ An entrepreneurial streak (because new product development programs really have no life of their own as do the ongoing marketing programs of a brand currently on the marketplace and, therefore, require a person who is a self-starter).

In many companies that utilize this organization, the new products manager may wear more than one hat; for example, he may also have responsibilities for an ongoing product. From my experience, this can work well. It is often not essential that the position be fitted by a full-time employee. If a split-function system is used, however, it is important that the person be rewarded for both activities. The annual bonus should be given for meeting new products goals as well as sales goals for on-going products.

The Staff Department

Many firms have a new product development department. As a rule, it is composed of people of various skills. Marketing and research and development people are usually in the majority. Of course, the new product department has access to the expertise of other members of the firm (for example, purchasing, the legal department).

My experience with this kind of structure has been, all in all, very good. It has the disadvantage, of course, of being a fixed cost that the firm must carry. Also, members of this department may be somewhat inflexible in terms of their skills. In times of financial retrenchment, it is not always easy to work them back into the regular structure of the firm. However, this organization does indicate a high level of commitment of the firm to the development of new products. It has the potential for the greatest output. There is one danger, however. On occasion,

I've seen the new product development department become a kind of refuge for people who, for one reason or another, are transferred from other departments. Some may be intending to leave the firm because their function has been eliminated. This is a mistake because new product development requires (a) professionals who are interested in this area, and (b) a long-run point of view.

Project Groups

Project groups are what the name implies—a number of people organized to develop a single new product or a group of new products. Commonly, the relevant departments (finance, marketing, purchasing, manufacturing, R&D, etc.) are represented with one or more persons devoting a portion of their work week to the project group.

As a temporary solution, or for a very specific situation, this kind of structure can work out well. As an ongoing thing, however, it can suffer from a number of problems: (1) most of the members continue to view the project group as a temporary thing and really never internalize its goals; they remain loyal to the goals of their department; (2) the members realize, quite rightly, that their success in the organization probably depends more on their behavior in their own department than their work with the project group, therefore creating a situation where the work of the project group becomes second-class work; (3) the work load, department-by-department, is uneven, and it is not uncommon for the work of the group to be held up because one of its members is unable or unwilling to devote the necessary time to performing his work within the group. All in all, there are too many problems inherent with this kind of structure to make it a viable alternative in the long run. However, if you wish to use it for a specific project, there are two requisites to making it work (outside of the obvious ones, which are selecting the right people, etc.). They are:

▶ One person must be in charge of the project. He must have both the responsibility and the authority. This must be known by all the members of the group.

▶ Top management must make it known to all the members of the group that they consider the work important and that it will be monitoring its output.

To Whom Should the New Product Development Function Report?

There are really only three viable lines-of-reporting for the new product function: (1) Top Management; (2) Vice President-Marketing; (3) Vice President-Research and Development.

My preference is the first: Top Management. This can be the President or an Executive Vice President, depending primarily on the size of the organization. This has the advantage of assuring top management commitment and lends the aura of importance to the function (no small thing when you consider that new products people constantly depend on other members of the organization for important work for them, even though they have no authority or responsibility relationship with these people). The only danger in this situation is that, by making the new products function a staff function in the overall organization, you take the chance that it can "get out of the mainstream" or become unresponsive to the needs and direction of the organization. I think this is a minimal risk if the reporting procedure is such that Top Management is cognizant of the activities of the function—but this danger still exists and should be guarded against.

My second choice is reporting to the Vice President—Marketing. Generally the marketing department has a number of skills that are important to new product development: a knowledge of consumers; a knowledge of the techniques of marketing research; a feeling for the role that the communications (positioning) values[2] play in the development of a brand. On the other hand, there are two potential problems: first, the marketing department is usually skilled in the maintenance and further development of brands; the development of a *new* brand usually requires a different orientation. This orientation and the time needed for new product development may not be available in the marketing department. (An example of this is how often the least experienced member of the marketing team is placed in charge of the new product development). Also, the marketing department is usually rewarded on the basis of its performance in meeting the sales goals of current brands, and it places most of its emphasis in this area; this can

[2]By communications values I mean all those things that the consumer knows about the product before he actually tries it. These are learned by the consumer from advertising, packaging, point-of-sale material, and so forth.

short-change the new product development function. I find the marketing department a more than acceptable choice but probably, in most situations, not the very best.

My third choice would be the Research and Development department. In fields where the product utilizes fairly involved technology, having the R&D department control the new product development function might work. Generally though, I find that the R&D department can suffer from problems that make it difficult for it to successfully develop new products: first, it is often more isolated from the Chief Executive than the marketing department (they are often viewed as "eggheads"); second, this department usually is unskilled in market research and unfamiliar with consumer data. Therefore, it often winds up working on products with which it feels comfortable, rather than on products for which it has evidence that there is a consumer need; and third, this department is usually relatively unskilled at working with the positioning of a product because its orientation is in the area of the physical product itself. All in all, I find having the R&D department control new product development for a firm to be the least attractive of the alternatives.

Decision Point

If you are in charge of organizing the new product development function, you now have seen that there are two organizational decisions you need to make. First, you need to decide which structure is best for this function in your firm. Second, you need to decide who in the corporate hierarchy has responsibility for this function.

Further, before you implement these decisions, you need to (1) provide a long-range plan so that the new product development can take place logically and (2) create an environment within which the risk-taking that is an inherent part of the end process must take place.

DEFINING THE ASSETS OF YOUR FIRM

For the first step toward setting some guidelines and objectives for the new product development program, you need to create a listing of (growth related) assets as they are viewed by the new product developer. (This is not in any way the Accounting Department's definition of assets.) This listing should cover both the present and the immediate future as you see it outlined in your long-range plan for the firm. It is important that this listing of assets defines these assets and includes only those assets that are useful from the new product developer's viewpoint. The following are some areas you should investigate:[3]

1 *Expertise in Certain Channels of Distribution.* This covers the kind of sales force your firm has; the kind of customers they call on; the kind of customers they will be calling on in the future. In other words, how are your products currently sold and how do you intend to sell in the future, because this is how your new product will ultimately get to the market.

2 *Patents Owned.* Does your firm own patents that will allow you to produce certain kinds of products with little or minimum competition? How long do the patents extend? (Note: patents really offer minimal protection in most industries because the products covered by most patents can be produced several ways. If you want, you can usually find a way to get around a given patent. Therefore, you must assume that your patented product is vulnerable, and you should not place great weight on this asset).

3 *Technologies Owned.* Each firm has areas of technological expertise. Usually this means that over a period of time this firm has solved all the large and small problems involved in producing and marketing a kind or various kinds of products. Quite often, however, this does not mean that these are protectable in the sense of being patented. But it does mean that you have spent the time and money to have your own little group of secrets—trade secrets that would take another firm some time to master. Like patents, these should not be over-rated, but they are a kind of asset that your firm owns.

4 *Under-Utilized Machinery.* Under-utilized machinery often presents the new product developer with a quandry. From an economic standpoint, this is a past cost and should not have a great effect on current thinking (and businessmen instinctively realize this). At the same time, they realize that its depreciation and servicing represents a fixed burden for the firm and the possibility of utilizing it (even in the extreme case where the utilization represents only a contribution to the overhead burden) is very attractive.

(Making a list of under-utilized machinery may give you some interesting insight into areas of new product development. But I must caution you, at the same time you must understand that the utilization

[3]For more detail, the reader is advised to consult books on strategic planning.

of this machinery should be the icing on the cake and should not force you into any new product development areas where there is not a clear consumer need).

5 *Brands Owned.* The brands your company markets are definite assets and often provide you, in new product development, with a very solid start in positioning your product. Your brand will already say a lot of things about you; for example, high quality, or low price, or involved technology, or durability, or whatever. This is a definite advantage if you are introducing a new product that needs the image of your current brands (and can meet it with its own performance). Therefore, the brands you own, or more properly, what the brands you own stand for in the mind of the consumer, are assets that should be considered when you are making your asset listing before preparing the guidelines for your new product development work.

6 *Economies of Scale.* If you look closely enough, you'll usually discover that your firm has what economists will call economies of scale. Economies of scale means nothing more than that, because of your size, you can do certain things more cheaply than many of your competitors. Economies of scale can involve anything from being small with low overhead to being relatively large and, therefore, capable of purchasing raw materials in larger quantities at a lower unit cost.

Usually, economies of scale are not something generally thought of by a firm as an asset. You may have trouble ferreting them out for your firm because most people won't be thinking in these terms. However, by talking to people in Purchasing and Manufacturing or the Controller, you might find your own economies of scale. If you can develop new products that take advantage of these, you will find often that you have price advantages, profit margin advantages, and the like.

7 *Personnel.* Often in a firm you will find experts in certain technologies or channels of distribution, whose area of expertise is currently untapped by the firm. In fact, it's not uncommon to find a whole department available with kinds of expertise that are not currently being utilized. You should recognize that people are an asset that can slip away from a firm very quickly. While they are there, they do represent a peculiar asset of your firm (from your point of view), and you should take account of them in preparing your asset listing before you do your guidelines.

8 *Financial.* The financial resources that a firm has access to sets the parameters for new product development not only from the point of review of the scope of the program but also the magnitude of investments possible for actual new product introductions. These resources might be limited to funds already available to the firm, or they might include the firm's borrowing power, including, if it is part of a conglomerate, other members. The new product developer should gauge the extent of these resources well into the future since that is when he probably will need them.

At this point you are ready to prepare your guidelines and objectives for your new product development program.

SETTING THE GUIDELINES AND OBJECTIVES FOR A NEW PRODUCT DEVELOPMENT PROGRAM

Now that you've taken into consideration the long-range business plan of your firm and put together a listing of assets, organized from the point of view of the new product developer, you are ready to prepare your new product development program guidelines.

The function of these guidelines is to set the parameters within which your activities will take place. These guidelines can differ dramatically by industry, but generally they contain provisions for the following areas:

1 *Financial.* The whole thrust of this book is that the new product development process is really a process of preparing investment alternatives for the firm. Therefore, the guidelines should include the financial expectations for a new product. My preference for this is a return on investment. However, some firms use different financial criteria for their investment alternatives; for example, payout, return on fixed assets, discounted cash flows, pay-back period, and so forth. Obviously, you have to deliniate the minimum performance of a prospective product that would make it acceptable to the firm.

Some firms also use maximum investment criteria in their new product guidelines. Although conceptually I am against this, in reality it's needed because some firms can handle investments only up to a certain level. You should determine what this is for your company, and make it one of the guidelines.

2 *Brands/Image of New Product.* Often a firm will include in its guidelines the mention that a brand currently owned by the firm must be utilized or, even more commonly, that the new product should fall into some quality or image area.

3 *Marketing.* The guidelines should include some reference to spe-

cific marketing areas. First, what kind of channels of distribution, or perhaps even product categories, the new products should fall within. Because the cost of setting up new channels of distribution can be expensive and lengthy, it is normal that the guidelines specify the current channels of distribution. Aside from financial guidelines, this is probably the most commonly found guideline.

Second, if the industry requires some minimum sales volume for maintaining distribution, this should be included as a guideline. If the product is to be distributed regionally because you cannot satisfy this requirement nationally, this should be made explicit.

4 *Manufacturing Facilities.* The guidelines must make it explicit whether it is acceptable to manufacture products outside or whether it is necessary to utilize the firm's own facilities. Acceptable investment levels for new equipment should be specified.

At this point I would think this is all reasonably obvious. An example at the end of the chapter should help put this in perspective for you.

Setting the Objectives

Setting the objectives for your new program should be quite simple. Generally, objectives cover, at least, the following points:

1 A reference that the agreed-to guidelines will be observed, and a restatement of the financial parameters for an acceptable product.

Example. The new product development program will concentrate on developing products that fall within the agreed-to guidelines and will attempt to develop products that exceed the required 15% return on investment.

2 You should make a statement showing the number of products that you intend to ready for the marketplace (either test marketing or full scale marketing) and the time period within which this will take place.

Example. During the 12-month period beginning May 1, we will complete all development work and have ready for test marketing two products. One of these will be ready for fall introduction and one put into production in the spring.

3 You need to show the other activities the new product program will be involved in in order to provide market-ready products in the next year.

Example. During the current year, we will procure and evaluate for their investment potential a minimum of 75 new product concepts. Utilizing historical data, this should allow us to complete our concept thinking and have begun actual R&D on two or three of these concepts with the objective of marketing them next year.

Some firms utilize objectives statements that are somewhat more involved than this, but it is my impression that the simpler the better. If you have included the above areas, I think you've set the stage properly.

Let's look at a case study. As we move through the book and explore our system for developing new products, we will stay with the same case and use it to demonstrate the application of the issues discussed in each chapter.

A CASE STUDY—THE MIDDLE SOUTH MILLING COMPANY

Middle South Milling was started in St. Joseph, Missouri, in 1932 by a farmer who wanted to control, and take the commensurate profit from, the distribution of some of his wheat production. Initially, Middle South marketed only a flour. Most of its distribution was in Missouri, Kansas, Tennessee, Arkansas and eastern Oklahoma. In 1935, Middle South was acquired by a wheat grower's cooperative. From 1935 through 1947, Middle South remained pretty much the same. Sales of flour grew modestly, but steadily, until, in 1947, sales of their Mother's Secret brand flour were at $12 million. Mother's Secret was a standard bleached flour which sold, at retail, for a slightly lower price than the brand sold by the national marketers (e.g., Gold Medal). Often this difference amounted to only a penny or two. No attempts were made to advertise Mother's Secret. Middle South did provide trade deals to retailers on a continuing basis. This was its main promotional effort. Middle South distributed Mother's Secret to its retailers through a system of food brokers.

In 1947 Middle South was purchased by J.R. "Red" Jackson who moved the headquarters to Memphis, Tennessee. "Red" Jackson had worked as a salesman and in the marketing department for a food company that specialized in canning vegetables and fruits and selling them through the Southeast, and brought with him a fairly good knowledge of the food business. He immediately began to add broker-age territories, increasing the retail distribution area of Middle South. By 1973 Middle South sold at least part of its line of products in 30 states. Generally these were states below the Mason-Dixon Line.

During this 26-year period, two changes of particular interest to us occurred in the product line sold by Middle South. First, relying on his canning experience, "Red" Jackson acquired a company in Savannah, Georgia which canned and marketed a variety of fruits and vegetables. Second, based on the milling skills of Middle South, "Red" Jackson had broadened this portion of this product line by adding: a grit mix; a hot cereal; a cold cereal; and a pancake/biscuit mix.

By 1973 "Red" Jackson was preparing for his retirement. His eldest son, Jerome, had returned to the company two years before after spend-ing eight years working for a management consulting firm in Chicago. Jerome realized that, if Middle South was to grow and prosper in the next 26 years, a number of changes would have to be made. One of these changes that he envisioned was a more formal new product de-velopment program.

Jerome had not placed new product development at the top of his short-run objectives list because he felt that strengthening the distribu-tion system, among other things, would probably make a more imme-diate contribution to profits. However, the matter was brought to a head when Middle South was approached by Professor Carl Hartman, who was head of the Food Science Department of a southern univer-sity. Professor Hartman, and two of his colleagues, had been looking for ways to increase the consumption of some of the farm products of the region. They had been working specifically with wheat and soy-beans, and were looking for ways to make new food products from these agricultural products. The university had underwritten his initial work on new soybean or wheat products that would probably contain an unusually high amount of protein. Since both Professor Hartman and his colleagues felt that protein from vegetables would begin to displace protein from animals in the nation's diet, the future implica-tions of his work seemed positive.

Professor Hartman found that he could create puffs of wheat or soybeans that would be little globes up to an inch or inch and one-half in diameter. With a slight change in the process, he could make an inexpensive protein powder that dissolved easily in water. Professor Hartman felt, instinctively, that this process might have some application for cereals or snacks, or even powdered beverages, and at the urging of the university president he approached Middle South.

His proposition was simple: the university really did not expect royalties if the technology resulted in a commercial product, but did desire that, if Middle South wanted to pursue the project, the university be allowed to participate. Also, the university requested that Middle South fund a fellowship for any student working on the project. Jerome recognized immediately that the process could make sense for Middle South, already dealing in two of the commodities, wheat and soybeans, that Professor Hartman successfully used. Jerome also recognized that the process contained a very basic problem for Middle South. It represented an easy and obvious entry into the new product area, but it would be very easy to become enamoured with the process and develop the new product program based on this specific piece of technology. Jerome had seen the potential error of this during his consulting time in Chicago and decided that the best approach would be to ask Professor Hartman for a two month right-of-first-refusal. This would give him time to develop a series of guidelines for a new product development program at Middle South before any commitments were made. Professor Hartman agreed to this.

Jerome realized that, in its own way, Professor Hartman's visit had brought into focus the new products program. He knew from his consulting experience that the organization of a new product development program would not be a large problem and that the monitoring of it also would take very little time each month. It was his experience that, once a basic system was in place and running, new product development should not be a problem for him.

He also realized that he had, in the near future, several decisions to make. First, he realized that he would need someone to guide the program, and that he would have to decide to whom in the organization this person would report. Further, he knew that it would fall to him to put together the guidelines and objectives of the new products program since he didn't feel that anyone currently with Middle South was capable of this. He knew that anyone joining Middle South would require several months to become comfortable with the situation and be capable of performing a task like this.

As a first step, Jerome decided that the best type of organization for Middle South's new product development program would be to have one person in charge, reporting directly to him. This person would have free rein to tap the various departments at Middle South and, if needed, to use the services of outside specialists. Jerome also knew that this person would need to be experienced in the area of new product development since he would be on his own much of the time. Because no one currently at Middle South qualified, in his mind, he contracted with a personnel firm in Chicago to conduct a search. He stipulated only that any candidate have four to five years' experience in the development of new products in the packaged goods business. Experience in food was desirable. He stated that experience in marketing products already in the marketplace would be valuable (since he felt that the new products effort might not be a full-time job for this person), but said that this was not an absolute requirement.

Jerome also knew that he had some serious thinking to do about the company. During the next five years, he and his father had agreed that the company would (a) attempt to expand its distribution to all 50 states and Canada; (b) attempt to market products in more categories (particularly those categories that were a little less commodity-oriented than their current ones); and (c) attempt to achieve some balance between investment in manufacturing facilities and investment in marketing—in other words, Middle South was to reduce its emphasis on owning manufacturing facilities and be more willing to use outside processors to produce the goods for them. Although this did not constitute a five-year business plan, Jerome felt he had enough to put together a set of guidelines for the new products program.

As a first step toward preparing some guidelines, Jerome decided to make a listing of the assets of Middle South. He ruled out any preemptive patents or technology. Middle South owned no patents and used technology that was common in the food business. A question in this area was Professor Hartman's technology. Although it was unlike anything that Jerome was aware of on the market at the moment and did seem attractive, some questions remained. How would the consumer react to products using this technology? Would Professor Hartman's technology be easily transferable to manufacturing? Also, how easily could Professor Hartman's cost figures be translated for his firm? Regardless, Professor Hartman's technology, he decided, should be considered a potential asset of Middle South.

He also decided to rule out a couple of other areas. Since he was familiar with his manufacturing operations, Jerome knew there was little under-utilized machinery and could see no economies of scale potentially available. Also, because he was familiar with the Middle South employees (many of whom he had known from boyhood), Jerome did not feel that any of them had specific skills appropriate to constitute an asset for new product development. Jerome reflected that this was an irony of Middle South's employment policy. Many of the managers and skilled workers had been with Middle South for most of their careers making a harmonious, well-oiled operation. It also made for a homogenious point of view and a Middle South way of doing things with very few outside ideas or different points of view.

Jerome further decided there were two other assets useful in developing the new product guidelines. First, there was the Middle South sales system, a small sales force which called on 47 brokers in the 30 states in which Middle South currently distributed its products. Second, although its products had never been advertised, Middle South did own two brands (Mother's Secret and Southern Delight) that seemed to have consumer respect and a fair level of awareness. He thus listed three corporate assets for his guidelines: (1) the distribution system; (2) a consumer franchise shown by the brands, Mother's Secret and Southern Delight; (3) with a cautionary note . . . Professor Hartman's process. Using these assets, Jerome put together the following guidelines for the new product development program at Middle South:

Financial/Marketing
► Any new products should have the potential for reaching a break-even sales volume by the 24th month after a full-scale introduction; a payback of no more than 36 months; and a return on investment of 10%.
► Manufacturing start-up costs should not exceed $100,000 if we have to use our own facilities. If we are to use an outside processing plant, there must be more than one available.

Marketing/Product
► The product should have no ingredients that might eventually become very difficult or costly to obtain.
► Any new product should have an estimated life cycle of a minimum of five years.
► New products using one of the current brands are preferable, but this is not a mandatory guideline.
► Any new product should have, as a minimum volume, a sales po-

tential of one case per store per month. (Jerome knew this was the industry's rule of thumb for maintaining distribution).

▶ The current distribution system of brokers and retailers must be used by the new product.

From these guidelines Jerome set the following objectives for the program:

1 We will develop a systematic approach toward the development of new products. This approach must contain provisions for (a) the generation of ideas; (b) the evaluation of these ideas as potential businesses; (c) the refinement of these ideas by consumers.

2 We will have one product ready for introduction into test markets within 18 months.

3 We will stagger our consumer research and product R&D so that we will be able to test market a new product on the average of every six months following the introduction indicated our first new product.

4 All new product development will fall within these agreed-to guidelines.

At this point Jerome, after interviewing several candidates for the job, decided to hire you. You accepted the Middle South offer, and assumed control of its new product development program, reporting directly to Jerome Jackson.

3 Organizing the Generation of New Product Concepts

At this point, we should take stock. First, we have an idea of how to set the stage for a new product development program; how to organize it; what the guidelines should be; what the objectives might be, and the like. Second, we have an idea about how to set up a system that will enable us to start with the guidelines/objectives and proceed logically, in a risk-reduction manner, to develop a product (or service) that we will ultimately market. This system was discussed in the previous chapter and with some modifications that reflect your special needs should be appropriate to your case.

The purpose of this chapter is to cover the next step—the preparations preceding new product concept generation.

CONVERTING THE GUIDELINES/OBJECTIVES INTO LANGUAGE APPROPRIATE FOR IDEATION

In Chapter 2 we discussed the setting of guidelines and objectives for a new product development program. Of course, these vary from firm to firm, but generally the guidelines include financial, marketing, and manufacturing constraints. The objectives use similar language: they cover the number of products to be produced through the year and the financial objectives that each new product must meet. This language is appropriate within the context of financial/marketing discussions that are the basis for setting corporate objectives, strategies, and allocating funds. It might be useful, at this point, to repeat the key guidelines and objectives from the Middle South Milling Company case as they were stated at the end of Chapter 2.

Guidelines

Financial/Marketing

▶ Any new products should have the potential to reach a breakeven sales volume by the 24th month after a full-scale introduction; a payback of no more than 36 months; and a return on investment of 10%

▶ Manufacturing start-up costs should not exceed $100,000 if we have to use our own facilities. If we are to use an outside processing plant, there must be more than one available.

Marketing/Product

▶ The product should have no ingredients that might eventually become very difficult or costly to obtain.

▶ Any new product should have an estimated life cycle of a minimum of five years.

▶ New products using one of the current brands are preferable, but this is not a mandatory guideline.

▶ Any new product should have, as a minimum volume, a sales potential of one case per store per month.

▶ The current distribution system of brokers and retailers must be used by the new product.

Objectives

▶ We will develop a systematic approach toward the development of new products. This approach must contain provisions for (a) the generation of ideas; (b) the evaluation of these ideas as potential businesses; and (c) the valuation and refinement of these ideas by the actual consumer.

▶ We will have one product ready for introduction into test markets within 18 months.

▶ We will stagger our consumer research and product R&D so that we will be able to test market a new product on the average of every six months following the introduction indicated the first new product.

If you took these guidelines and objectives and began to develop new product concepts, you probably would be able to begin working immediately—after all, even though this language is chiefly that of the finance/marketing man, it would be meaningful, and you would have some ideas already in mind about the kind of categories/products you wish to explore.

However, most likely you are involving other people, some of whom have very strong ideas about new products. These people may use an entirely different language than yours in your guidelines/objectives and, therefore, may not know exactly what you mean. Further, you probably will involve people from outside the firm and, whether they understand your business, they will still bring their perceptions to the situation. These may not coincide with yours. The point is that the language is too abstract—too open for interpretation. When you get down to developing new product concepts, you need to speak in concrete terms. However, you must avoid the danger of being so concrete that you allow no running room (we will discuss this a little later in the chapter); but be concrete in a directional way. In other words, show the direction and the area you would like to explore without being too specific about the nature of the explanation process, and without being too exact in defining specific end results. The following are some examples of language appropriate for ideation.

Aiming at Developing a Certain Kind of Product

By using this kind of direction, you show the kind of product that you would like to develop—but not its specific attributes. For example, you might aim at developing a shampoo, specifically designed for senior citizens. You would need to give more information, of course, but stating a direction this way should allow most of the people helping you sufficient latitude to play with things like the consumer end benefits, product form, and delivery system, to enable them to provide a wide spread of concepts. And yet, you are assured that the end result will be in the area in which you are interested.

Aiming at a Category

Using a category rather than a product allows for a wider spread of ideas. For example, if you are a company that markets mechanical office supplies—staplers, paper-cutters, punches, and the like, it would be appropriate to set as a direction "any type of electric/mechanical office equipment, not to include paper and writing instruments—for large and small offices and home use, with the product to retail between $2.00 and $14.95." Keep in mind that the broader the direction you give, the more you will receive some ideas that are unusable. This cannot be avoided and you should not worry about it. There is a certain waste in concept generation (and much that appears like waste early on really is not, but we will discuss this in more detail later), and you should accept it as a cost of doing business. You need to make sure that you have developed a large enough bank of ideas to ensure that you have, at the end, a number that are on target. Again, we will investigate this area later in the chapter.

The Use of a Technology

Use of technology usually occurs after a laboratory discovery. When a technological discovery is made, it is usually impossible to decide whether it is commercially feasible without first deciding what it might look like in a saleable form, or what its market might be. Therefore, the next step is to convert it into new product concepts. You then can compare them (using your business analysis system that you will develop later) to existing markets. It may be that once you have developed the new product concepts, you will find that no known market for these is in existence. At that point, you must move to some kind of consumer research to judge the commercial viability.

An example of this might be the discovery by a pharmaceutical firm of a chemical that inhibits the growth of mold. Immediately a number of possibilities come to mind: protection of carpeting; protection or lengthening the life of grain in storage; protecting growing plants. You might even reverse your chain of thought and consider the development of a very durable mold that would act as a roofing material. Your discovery would be used to keep it from spreading off the roof into other areas. Regardless of what direction you take, the idea just sits there until you can develop concepts that use it.

Aiming at Providing a Specific End Benefit

You can aim at providing your customers with a specific end benefit. Very often, this is done within the text of a specific product category (you would like to develop a shoe polish product that is easier to use than anything on the marketplace today: it will allow the completion of the entire shoepolishing task in less than 60 seconds). But this does not have to be the case. For example, a bank might be looking for ways to provide its customers a greater security, using any of its services (or really, products). In this case, the direction of the concept generation might be as follows: any device, process, or service that will provide our customers with a greater security, including credit cards, checking accounts and time deposit accounts.

The Use of an Asset

You will remember from our previous chapter when we talked about assets from the new product developer's point of view we included things such as expertise in a channel of distribution, or a brand name that has high consumer recognition, in addition to items that might more normally be considered assets such as machinery, and the like. It is commonly the case that a concept project aims at using one or more of these assets, and this is the stated objective of the project. For example:

- ► We will develop a group of new product concepts that take advantage of our resources and expertise in paper-making technology.
- ► We will develop a group of new product concepts that are based on the positioning of our brand "X" which will help us expand our franchise in the area of industrial cleaning/light maintenance products.
- ► We will develop a group of new product concepts that will be sold through mass-merchandising and that use our current distribution system of selling through registered representatives to mass merchandisers.

This will give you an idea of how you might translate objectives into language useful for developing a group of ideas. In practice, it is quite normal to use several of these to set the parameters for technology, channels of distribution, and product category in order to obtain the kinds of new product concepts that you are looking for.

Again, I must remind you that it is better not to set the parameters too tightly, because ideas that are just a little bit too much off target can often be reworked and become useful. This is merely another step at a later stage.

DEFINING THE COMPETITIVE ENVIRONMENT AND UNDERSTANDING YOUR POTENTIAL CUSTOMER

Before beginning the concept generation process, it is necessary to make a complete review of all data available about the kinds of products you are interested in developing. Generally, this data will be one of three types:

1 Secondary data.
2 Primary data owned by the firm.
3 New primary data.

Secondary Data

In most industries, a good deal of secondary data is available, although some industries are much better reported on than others. Regardless, it will not be very much trouble to find out in a very short time what is available. The places you should look are:

1 *Industry Publications.* Almost every industry has a number of publications that serve it. Typically, they specialize in that some tend to be concerned with manufacturers' points of view, and others with the point of view of suppliers or people in the channel of distribution. These publications are often very useful in that they report trends, or sometimes report sales figures, etc. But do not limit yourself to the published data. Make it a point of talking to the editorial staff. If has been my experience that very often they have a great deal of data available that they have not reported.

2 *Advertising Agency.* Most advertising agencies keep information files that relate to their client's activities. Most larger ones contain a library in which a wealth of data on business is filed away. It is a good

start to let your agency know immediately of your needs so they can be most helpful. You may be in a situation where you do not have an advertising agency relationship, or yours does not contain such an information source. In these cases it is very often possible to buy the kind of data you need from larger agencies by contacting the correct person at that agency. I would start with the very large first, because the larger agencies are generally better equipped in the information-gathering area.

3 *Government Data.* The U.S. Government publishes data on various industries. In some industries it is the prime source of information. The best place to start is the public library. If this is no help to you, you should write to the U.S. Department of Commerce and state your needs. Also, in some cities, there are government offices where you can ask for information.

4 *Internal Sources.* It is likely that your firm already contains a great deal of data. It may be in a company library; or it may be information that people are carrying around in their heads. If it is the latter, you have to be careful that you separate facts from personal opinions, since anyone working in an industry for a period of time quickly forms opinions on what is important, what the trends are, and so forth. Often, people carry around data in their heads in the form that is useful to them (for example, the people who see trends from their point of view). Therefore, you will need to translate it into the language of the new product developer. Regardless of the potential problems, internal sources cannot be overlooked. If you talk to enough people, you should be able to get a composite picture that will be helpful to you.

5 *Professional Firms.* There are a number of professional information firms. One that I am aware of in New York City is FIND. Another is The New York Times. These firms either gather data and keep a large amount on hand, or know where the kind of data you wish is available (if available at all). In addition to gathering data, they will also prepare reports for you which summarize the data they have gathered. Working with these firms can be expensive. Some work on a flat-rate basis. Some prefer a contract that gives you the right to tap their resources a certain number of times in a given period. Before you make a commitment, you should check out more than one, because the cost of data can vary quite a bit. The quality can too. Make sure you are comfortable with the expertise of the firm before you deal with them, because thoroughness is necessary in this area. But if you do not have access to the information gathered by a large advertising agency, or do not have your own company library, these kinds of firms represent the best single source of data available to you and are almost always worth the

fee that they charge. They can provide you with a reasonably thorough search within a short period of time.

Primary Data Owned by the Firm

Very often your firm will have done research about its markets. In some industries this can involve a wide range of research. For example, in the food industry you might find that there is retail movement data (for example, Nielsen's measurement of sales through retail stores); usage and demographic studies (the kinds of people who consume the product; how they consume it; when and how often they consume it, etc.); consumer attitude data; tests of advertising and promotion, and the like. From this kind of data you can synthesize and provide the people who will help you develop your new product concepts with a great deal of information on trends, consumer preferences and attitudes, and so forth.

On the other hand, it is not uncommon for the new products developer to lack this kind of information. Some firms have not acquired this kind of data. Or, the task the new product developer is facing is much different from the area(s) in which the firm currently works. In this case, the new product developer must acquire relevant secondary data, or he must develop his own primary data—or perhaps may have to do without any at this point. Frankly, the last two situations are the most common.

Developing the Appropriate Primary Data

Developing your own primary data should be no problem and need not be expensive in time and money. In industrial products it is possible to generate good data by interviewing a small number of customers, as few as 20 or 30, but this will vary depending on the size of the market (usually in terms of decision-makers). For consumer products it is usual to run personal interviews or focus groups during which consumers are asked to discuss the kinds of products they are currently using; what problems they have had; what improvement they might like; and, most importantly, the framework (attitude, product's attributes, etc.) in which the whole product category exists in their mind.

The specific research techniques are not important here, because your market research people will be able to help you to set up the proper research, and analyze the data. What is important, though, is that you are very careful to define the kind of information that you want ahead of time.

The kind of information you will want will vary from industry to industry and problem to problem—but only slightly, because there is a similarity that I believe extends across practically every situation. What you need are answers to questions like:

How do people see the products currently in the marketplace? . . . . What brands are they aware of? . . . . What brands have they tried? . . . . What brands do they currently use? . . . . How do they use these brands in terms of time of day? . . . . Time of year? . . . . Usage occasion? . . . . Are these brands used in more than one way? . . . . What attitude do they have toward products in this category? . . . . What product attributes are important for the brand they use most often? . . . . What attributes are important for other brands they are aware of? . . . . For brands that they tried? . . . . Why did they reject them? . . . . How do they think they go about deciding which one to purchase? . . . . Who in the family actually makes the decision to buy products of this kind? . . . . Who in the family will make most use of the product? . . . . What improvements should be made in current products?

All of the above will give you an idea of the information you should gather. When you are done, provided the work is done properly, you should have a fairly complete idea of how your potential customers feel about the marketplace. Of course, if you are dealing with a product that is still new, then what you need is to question consumers about products for which they will substitute your new product. This makes it a little more difficult to get the kind of information that will give you a "perceptual framework," but it is still a far distance from starting with nothing.

Once this information is gathered, you then need to synthesize it into a presentation for those who will do your new product concept generation for you. Ideally, the information should be delivered to them in a terse enough form so that they can absorb it and refer to it often without becoming immersed in the details. My favorite way of doing this is to prepare a presentation of about 30 minutes on the results of the research with a small document that summarizes these points. That way, they can refer to the document often and, in doing so, evoke more detailed memories from the presentation.

I must caution you here that you should not expect new product ideas to come from this piece of research. On occasion they do. More often some strong hints are given that lead you down some solid paths —and that is the purpose of research. But actual new product concepts almost never will come from this step. The people you are talking with are not trained to think in terms of new product concepts. For most, what you are asking them about is only one small part of their life or daily work experience. Very often, the product is purchased or used infrequently, perhaps as little as once every three or four years—or even longer. They do not have proper (mind) awareness of the product or of the category or of the attributes of this product. Therefore, you must not expect (in addition to having to do a lot of probing during this first stage) that people will be telling you how to create the next good new product or category. It may happen, but it is unlikely.

Of course, there is always the situation in which you have no data and for some reason are unable to obtain any primary data. In this case, my advice is that you should use what I call the combined best guesses system. In the combined best guesses system you need to assemble the opinions of a number of people in the firm who you consider to be knowledgeable about the market and the problem you are facing. Ask them to play the role of the customer (this is best done in small groups, since people in large groups from the same firm are very often unwilling to make what they feel are wild guesses). Once you have done this, then assemble the data as if you had interviewed your actual potential customers. My experience is that this data can be very good. After all, you are dealing with people who supposedly have had experience with the product and the market for a number of years and have ingested a good deal of data about it. In fact, what they are giving you is their synthesis of probably quite a few experiences with the area.

There are only two problems with this approach. First, it may be that the market you are exploring is so far away from your firm's efforts that these people may have only the vaguest idea about the products and market at which you are aiming new product concepts. Second, it is possible that people working in a firm for a number of years have developed fairly strong biases about the firm's markets, its products, and its competitors. Therefore, you have to exercise judgment in interpreting their responses. All this aside, it still can produce useful data and, formally or informally, is a very worthwhile step at this point.

SOURCES OF IDEAS FOR NEW PRODUCTS

The following is a listing of sources for new product ideas. Generally, you are going to have to develop your own portfolio of new product concepts. The next chapter is about this process. However, before we get into techniques for generating new product concepts, we should look at a list showing the sources of ideas for new products. I will differentiate between a concept (which is a well-formed thought for a new product, including a reasonable description of what it would look like and how it would act), from an idea (which is simpler and is usually not much more than a bare-bones thought about a possible new product). Some good sources of new product ideas are:

Advertising Agencies

Generally, the advertising agency is staffed by persons who are trained to see things in an innovative way. Very often they will have suggestions for improvement or modification of your current product. Just ask. Given proper direction, they are also a good source of new product ideas. This is a resource that you should never overlook.

Consumer Research

Occasionally, when you are doing some pre-concept generation research, someone will come up with a new product idea. Also, sometimes when you are doing other kinds of consumer research, a consumer may suggest an improvement in a product or new product for your company. You should alert your Market Research Department to your interest in these kinds of ideas and periodically ask them if they are engaged in projects that might generate these ideas, or which might be modified to increase the probability of an idea.

Your R&D Department

The R&D Department is a rich source of ideas. To begin with, they often have potential suppliers talking to them about new technological developments, and the like. Also in the process of their normal R&D

efforts, they will come across ideas or developments that you will find useful. It is necessary for you to establish a strong liaison with this department. You should be frank with them about the goals of your program and the direction that you are taking, and ask them to forward any ideas or pieces of data that seem relevant.

Firms Specializing in Creating New Product Concepts

There are a number of firms that specialize in creating new product concepts. These firms span a wide range of techniques and philosophies (and costs, too). It is useful, therefore, to interview several before you decide to use one. You can obtain the names of some responsible firms through your advertising agency or through other new product development practitioners. Generally these firms have some new business development program and your fellow practitioners will have heard of several of them. Later in this chapter we will cover, briefly, some criteria you should use in selecting these firms.

The Company's Marketing Department

Alert all members of the Marketing Department to your program's aims and the kind of new products that you are interested in. This has two advantages. Many marketing people are innovative and will often have a whole host of ideas for new products that they have been tucking away. Further, once they understand your needs, they will help you keep track of potential competition by telling you of rumored or actual products that have entered the marketplace. This is a particularly important area, so that you should plan to periodically update everyone in the Marketing Department on the status of your projects.

R&D Consultants

Most industries have outside firms that will do R&D work. Often these firms independently produce a new product and then attempt to sell it. They may approach your own R&D Department, and you should let it be known that you are receptive to new ideas. But it does little good to actively solicit these firms. Their new products are usually the result of experimentation. You would not want them working with the thought of selling the product to you at the end. Therefore, letting your R&D

people, and those in the industry, know that you are receptive to ideas, is an excellent course of action.

Customers and Other Outside Individuals

It is not uncommon for customers to mail in ideas on product improvements, and for outside individuals to submit new product ideas to your firm. It is probable that your firm has a method of handling those already because of the legal implications. Generally my experience has been that few, if any, worthwhile ideas ever come in this way. There is just too much working against these ideas. Further, acknowledgment of an acceptable idea leaves you open to legal action. Discuss this with your legal department. It is usually best to have a formal system that tells the person submitting the idea that you cannot accept or consider his ideas (but thank them).

Selecting a New Products Consulting Firm

One good way to obtain new product ideas is through a professional new products consulting firm. Dealing with a firm like this can have a number of advantages. First, often you can effect cost savings. For many firms, the new products function is not a full-time function, and therefore employing someone in house with expertise in this area can be wasteful (this is particularly true if your new product problems are short-term).

A second advantage is the objectivity that a professional consulting firm can bring to your problem. The fact that your own people can sometimes be too close to the problem to be perfectly objective, will come as no surprise to you. A professional consulting firm, by viewing the situation from a detached and fresh viewpoint, can be most beneficial to your firm. When you hire such a firm, you are obtaining the benefit of many years of experience in the new product process, including work on many successful and unsuccessful new product ideas. Generally, you will find their judgment to be quite good—perhaps saving you from wasting time and money by pointing out hidden risks and assumptions, unanswered questions, and the like.

The third advantage is a wider range of imaginative ideas. If you select the company correctly, they should be quite skilled in the area of concept generation and concept refinement. As a rule, manufacturers do not keep experts in this field on their staff. Therefore an outside firm should not only be able to provide you with a wider range of imaginative new product concepts than you could generate internally, but also be better able to assess these concepts as business propositions than you can. (If they cannot, you have selected the wrong firm.) A final advantage of dealing with new products consultants is their range of contacts. A firm that has been in business for a number of years should have a good grasp of what the industry is doing and what the trends are. They can often suggest an acquisition or the purchase of a brand from another company. They can obtain data from the industry with anonymity, thereby protecting your own firm from exposing its area of interest, perhaps, even its new product development thrust. Although this advantage is not necessarily the reason you would select a new products consultant, if you establish a relationship over a period of time, you have every right to expect this kind of help. The good firms will provide it.

Selection Criteria

Selecting the proper consulting firm is an important decision. Although many of these decisions are based on "chemistry," let me suggest the following criteria by which you can at least narrow your list to a few acceptable choices. "Chemistry" is probably as good a way as any in making the ultimate decision.

1 First you should look at the number of years they have been in business. New products consulting firms often start up when people are between jobs. They last only as long as it takes to find another position. The firm should have been in business for at least three years, but 5 or 10 years will give you a higher level of assurance.

2 You should look at their client list. This includes (a) the quality of the clients, (b) the amount of time the client has been with the consulting firm, and (c) if the firm works on a project basis—how many times each client has been a repeat customer.

3 You should analyze the qualifications of the principals of the consulting firms and particularly of the people who will be assigned to your project.

4 You should ask for a written proposal and then, on the basis of the proposal, judge whether the consulting firm appears to understand your problem and whether their method of attacking the problem seems to be appropriate and sufficiently sophisticated for you.

5 The cost of the project is always a criterion. View it as important but not the sole basis on which the sorting among alternate firms is done.

6 After completion of a project you will often require some additional time from the consulting firm to help you interpret the project results and plan the next steps. Make sure that the firm has made provisions in its proposal for this, or, that you can obtain this help separately, and for a predetermined price.

Once you have determined this, it should be no problem to find a group of firms (through friends, contacts, etc.) that you can review. But before you start this process, make sure your whole development team is in agreement with your evaluation system—they all must accept the work of the firm you select.

Keep in mind that many of these firms are specialists. Some specialize in an industry. Others specialize in a function (concept development, concept research, product development, advertising development, etc.). Make sure that you define your problem ahead of time to find the firms that seem to be best suited for your need.

At this point, you should have a good understanding of the problems of concept generation and how these problems can be solved. Obviously, the area is a bit complex, but it need not be extremely complicated. There are many times you'll require the services of experts. However, there are times when you will want to do the work yourself—including the actual concept generation. The next chapter will introduce you to some creativity tools that will prove beneficial to you in this process.

CASE.   THE MIDDLE SOUTH MILLING COMPANY— GENERATING NEW PRODUCT CONCEPTS

Upon assuming the position of Manager of New Products of Middle South, you realized that Jerome has set the stage for you to do some very interesting work. You find yourself in agreement (with one reservation) with his definition of the assets of the corporation and, further, find the objectives and guidelines to be reasonable and sufficiently ambitious. The reservation you have is with his viewpoint of Professor Hartman's work. Although Jerome has been cautiously optimistic, your assessment is that Professor Hartman's work is solidly based and represents an opportunity for Middle South to tap segments of certain markets that it has not tapped or has serviced at a low level. You decide that the first step is to get a better fix on the feasibility of Professor Hartman's discovery. Obviously, doing this requires technological expertise in addition to expertise in commodity forecasting and pricing. You recommend to Jerome that a consulting firm be employed to conduct a research project with the following objectives:

1 Double-check Professor Hartman's work to make sure that his processes really can be converted into manufacturable new products.
2 Provide a preliminary economic forecast for the necessary manufacturing machinery, and ascertain the availability of outside contract packers that already have machinery of this type.
3 Forecast, for the next 5 years, the price of wheat and soybeans.

The cost of the project is $20,000 ($10,000 per month), and Jerome gave you the green light, agreeing that, if Professor Hartman's work is as solidly based as it would seem, it represents a special asset that might give Middle South an advantage in new product development.

At the end of two months, the consulting firm issues a favorable report. The machinery required for implementing of Professor Hartman's process is relatively common in the food industry, and a number of contract packers are available. The purchase of machinery, either new or used, is also possible, but is not recommended as being necessary initially. Further, the consulting firm states that it could find no problems with Professor Hartman's work. Indeed, they state that the work was above average for product development. Forecasts for wheat and soybean prices showed no specific cause for concern. On the basis of this report, Middle South entered into an agreement with Professor Hartman and the University.

While this was going on, you prepared to take the next step. You realized that you needed a portfolio of new product concepts for the next few years. To obtain this, you know that you would have to go to an outside new products development firm. You also know that this requires two steps: first you have to select the firm; second you have to be prepared to provide them with directions in a language that would enable them to do their best job.

Deciding that professional recommendations would be the best way to construct a list of potential consulting firms, you called three friends who were active in marketing products similar to those marketed by Middle South. From these friends, you obtained a list of potential consulting firms and, based on their comments, narrowed this list down to three.

After interviewing the three, all of whom seemed to meet your criterion of having been in business for more than 5 years, and for having obtained repeat business from their clients, you decided to recommend the use of Ryan & Ross (called by its principals, "R&R"). In explaining your rationale to Jerome, you state that the selection of R&R was based on three factors: (1) R&R had a disciplined philosophy; (2) they had a successful track record in developing imaginative new product concepts; and (3) they seemed to have expertise in the market research and consumer research areas.

The other two firms differed a lot from R&R. Alfred Jones, Ltd., also a viable alternative, leaned more toward the traditional consulting role. This involved setting up systems, making sure the objectives and controls were correct, and so forth. Although you viewed this as a valuable asset, it seemed that Jerome had already made some good strides in this direction. The third group, New Products Design, seemed to have more of an advertising orientation. They appeared to be quite good in the area of concept generation, and particularly in the translation of a concept into finished advertising. However, they seemed to have no established philosophy or concept research, and you viewed this as a potential problem, since Middle South had no internal facilities in this area. For these reasons, you and Jerome decided that R&R represented the best alternative and made appropriate arrangements to work with them.

While the selection process was going on, you decided that, in this instance, the best specific directions to give to the consulting firm would be product categories in which you wanted your new product work to concentrate. These categories would have to represent reasonable sales growth (at least 3–5% per year for the last five years on the average), and would have to be large enough to assume that there were market segments that might not be fully tapped. Further, they would be categories in which Professor Hartman's discovery could be applicable. This way, you reasoned, you might be able to start with a special advantage, Professor Hartman's work, and convert it into a product concept that would represent viable economic opportunities. You selected on these bases the following four categories:

1 Cereals
2 Powdered Drinks
3 Cookies
4 Snacks

The concept generation project at R&R took five weeks to reach the first checkpoint. To start the process you reviewed the objectives of the program and the guidelines with R&R. You specified, however, that R&R should not be too concerned with the specifics because a solid idea should come first. If the idea did not meet all the objectives, there might be a way of changing it to meet the program objectives and still represent a solid opportunity. You also indicated that the four categories should represent 90% of their work (10% could be "blue sky"). As a third constraint, you required that at least half the ideas should take advantage of Professor Hartman's work (and to this point arranged for them to visit Professor Hartman in his laboratory).

At the end of the fifth week, R&R invited you for a preliminary review session. During this time period, you were exposed to 143 ideas in rough (a few sentences) form. Making a few broad guesses about feasibility, and using the combined best judgments as to whether it seemed like a fairly good idea, the group reduced this figure to 82 concepts as follows:

Cereal	24
Powdered Beverages	17
Cookies/Desserts	19
Snacks	18
Remaining	4

R&R agreed to put each of these 82 concepts into a single paragraph. This paragraph would state what they felt the consumer benefit of the product was and what it looked like. These were to be reviewed by Middle South management.

Jerome agreed that a decision had to be made: 82 concepts was far too many to be researched with the consumer. Further, you both agreed that further culling would undoubtedly involve a great deal of personal subjectivity. Therefore, it was agreed to use R&R's system for evaluating concepts as potential business propositions. You agreed that this would reduce the concepts to a more manageable number and, further, should point the way to the better economic opportunities. As preparation for this task, you began to gather economic data for the categories involved, and requested that Professor Hartman spend a day with you reviewing the feasibility of the concepts from a technical standpoint, and also to help you make some estimates as to the cost of goods.

4 Generating New Product Concepts

Any new product that is brought to the marketplace has been through a series of evaluations and refinements. The better the initial idea, the greater the likelihood of a successful new product. Of course, if you can deal with many concepts at the same time, the probability of a successful outcome will increase.

This is why new product developers see themselves as portfolio (of new product concepts) managers. Since our basic philosophy is providing investment alternatives, it is useful to think of your group of new product concepts as a portfolio of potential investments. You'll agree that any stock portfolio is the result of many high-quality ideas. In this chapter, we will investigate some methods for generating high-quality new product concepts.

PUTTING TOGETHER YOUR OWN CONCEPT PORTFOLIO—SOME RULES

When you put together a concept portfolio or bank of ideas, there are a few rules that I have evolved. I use the word rules with caution, because they are not laws. Rather, they are rules of thumb evolved over time and tested in my mind by project after project. I am satisfied that they are true more often than not. Like most rules in the social sciences, there are exceptions to them.

1 The more ideas you start with, the better will be the final concept(s). What this means is that if you start with 100 ideas, your chances of winding up with a single good one are better than if you

54

start with one. After all, with 100 ideas, once you have had a chance to reflect on them, perhaps expose them to consumers and do some refinement, you can make improvements on them based on your knowledge and any consumer data that you might have, and then build on them by thinking of how they might be improved or strengthened. In other words, you get the pick of the litter. I do not mean to imply that if someone comes up with an idea that seems good that you should reject it or minimize its importance. What I am saying, though, is that by working with one, or a small number, of ideas early in the process, you may not be working with a really strong idea, and you take a chance that you will lose the idea later because of other constraints. Let me suggest a rule of thumb to you: if you start with 100 rough ideas, you should be able to come up with 25 that seem acceptable after you apply your business analysis system. From there, you should wind up with three to five concepts that represent potential good businesses when you finish the quantification stage.

It is my opinion that the violation of this rule is one of the biggest causes of problems with new product programs. There seems to be a good many firms that get caught in the trap of working with three or four ideas—having started with five or six, and then picking the three best through some consumer research technique. Quite often, the six ideas are chosen because the firm was certain they could produce the product, not necessarily because they were the best consumer ideas. The scene is set for something less than optimum results in a new product development program.

Remember that in product development, just like in mathematics, there is a law of large numbers. You must start with a group of concepts significantly larger than the number you ultimately would like to develop and ultimately market. Starting with a few puts severe limitations on your efforts in the very beginning—limitations that are almost impossible to overcome later in the process.

2 It is not advisable to count on consumer research for the generation of ideas. The people you will be dealing with will probably not view the area as seriously as you because it represents a small, and insignificant part of their life. You should utilize these people for the evaluation and refinement of concepts later on—but you cannot count on them for the generation, and you should not make this an integral part of your system for developing a bank of ideas.

3 Do not set the parameters too tightly. Aim at providing guidance, direction, and certainly the outside limits of useable ideas. But avoid the tendency to set tight parameters so that you wind up with the great idea at the end of the first part of the idea-making process. The great

idea will evolve later, after feedback from consumers and additional massaging of the concept. At first, your job is to provide data and guidelines that give direction but that do not unnecessarily bind the hands of the people that are doing your work.

GENERATING A PORTFOLIO OF NEW PRODUCT IDEAS: THE PROBLEM WITH STRAIGHT LINE THINKING . . .

From childhood we are trained to solve problems in a logical manner. For most of us this results in a propensity for straight line thinking. In straight line thinking, we usually go through the following steps:[1]

Step	Process
1 Orientation	Problem Definition
2 Preparation	Gathering Material
3 Analysis	Breaking Down Material
4 Hypothesis	Idea Making
5 Incubation	Inviting Illumination
6 Synthesis	Putting Pieces Together
7 Verification	Evaluation

As you read this, you undoubtedly said to yourself, "Yes, that is pretty much how I go about solving problems." And this is fine because most of our life we are in problem-solving situations. This can involve our work (e.g. how best to handle certain kinds of paperwork at the office) or our personal life (which car to buy, or how best to make a make-shift repair of something that is broken in the home until you can get professional help). It will sound like heresy, but under these conditions it is not necessary to be overly creative in your solutions. What is necessary is that the solution is logical, that you can arrive at it quickly, and that is it do-able. This brings to mind the old bromide often used by people in concept generation that, when you are driving down the street and see a red traffic light hanging above your lane, it is not necessary to go

---

[1]This is sometimes referred to as historical method. A number of thinkers who have tried to discern and understand the steps of historical method have put together the sequence that more or less is the same as the one that follows. This particular method, if my memory serves me correctly, was put together by Alex Osborne of my alma mater, BBD&O.

through all the things that a red light means, or the alternative ways of hanging lights above streets, or . . . what your mind needs to do is to go quickly to the meaning of that traffic light and to indicate to your body the necessary reaction to it.

Developing a bank of new product concepts (or looking for creative solutions to any kind of problems, for that matter) is a whole different kind of problem. Here, the historical method of thinking can present a problem. Using it will result in a lot of solutions that are not terribly creative.

My favorite example is a meeting that I attended the objective of which was to look for new uses for a chemical product that had been in existence and had been sold for a couple of years. As a warm-up, we began talking about the problems that are involved with cigarette ashes. The discussion went quickly to the point that an ashtray was an unsightly item when it was full, was messy, and possibly often unhealthy, since it often resulted in ash particles scattered in the air and inhaled. The problem as we stated it was, "What is a better way to handle cigarette ashes?" For about ten straight minutes all the conversation revolved around receptacles—really ashtrays, which we already had. Now some of them were more clever in that they had self-closing tops, or were small pocket-type items that you would carry away with you and empty in your office or in the lavatory—any one of a number of similar solutions. But the point was that all we were doing was redesigning the ashtray. At that point I suggested that we spend some time looking at the problem of cigarette ash disposal from different points of view. How are substances disposed of by nature was one tack that we took. We went through the various ways nature disposed of a thing. For examples: How does nature dispose of the carbon dioxide generated by animal breathing? How does nature dispose of the excrement from animal metabolism? I will not get into the details here, because we will see how this works in a later example. But we eventually were able to come up with a whole host of alternative approaches for handling the disposal of cigarette ashes.

The point here is simple. The straight line method of thinking is fine for solving problems in your daily life. It can also result in new product concepts. But you cannot depend on it for the sole support in your idea process. You must go beyond it and use tools to free the thinking of the people you are working with to obtain some truly innovative concepts.

A TOOL KIT FOR ASSISTING IN CONCEPT GENERATION

Before we get to discuss the creativity tools, it is necessary to discuss the rules of brainstorming.[2] It is necessary to discuss this topic before we touch on any specific creativity tools because brainstorming is the setting in which we are best able to make use of the creativity tools. In itself, it is not a special technique but a special atmosphere that encourages the application of the principles and the techniques . . . of conceptual ideas. Brainstorming, with any of the creativity tools to be discussed later, can be done either within the context of the group, or by oneself. In this book we will speak always of use within the group, but, with very little imagination, you can make the translation for individual use. Basically, brainstorming is a free-wheeling situation in which the participants feel free to say anything that comes to their mind with even the vaguest relation to the problem being discussed. This does not mean that brainstorming is an out-of-hand situation—actually, in some ways, it is tightly controlled. What it does mean is that most of the constraints of normal group work are relaxed. Basically, some important facets of brainstorming are:

1 *The need for a Leader or Moderator.*[3] It is important in a brainstorming session that someone takes charge. This person needs to make sure that the problem is defined and that the relative information is disseminated. Also to make sure that the rules of brainstorming are followed and that the group generally keeps moving toward the areas of interest. The moderator should view this rule very loosely. He should not impose his views on the group, nor constrain the activity too much. Rather, he should assume the role of a benevolent leader and the jealous protector of the right of strange ideas to exist.

2 *Definition of Problem.* It is important in a brainstorming session that (a) everyone have an idea of the problem to be discussed and (b) everyone has an adequate grasp of the information that is generally available. In some way, both these functions must be fulfilled or arranged for by the moderator.

3 *Size of Group.* Generally, brainstorming requires a group of somewhere between 5 and 10 members. This gives everyone an adequate

---

[2]Brainstorming, to my knowledge, originated with Alex F. Osborn (*Applied Imagination*), New York: Charles Scribner's Sons, 1953.
[3]Later in this chapter, we shall see how someone trained in the synectics system handles a meeting whose objective is a creative solution to a problem.

chance to participate and to feel involved. Any more is very unwieldly. Less than five is usually inadequate because it puts too much pressure on the participants, although I have run brainstorming sessions with fewer people and, if they feel comfortable enough with one another and the idea of brainstorming, it can work.

4 *Openness to Ideas.* The most important thing about brainstorming is that the setting must be made so that every member feels perfectly able to say whatever he thinks might relevant to the issue(s). The moderator must maintain this right of each member and should make it clear ahead of time that this situation exists. "The brainstorming session provides a formal opportunity for people to make suggestions that they would not otherwise dare make for fear of being laughed at. In a brainstorming session, anything goes. No idea is too ridiculous to bring forward."[4]

5 *The Suspension of Judgment (the Avoidance of Criticism).* It is absolutely essential in brainstorming that no criticism of anyone's ideas be made. This is called suspension of judgment and is the most difficult for first-time brainstorming group members. The moderator must be cautious about comments that begin with any of the following:

"That would never work because . . ." "What would you do about . . ." "It is well-known that . . . ." "How would you get that to . . . ." "You are leaving out the vital points of consideration . . . ." "This is a silly, and impractical idea . . . ." "It wold be much too expensive . . . ." "No one would accept that . . . ." "We have tried that . . . ."

These are very natural comments, but if they are allowed, then the brainstorming session is useless. Not only is one forbidden to evaluate the ideas of others, but also his own ideas. It is the job of the moderator of the session to stop any attempt of evaluation. He must make this quite clear at the start of the session. After that, he need only say 'that is an evaluation' in order to put a stop to it.[5]

It is, however, possible to build on someone's ideas. By building on, you take someone's stated idea and, in your opinion, improve on it. In doing this, it is essential that you start by making one or two positive statements about the idea and then making whatever addition to it. For example, if someone has just put forth the idea of a pocket ashtray (the example we talked about a few minutes ago) that is: (a) disposable and

[4]Osborne
[5]*Ibid.*

(b) has a spring-loaded top so that the ashes do not fall out, you might say,

> "I like the idea that you can keep it in your pocket so that is it not necessary for people to come around and empty it, and that the spring-loaded top will keep ashes from flying around the room. I would like to build on that by suggesting a device that allows it to be attached to the wastepaper can as you leave your office and, when the can is emptied, the ashtray is automatically emptied also . . . when you return the next day, you can start using the same ashtray again and need not throw it away . . ."

Here, one person clearly took the idea of one of the group members and attempted to improve it (as he saw it). From his tone, and the fact that he pointed out some useful facets of this idea, he did not make that person feel that it was rejected. In fact, the opposite took place, and he felt the idea has some merit. The moderator should explain the idea of building on someone else's idea as the session starts.

6 *Challenging Assumption.* The moderator should make clear that every assumption implicit in the problem and the information given is challengeable. There are no sacred cows, and every member should feel very free to say why he feels uncomfortable with an idea and suggest modification.

7 *Cross-Stimulation.* An important facet of brainstorming is that people get a chance to see a problem from a new point of view. This new arrangement of information provokes some interesting effects. In a brainstorming session, the provocation is supplied by the ideas of others. Since such ideas come from another, it stimulates one's own ideas. (Building on). Even if one misunderstands the idea, it can still be a useful stimulus. It often happens that an idea may seem obvious and trivial to one person, and yet it can combine with someone else's ideas to produce something very original. In a brainstorming session, one gives stimulation to others and receives it from others. Because of the different people taking part, each tends to follow his own line of thought, and there is less danger of getting stuck with a particular way of looking at a situation. Although the ideas in a brainstorming session are related to the problem under discussion, they can still act as random stimuli.

The moderator should promote as much cross-stimulation as possible, asking one member to build on another's idea, or asking one member to follow the same train of thought (even if he must force himself to) that another has just started. Cross-stimulation is an essential ingredient is a brainstorming group.

8 *The Need for Creativity Tools in a Brainstorming Group.* Unless you are very fortunate, the brainstorming group will, on occasion, get stuck. It will not be able to proceed further, and no one will be satisfied with where it currently is. In this situation, the moderator can do one of two things. He can move back to an earlier phase and ask to develop ideas in a different direction. Or, he can use some game or creativity tools to stimulate the group to think in new areas. These tools are absolutely essential for the new product developer whether he's working by himself (to get a new or fresh look on a problem), or when he's running a brainstorming group.

The next part of this chapter is an attempt to give the reader an idea of what some of these tools are, and how they are used.

SOME CREATIVITY TOOLS THAT I'VE FOUND USEFUL

There are some tools that I prefer over others and use most of the time. If you experiment with them, you will soon find that you have preferences for some that just seem more "natural" than others. Where it is possible, I've indicated a source where you can read more about them.

Attribute Listing

An attribute listing is a technique in which you break down the product that you would like to improve or the new product that you would like to develop into its attributes. Then, you select one or several attributes, and the group develops new products or improves the current product by changing only these attributes (all others remain constant or disappear, if necessary). It allows some focusing without any real rigidity, and you will soon find groups are more able to handle one or a couple of areas than completely reformulating or changing a whole product. The following was written by John E. Arnold as an article in a book on creativity.[6] It takes a relatively simple item and breaks in into attributes with an eye toward changing one and improving the end product.

[6]John E. Arnold, "Useful Creative Techniques" in *A Source Book for Creative Thinking* by S. Parnes and H. Harding, Charles Scribner's Sons, New York, 1962.

As an example of attribute listing, one might take the old woodenhandle screwdriver of a few years back. These attributes are the descriptive phrases that would completely define the object under consideration, and are:

1 Round, steel shank.
2 Wooden handle riveted to it.
3 Wedge shaped end for engaging slot in screw.
4 Manually operated.
5 Torque provided by twisting action.

Now each one of these attributes has been changed, not once, but many times, and each change has supposedly resulted in a new and better screwdriver. The round shank was changed to a hex shank, so that a wrench could be used to increase the torque. The wooden handle has been replaced by a molded plastic handle, thereby cutting down on breakage and danger from electrical shock. The end has been modified to fit all kinds of screw heads. Pneumatic and electric power have been substituted for manual power, and the 'yankee' type driver provides torque by pushing.

Perhaps another example will help you understand this technique better. Let us assume that you are going to invent a new cereal. This cereal would be positioned as a light evening meal, or perhaps a late snack. Its target will be the general population currently consuming cereals that are often described as all-family cereals (such as Kellogg's Corn Flakes, Cheerios, etc.). You might make the following listing for cereals in general:

Attribute Listing—Cereals
Shape
Color
Size
Smell
Nutrition
Flavor
Price
Package
Texture

We see that we have a list with nine attributes. For an example, let's take three: size, nutrition, and smell. Now let's force ourselves to invent new products that are basically cereals, using only these three factors. The following are a couple that I made up as this chapter was being written:

1 A low-nutrition cereal (possibly with some cellulose) that would not be fattening, which has the smell of fruits, and which comes in nibble-size pieces so that you can eat it dry while you are watching T.V.

2 A cereal for dieters that represents a light evening meal. The pieces are big so that you can hold them in your hand, and eat them like a small sandwich alone with a glass of milk. (Or, you can put them in a bowl with milk.) The nutrition is high and complete so that even though you have not eaten properly during the day, this completes the nutrition that you require for a 24-hour period (of course, you should use skim milk). It is low in calories and has the smell of a bacon, lettuce and tomato sandwich. It's very chewy to give you the satisfaction of chewing and swallowing.

3 A cereal for people on a low meat and dairy diet (either for medical reasons or personal preferences). The pieces will be various sizes (not much different than cereal sizes now) and chewy. It will be low fiber—assuming that the fruits and vegetables that are forming the bulk of the people's diet are already giving them adequate fiber; it would be high in vitamins, particularly B, which you would normally get from dairy products; and it would have the smell of a cheeseburger.

These three ideas may or may not be attractive to you. They literally were the first three that came to my mind, as I forced myself to develop new products using just these three attributes. In the space of an hour, you or I, once we got our thinking freed, could probably develop 10 or 20 more like it. They would be of various levels of attractiveness, but they would be a start and we could use (probably by adding more attributes) many of them to create some fairly attractive concepts.

When you first try attribute listings, you might run into a problem. Basically, the problem is that you are too familiar with the subject. Mr. Arnold, in the same article, points out this danger.

In trying this technique out with various groups, I have discovered something that at first appears to be a strange phenomenon. The more familiar the members of the groups are with a certain product, the more difficult it is for them to agree on the basic attributes of that product. The group at the A.C. Spark Plug Division of General Motors, for example, had no difficulty in lisiting the attributes of a hammer or a bicycle, or still more complicated products, but they could come to no agreement on the basic attributes of a spark plug. A group of top designers from the Farrel-Birmingham Company, manufacturers of heavy machinery for the rubber and plastic industries, had no trouble with the spark plug, but failed to describe to the satisfaction of the majority the attributes or essential features of their Banbury Mixers which they had been designing, redesigning, and manufacturing for thirty or more years.

On second glance, this is not so strange, and it points to a danger that we are all susceptible to, but of which we are probably completely unaware. Familiarity need not breed contempt, but it certainly places things in the classification of 'obvious,' and from then on we can neglect questioning or observing them. At least it certainly has the effect of limiting the flexibility and originality of our thinking along certain lines. It establishes a very limited number of fixed approaches, and it prevents us from standing back and viewing the object in its entirety from new vantage points and in new lights. This is exactly in line with the statement that has been quoted many times that "it is only the amateur or tyro who invents anything; the expert knows too many reasons why something can't be done, so he never tries." [7]

Okay. Now one of the big problems with Attribute Listing is now known to you. The fact that it is obvious may not help you avoid it the first few times you use it, but with a little practice, you will. I think Attribute Listing is an absolutely brilliant creativity tool, and is one of my favorites.

Morphological Analysis

Another idea tool that I'm fond of is Morphological Analysis. It is, like Attribute Listing, another way of bringing together attributes that would not normally be related—and this new combination then allows you to think in previously unexplored areas.

Morphological Analysis, as described by Dr. Zwicky, is a very useful tool for organized creative activity. [8]

[7]Ibid.
[8]Ibid.

It replaces check lists and attribute listings, although both can probably be useful in setting up a Morphological Chart. The procedure is as follows: "The statement of the problem should be as broad and general as possible, and then all of the independent variables must be defined as broadly and completely as possible. Each one of these independent variables becomes an axis on the morphological chart, and if there are *n* independent variables, we will have a chart of *n* dimensions. Each of the independent variables can probably be expressed a number of different ways, and these are laid out with unit dimensions of each of the *n* axes.

This all can be best explained by following a simple example and developing a morphological chart for a problem that we have already mentioned, that of the Harvard Bridge Case.

Figure 4-1 shows this chart partially worked out. The statement of our problem will be as all-inclusive as possible, and we will list it as The Problem of Getting Something From One Place to Another Via A Powered Vehicle. Certainly, one of our independent variables would be the type of vehicle used and we could subdivide that into (1) some kind of cart, (2) some kind of a chair, (3) a sling, and (4) a bed (we could list many others, but this will be enough for our example). A second independent

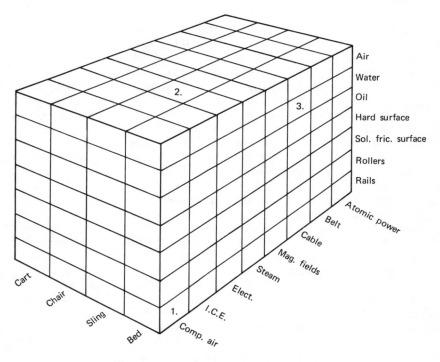

Figure 4-1   Morphological Analysis Grid

variable might be the media in which our vehicle operates, and here we might list air, water, oil, hard surface, rollers, rails, and a solid friction-less surface. A third independent variable would be the power source, and this could be broken down into compressed air, internal combustion engineer, electric motor, steam, magnetic fields, moving cables, moving belt, and atomic power.

Let us assume for the moment that these are the three independent variables that will completely describe some device for getting some-thing from one place to some place else. This may be an over-simplifica-tion but it helps make our chart-making much easier, for a three-dimen-sional body is easily visualized and sketched on a two-dimensional sheet. Our chart then becomes a three-dimensional body which can be thought of as a filing cabinet with drawers operating or opening in all three directions. The contents of each of these drawers will be defined by one of the variations of each of the three independent variables. Note the three drawers arbitrarily singled out on the chart. Drawer #1 is charac-terized by a bed-type vehicle, moving over rails, powered by compressed air. Drawer #2 would be a sling-type vehicle, moving through air and powered by electricity, and Drawer #3 would be a bed-type vehicle, moving through water and powered by a moving cable. With the subdivi-sions we have chosen for the three independent variables, we have con-structed a morphological chart that contains 224 drawers, which is more combinations than the average person could produce by any process of free association or than most groups could assemble by brainstorming. We could, of course, easily increase the number of variations along each axis and thereby greatly increase the possible number of combinations.

On opening up some of these drawers, we will find that they are filled with some already invented transportation device; for example, the cart-type vehicle, powered by an internal combustion engine and moving over a hard surface, is our automobile. A chart-type vehicle moving over rails and powered by electricity might be our street car or subway or electric locomotive. And the sling-type vehicle moving through air and powered by a moving cable would be a chair lift for a winter ski resort. However, the great majority of these drawers will be empty, mainly because the combinations themselves are absurd or impractical. (For example, a sling-type vehicle moving through oil, powered by a moving belt). But some of the drawers may be empty because no one has ever thought of combining the variables in just that fashion, or, if they had thought of it, their first reaction was to apply judicial thinking and be-cause the combination seemed silly, they gave it no serious considera-tion. While this chart provides you with a mechanical aid for listing alternate approaches for solving any specified problem, it will take a great deal of imagination to take the specifications for any given drawer and work them into a worthwhile, practical, economical solution to the problem of getting people across Harvard Bridge safely and comfortably. It will also require a great deal of daring and a great deal of persistence.

The aim, of course, should be to come up with the best possible solution, not just something different.

One more word about morphological analysis—should you find as you go through the drawers in your n dimensional model that some of the drawers contain two or more quite distinct solutions, you will have a clue that you had not chosen enough independent variables. The feature that distinguishes the two solutions in one drawer will be a variation of the additional independent variable needed. The new model should be constructed with this new variable in mind. This morphological analysis is the most comprehensive way that I know of to list and examine all the possible combinations that might be useful in solving some given problem. I recommend it highly.

Let me give another example of how morphological analysis might be useful. Let's return to the cereal example. As you recall, we were trying to invent a cereal that could be used as a snack or light evening meal, and so forth. To make things simple, let's construct a two-dimensional morphological analysis grid with five end benefits (the satisfaction that the consumer receives by using the product) and five product attributes (see Figure 4-2).

As you can see, we've taken five product attributes . . .

Shape
Color
Size
Smell
Texture

and we selected five end benefits . . .

Nutrition
Flavor
Eat Wet or Dry
Easy to Digest or Eat
Nonfattening

Now, for the sake of an exercise, let's think of one new product idea for each of the blocks. The listing below is coded to match the number in

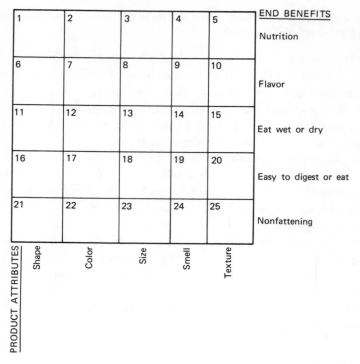

Figure 4-2

the upper left-hand corner of the block. For each number, the product attribute must be related to the end benefit in the concept.

1 Nuggets of hard whey (dairy protein) that you mix into other cereals. They add protein (Shape/Nutrition).

2 A multicolored cereal (because it is made with various fruit essences and colorings) that kids would eat as a dry snack after school (Color/Nutrition).

3 Slurpo—the nutritious cereal that is as big as a child's fist and which slurps up all the milk in the bowl—you can eat it like a dunked cookie (Size/Nutrition).

4 The cereal snack that smells like fresh vegetables. Made from cellulose, and high fiber grains, this cereal smells like fresh vegetables. It is shaped like a stick pretzel so that it can be used for dipping, and so forth (Smell/Nutrition).

5 This is a cereal that helps you keep your gums healthy. It is chewy, and it also helps to keep plaque from forming (Texture/Nutrition).

6 This is the fruit salad cereal. Different pieces look and taste like various fruits (Shape/Flavor).

7 This is a cereal that has very little color (it is almost transparent) and very little flavor. It can be added to other snacks, however, to add fiber, vitamins and the like, and, therefore, increase their food value (Color/Flavor).

8 This is a very concentrated cereal. It comes in nugget form. You add it to your regular cereal to give it a concentrated burst of taste (Size/Flavor).

9 The dessert cereal. It tastes and smells like chocolate-covered mints (Smell/Flavor).

10 This cereal is shaped like fruits and nuts. Each piece has the flavor and texture of the fruit or nut that it is supposed to be (Texture/Flavor).

You may have noticed some of these concepts are a little shallow. That's because we're working with a two-dimensional matrix. Later we'll try a three-dimensional matrix; normally this results in fuller concepts. We are really developing core ideas at this point. Later in the chapter, we'll show you how to build on a core idea and to change it and make it better.

11 Cereal nuts. They look like normal nuts (cashews, walnuts, etc.), but they are made from cereal protein. You can eat them wet or dry— they won't get soggy (Shape/Wet or Dry).

12 This is a cereal that changes (into fruit flavored) colors when you make it wet (Color/Wet or Dry).

13 This cereal comes in big chunks (like a chunk of caramel corn). You can eat it like a dry snack. But when you add milk, it becomes a thick stew-like cereal with chunks in it (Size/Wet or Dry).

14 This cereal has no smell when it is dry. You can carry it for lunch, and so forth. However, when you add orange juice, it becomes a fragrant dish that smells (and tastes) like fresh fruit salad (Smell/Wet or Dry).

15 A dry cereal that looks and smells (and it is moist) like cooked hamburger. It is good for snacking; to sprinkle into salads, and the like. (Texture/Wet or Dry).

16 This is a cereal that comes in a stick. It is an easy-to-eat snack (Shape/Easy to Digest or Eat).

17 This cereal consists of small, soft, easy-to-chew and digest pieces. It is easy to eat, and you can carry it for lunch, and so forth (Color/Easy to Digest or Eat).

18 This cereal consists of small, soft, easy to chew and digest pieces. Obviously, as in the use of some of the drawers of the previous example, this has already been invented, and a number of examples are on the marketplace (Size/Easy to Digest or Eat).

19 This is another problem drawer. At the moment, I can think of no cereal concept that relates smell and ease of digestion or eating (Smell/ Easy to Digest or Eat).

20 The cereal with four different textures. Some pieces are crisp; some are chewy; some are crunchy; some are soft, like marshmallows. It is easy to eat—you can eat it like a dry snack, or with milk (Texture/ Easy to Digest or Eat).

21 This cereal is a snack. It is meant to be eaten dry. The pieces have reminders on them—short sayings reinforcing weight-losing behavior. Of course, the cereal is low in calories itself (Shape/Nonfattening).

22 This is another problem drawer for me. I can't think of any cereal product relating the attributes and nonfattening (Color/Nonfattening).

23 This is the time-release cereal. It is composed of different sized pieces which also are digested at different rates. This means that the full feeling remains longer. As much as possible, this cereal is made of low-calorie materials (Size/Nonfattening).

24 The cereal is based on the fact that smell is a good part of the eating experience. This cereal (unlike most others) has an intense satisfying smell. You really feel as though you're eating something good and satisfying. It is nonfattening since you can get by with a smaller portion (Smell/Nonfattening).

25 This cereal is extremely chewy. You get so much satisfaction from chewing it, that you eat less than normal (Texture/Nonfattening).

At this point, we've gone through the grid and have a number of ideas. Frankly, none of these ideas are ready to be seriously considered as a new product concept. Later in the chapter, we'll finally take partial concepts and improve them. However, to take this exercise a little further, let's convert this cereal project into a three-dimensional grid (see Figure 4-3). We've worked so far with two interesting variables, product property and end benefit; let's add a third variable, means.

All right, let's begin to look at some of the drawers in this three-dimensional grid:

Drawer #1 is a cereal that's easy to digest or eat, which has some peculiarity about the size particle and which can be made of standard cereal grain. It's probably already invented. A great number of cereals, both hot and cold, that are on the market would fit this box.

Let's do one or two more to show you this technique more clearly. But, as an aside, you probably have noticed one of the problems in working with a three-dimensional grid—mainly that some drawers seem to be hidden from your eye because they are not on the surface (given the way you view the grid). For example, a cereal that was made at least in part of dairy protein that you could eat wet or dry, and that

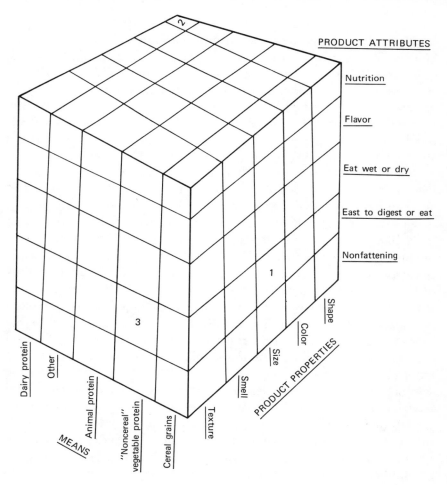

PRODUCT ATTRIBUTES

Nutrition

Flavor

Eat wet or dry

East to digest or eat

Nonfattening

Shape

Color

Size

Smell

Texture

PRODUCT PROPERTIES

Dairy protein

Other

Animal protein

"Noncereal" vegetable protein

Cereal grains

MEANS

Figure 4-3

had some peculiar smell property, would not be obvious to you the way this grid is drawn. It actually would be on the back-side of the grid. Regardless, once you see the attributes and properties and means, or whatever the three variables are that you are dealing with, you can still define the parameters of the concept that you want. You need not really see the drawer.

Let's go on to another example or two. To keep it obvious, we will use only those drawers that are on the surface and observe them from our perspective.

Drawer #2 is a cereal made out of (at least partially) dairy protein; it has nutrition as an important attribute, and it has shape as an important product property. Now let's think of a cereal that fulfills this requirement. Okay . . . one quickly comes to mind. This should be a freeze-dried yogurt with pieces of granola in it. It would come in sticks or bars, so that you could crumble them, put them in milk, have the yogurt reconstituted (to some degree), and then have a dish of reconstituted yogurt with pieces of granola in it. Or, you could use it in the stick form and carry it with you as a quick, nutritious snack.

Let's look at Drawer #3. This would be a product made out of vegetable protein; it would have some interesting texture properties and would be easy to digest or eat. Let's assume the vegetable protein is what we call a meat analog. By meat analog, we mean something that looks like meat, has many of the properties of meat, but is really made out of vegetable protein. There are a number of products in the marketplace today that are made of vegetable protein and meat analogs. One of the better known ones is produced by General Mills and is called BAC°OS®. It is a bacon analog. In this case, we might decide to make a Breakfast Stick. The Breakfast Stick would have vegetable protein that looks like bacon in it, and the rest of the stick might be a grain cereal that has the taste and texture of a whole wheat bread. Therefore, you would be able to have a bacon/whole wheat sandwich in the morning without frying the bacon, toasting the bread, or whatever. You could have it as a quick breakfast that would enable you to eat while you are getting dressed, shaving, preparing to leave home, or you could carry this with you. Again, we could go on and on. In each drawer we could create many ideas. You must now see that once you begin using the disciplined tools of creativity, a whole host of opportunities open to you. What has really happened is that you are no longer stuck with your old perceptions in your old cultural rut.

Let's discuss one other tool.

Synectics[9]

Putting Synectics third in a list of creativity tools is not at all fair. It is not fair for several reasons. First, it isn't a tool: it is a system for practicing creativity. Second, it is, in my opinion, far more important than any other tool in this section—as far as being useful goes.

But this was intentional. Synectics is much too broad a subject to be covered in the space we can allot for it. Therefore, I have limited this section to two areas:

1 An excerpt from an article by George M. Prince which succinctly covers running a meeting in which creativity will be important. In a palatable way, Mr. Prince provides you with some of the underpinnings of the Synectics System—displayed in a way that you can use in your next meeting.

2 A brief excursion into excursion techniques—which will provide you with a new tool or two.

To the first point, let's talk about chairing a meeting in which new product concepts are to be generated. The following is a portion of an article that appeared in the Harvard Business Review[10] by George Prince.

> To the interested observer, a meeting is a kind of fishbowl in which he can watch the birth and early development of an idea. A good many of the new ideas in business today are born in meetings; and as a member of a company whose main interest is the creative and inventive processes, I am associated with a group that has studied the dynamics of literally hundreds of meetings over the last eight years. Our usual practice is to tape-record the proceedings and then to replay the tapes to discover what has actually been said by each member of the meeting at various junctures, the tone of voice used, and the results that followed—in much the same way that a football coach studies motion pictures of his team's games and practices at slow projection speeds to analyze the team in action.
>
> Certain facts about meetings are obvious. Foremost, for my present purposes, the chairman of a meeting is its heart and will. His function

[9]Synectics Inc. is a Cambridge, Mass., consulting firm named after the system.
[10]"How to be a Better Meeting Chairman" by George M. Prince, *Harvard Business Review*, Jan.–Feb., 1969, page 68, Mr. Prince is President of Synectics, Inc. I spent one of the most delightful weeks of my life studying with them, and I recommend their courses to anyone interested in new product development.

and object is to run a productive operation; and to the extent that his group discusses what they are supposed to discuss and the extent that decisions are made and projects and deadlines are assigned to individuals and teams, the chairman is a successful leader.

Our experience indicates, however, that even the successful chairman usually has serious problems and deficiencies of which he is often unaware. Some of our observations on this point have been quite surprising and have made us question many of the assumptions commonly made about the proper role of the chair; and, taken as a whole, our observations strongly suggest that the chairman of a meeting must apply certain novel operating techniques if he wants the people he has gathered together to generate their full voltage. I shall try to show what these techniques are and how they can increase the productivity of the group.

Most of my company's research is done with businessmen. We observe meetings sometimes in company offices and sometimes in our Cambridge experimental environment; the environment seems to make little significant difference to behavior. Usually the group is working on an internal problem, one that is important to its company. Also, since we find seven to be the maximum number of people that can work together productively in a meeting, our work has for some time been limited to groups of seven people or fewer. It is the small business meeting, then, with which I shall be concerned.

FOUR MAJOR STUMBLING BLOCKS

First, meetings are often used very casually. In many cases there is only a vague notion about the objective of a meeting, and quite often objectives are mixed. This is likely to be true where the chairman wants to give information, get ideas, or see how members react to some ideas of his own. One of these objectives, clearly enough, is wrong in itself; but unless the chairman provides precise knowledge of what he expects, the members can easily become confused. An agenda alone does not solve this problem.

Second, meetings are frequently used to solve problems, to plan, and to help make decisions. Creativity is a vital component of such meetings because it develops alternatives, enriches possibilities, and projects consequences. There is evidence, however, that chairmen habitually, albeit unwittingly, discourage creativity and free speculation.

Third, the chairman is likely to use his power unwisely. He is often the senior member (the boss), and he therefore has influence that transcends the meeting. It is accepted practice for him to exercise this power and for other members to play to it. The consequence is that his prejudices can inhibit the open proposal of alternatives and new ideas.

Fourth, we find in almost any meeting that there is a high level of antagonism toward ideas. For example:

One participant (call him Mr. A) says, "I think it would be a good idea to shape our new dog food like a bone and make it chewier." A second objects, "But there is already a dog bone on the market. . . ." And a third adds, "And one of the strengths of the leading brand is that it's like hamburger—it's not chewy." And so on.

When ideas are subjected to this kind of exchange, their value and potential are easily destroyed. The ideas of a new shape and a new texture are at least worth exploring, since they suggest possibilities for alternative paths of development; but the negative reflex one customarily observes against a new idea foreshortens these possibilities. The negative reflex also has a further effect: the person who has advanced a new idea or suggestion is a human being, and as such he identifies with his own suggestion. He perceives a negative reflex response as a personal put-down.

In many circumstances Mr. A will be too mature and sophisticated an individual to acknowledge this attack, a fact which merely compounds the problem. We have asked many Mr. A's how they feel about such criticism, and most protest that the do not feel personally attacked. If you follow Mr. A on a tape recording, however, you will note that at the earliest opportunity he gives his critics as good as he got. Thus he himself contributes to the foreshortening effect. The extent and effects of this kind of early negative response are quite remarkable. Not the least remarkable aspect is that if a member is polite, his negativity is considered acceptable by all; it is considered part of the ordinary give-and-take of daily meeting life.

There are other stumbling blocks built into the traditional meeting, but the careful and conscientious chairman can reduce or eliminate all of them. His first step must be to recognize subtle destruction when it occurs; then he will know better how to use it to general advantage or to discourage it.

NEW FRONTIER FOR THE CHAIR

We have asked hundreds of chairmen of task-oriented meetings about the responsiveness of their groups. Their most common remarks are revealing: "It's hard work to get good suggestions from my people," or "I find that the group depends on me for most of the ideas." Our observations tell us that very few chairmen are able to recognize and sort out helpful responses from those that, in fact, are valueless, negative or damaging. This is true not because they are not capable of doing so but because they are not in the habit of doing so. This chairman usually does not realize that his role includes being a careful, judicious listener.

Furthermore, it appears that most of the time the leader does not appreciate the possibilities of his role. The traditional image of the strong chairman is that of an executive who guides the discussions, hews to an agenda, makes instant judgments of relevance and usefulness, and parcels out assignments. He has a general goal; namely, to get things done. He assumes that the present structure of the chair, agenda, and guided (or perhaps free-wheeling) discussion is an effective one, indeed, the *only one;* his assumptions on this score go by unexamined because things do get done and goals are accomplished. The result is that the old-fashioned chairman wastes talent, both his own and the group's, and therefore time and money as well.

The meeting that is "sabotaged" by the traditional image of the chair and its application has certain familiar symptoms: boredom and impatience, obviously, and more subtly, hostility and rivalry. Perhaps the worst symptom, as I have already suggested, is immediate negativity to new ideas and the consequent need to defend one's point of view and oneself; and the worst indictment of the traditional system is that negativity is commonly accepted as useful and realistic.

Our experiments with creative group leadership make it clear that the chairman can multiply the effectiveness of his people. To do so, however, he must adopt a nontraditional attitude. He must come to view himself as the servant of the group (in the same way that the group views itself as the servant or the objective of the meeting), and as such as he must devote his entire attention to helping the group use its wits. Later in this article I shall make a number of concrete suggestions as to how he can do this.

The Rotating Chair

There is quite a bit of evidence that the traditional chairman is self-serving and manipulative. For example, he is likely to see to it that his own ideas get special treatment, and usually he has developed a sensitive ear to responses that support his own preconceived notions. It is also quite clear that members recognize this, resent it, and struggle against it —sometimes openly, but more often subtly. When we have questioned participants about the behavior of the chairman in task meetings, common responses are: "He doesn't listen to my ideas," or, "I think I could run a better meeting than he does."

A habit of egocentricity in the chair severely limits the productivity of a meeting, and our recommendation is commensurately radical—rotate the chair. We believe it is important that every member of a meeting group regularly have the opportunity to lead—to test and shape his capability, and to taste the responsibility of sitting at the end of the table.

EXCERPTS FROM A MEETING

We assume that the purpose of a meeting is to make the fullest possible use of each participant, and we believe that the traditional chairman must redirect his energies and skills if he is to achieve this goal. He must first of all create an atmosphere in which a participant need never defend himself or his idea. When relieved of the burden of self-protection, a member can wholeheartedly devote himself to speculation and support, to the processes that produce the rich variations out of which fresh alternatives are born and exciting decisions are made. How can the chairman accomplish this? Before developing my set of rules for conducting a meeting, I should like to develop a model or procedure and with it some concepts of good policy.

Stating the Problem

In small, task-oriented meetings, the conference room should be arranged so the chairman can keep notes that all can see. A blackboard is good; large newsprint pads are better, since one can save the sheets. Initially, at least, it is useful to operate within a loose step-by-step framework.

The first step is to write a brief statement of the problem. This need not be detailed, since there is or should be expert knowledge about the problem in the group. (By the way, these experts can be depended on to keep the group honest.) To illustrate, let us expand the case of the company which is entering the dog-food market:

The experts are Mr. B of marketing and Mr. C of R&D. Both men have been involved with the development of the new product. With their coaching the leader writes, "Problem: How can we enter the pet-food market with an advantage over the competition?"

The next step is for the chairman to ask the experts for a more detailed explanation of the problem. As they talk about their experiments and findings, the chairman and other members will think of questions. They should ask them. The experts will be more interesting when responding to questions than when lecturing, and usually they will enjoy it more, too. The chairman should listen to these questions with much more than casual attention.

Temporary Shelving

There is a great temptation, for a member to demonstrate his incisive, penetrating thinking at this stage:

Mr. D asks, "Is our problem to figure out an advantage? Aren't we really trying to capitalize on the acceptance that the leading brand has attained?"

The chairman does not devalue this question; but since he knows it can lead to endless discussion of opinions which do little or nothing to help with the problem at this point, he says, "Mr. D, if you believe the real problem is other than stated, will you please write down the problem as you see it, and we will take it up later as a subproblem."

Mr. D then makes a note: "How can we capitalize on the acceptance that the leading brand has received?"

Spectrum Policy

As the experts discuss the problem, both members and chairman may think of possible solutions. These should be voiced and treated with care, as should every idea. For example:

Mr. A says, "I think it would be a good idea to shape our dog food like a bone and make it chewier." Without evaluating this suggestion, the chairman refers it to the experts, Mr. B and Mr. C.

"But there is already a dog bone," Mr. B starts to answer.

"Just a second, Mr. B," the chairman intervenes, "first tell us what you like about Mr. A's suggestion."

Mr. B thinks hard for a moment before responding. "Well, this change in shape is a good idea. Mr. A, if I get his meaning, wants to use shape to make our product more appealing to the buyer. We know the buyer's view of the food is a key element—the dog doesn't care much. In fact, the dog would probably be happy if we made the product look like table scraps."

What the chairman has done is to force Mr. B to think about the positive value of Mr. A's suggestion. As I have said before, one can presume that Mr. B will think of negative points on his own, as a matter of course; thus Mr. B now sees a range of values in the suggestion, a range from good to bad—a spectrum of values. The chairman has enforced the so-called spectrum policy, and by so doing he has accomplished more than may be apparent. Note that Mr. B has continued on to identify some approaches for the group that he himself finds acceptable. Note also that his approval signals Mr. A that he is considering the suggestion on its own merits, thinking about its advantages and disadvantages and not those of Mr. A. Let's return to the example:

"Now, what troubles you about the idea of a chewy bone, Mr. B?" asks the chairman. He replies, "I'm worried about the shape. Although the bone is traditionally associated with dogs and is good from that viewpoint, it isn't new to the market. One of our competitors is using it."

If the chairman is to use each participant to the full, he must see to it that everyone's views are considered. Another participant may have a contribution to make that will meet Mr. B's objection, and the chairman ought to encourage such contributions by making it clear that the meeting will respect and listen to any attempt to help. Thus:

Mr. D says, "Mr. B, your concern over the bone shape not being new suggests to me that we might go in a completely new texture direction: let's have an 'Instant Breakfast' dog food or a 'Metrecal' dog food."

If the experts consider this a possible solution, they say so and the leader records and saves it; if they don't then the chairman lets the discussion continue, with the spectrum policy, until everyone has a working understanding of the problem.

Restating the Problem

Next, the chairman asks that each member of the group write one or more statements of the problem as he, the member, understands it. The chairman then records these for all to see, adding any that occur to him.

It is at this point also that the various subproblems are recorded:

1 "How can we capitalize on the acceptance of the leading brand?"
2 "Why don't we devise a pet food that makes addicts out of pets?"
3 "How can we make pet food that perfectly fits the buyer's image of what the pet needs and loves?"
4 "Why can't we devise a pet food that the pet will choose every time in a taste test?"
5 "How can we make a pet food that the pet will eat and like so much he sends a message of thanks to his owner?"

I have deliberately chosen some of the more wishful subproblems. At first these may disturb practical people because they seem unrealistic and therefore useless. On the contrary, we have found that, at this point, the wilder and more wishful the statement, the more likely it is to evoke additional possible solutions. This stage gives each member the opportunity to make an official declaration of the problem as he understands it or of the goal he wishes to attain. The more of these, the better—and the more differences between them, the better. Imagination and temporary irresponsibility should be welcome.

Metaphoric Vacation

Next, the chairman selects one of the subproblems or restatements listed (never his own) and notes it—for example, the third one. He then applies a technique that outrages many people. I advocate it not for its shock value but because in thousands of experiments it has actually increased the probability that the group will ultimately develop a novel and profitable approach to its problem. The chairman creates *an artificial, instant vacation from the problem.* This technique is modeled after the practice of nearly every successful problem solver: when he has worked hard on a problem and no satisfactory solution has been forthcoming—when he has "gone dry"—he temporarily puts the problem out of mind with confidence that later, when his mind has rested, some new clue to solution will come to him. Thus:

The chairman instructs, "Please put the problem out of your mind. Now, can anyone think of an example of a striking image in the world of weather?"

"A thunderhead," answers Mr. A. Others also offer examples. The chairman records all of them and then listens to comments. He then selects one of the examples, and the members discuss it.

Mr. D: "A thunderhead is beautiful, but there are dangerous forces inside it."

Mr. B: "If aircraft had not explored them, you probably wouldn't know about the dangerous updrafts and downdrafts."

Vacation time should last from 5 to 15 minutes, depending on the members' skill in focusing off the original problem and the chairman's ability to sense the members' involvement in the vacation.

Toward the Solution

As his next step the chairman should bring the vacation to a close. In our example:

The chairman asks the members to return to the problem in question (Number 3) and to use the seemingly irrelevant comments about thunderheads to suggest unthought-of lines of speculation.

Mr. D comments, "This idea of hidden danger in the thunderhead—it makes me think of hidden meanings. Could we perhaps put some sort of hidden meaning in our product?"

The chairman supports the idea: "Do you mean that we should somehow put extra meaning in dog food?"

"Yes, but I don't know how."

Mr. B. then enters the conversation with the suggestion that they should treat dog food as though it is more important than dog food. To this, Mr. C replies, "OK, OK, we can treat it like people food!"

This discussion leads to the notion that a dog food exactly like hamburg could be marketed directly through the butcher. It would be put in the regular meat case and treated as meat in every sense. Members express concern about the stores' willingness to go along with this; but since the group can only guess about the stores' reactions, it is decided to test the idea.

A further idea comes out of this discussion, one that might have been considered out of order in a traditional meeting on dog food. One member suggests that the company market a completely synthetic "hamburg" for people. Mr. C believes that it is possible to achieve the correct texture and flavor, and Mr. B supports the idea because of low product costs, good storing qualities, and data suggesting that some people eat pet food.

Meetings in the style of the one just described make heavy demands on members and the chairman, but most participants thrive once they understand the rules of the road and feel the freedom to range.

Each suggestion receives the attention of every member; prestige derives from supporting any idea and thinking of ways to overcome the very elements that arouse concern; and each beginning idea is enlarged and modified until it reflects the constructive energies of the group. If a flaw remains, it is identified, and the idea is put aside, perhaps to be used later in a fresh context.

You've now observed a number of the problems (and suggested solutions) for running this type of meeting. Most were included in the brainstorming section of this chapter. But you also saw something important; that is, the use of creativity tools within the context of a meeting—in this case, the use of a metaphoric vacation.

This vacation is similar to what the Synectics people call excursions. Excursions are really just what the word means: flights of fancy but, in this case, for the mind. There are ways of allowing the mind to remove itself from the immediate problem; to remove itself from the constraints of being properly serious; then, perhaps most important, to enter into the problem from an entirely different point of view. In a sense, for a short period of time, you are creating a new reality.

As I mentioned previously, synectics is far too complex, and too important a topic to do more than cover it briefly in this section. Therefore we will limit ourselves to one example of how an excursion technique would work. I have chosen one that I'll call biological analogy. I am not certain that this would be the title that the synectics people would use, but I think it fits—the world of biology has provided me with a great deal of help in my concept generation work because nature seems to have solved every problem, in a host of ways, long before I even encountered it. To show you how this would work, I'm going to quote from another book written by Mr. Prince in which he addressed a group whose problem was to design a closure for a thermos bottle that was an integral part of the bottle.[11] The group had gone through all the obvious solutions, and the moderator realized that the time had come to look beyond the obvious.

Leader: Let's put down some goals that might answer this problem:

Goal Generation	Comments
1 How can we make a thermos that grows closed when we want it to?	All these "goals" involve good wishful thinking. We find that practical-minded people are often distressed by a Goal like number 2 They often say, "Let's face it, you can't teach a mechanism any-
2 Devise an integral mechanism that has learned to open and close on signal.	

[11]Prince, George, *The Practice of Creativity*, Collier Books, New York, 1970, pages 130–137.

3 Devise a closure that doesn't take up space.

thing. This is misleading and sloppy thinking." Strictly speaking, they are right, but our observations suggest that this is not the time for precision. The misleading and sloppy aspects of the statement are often stimulating and lead away from the familiar paths. Nearly every statement made in a Synectics meeting should be taken loosely, not literally. The time for precision comes in the final evaluation of a possible solution.

Now let us analyze an Example Excursion, concerning the thermos bottle closure problem we have already encountered.

Excursion	Comments

Choice of Goal

Leader chooses a "goal"—devise a closure that doesn't take up space—and writes: Goal #3.

This last goal appeals most to the leader.

Leader: Let's try to get the problem out of our minds. My Question is for an Example.

The leader selects an appropriate key part of the Goal (he does not ask for an Example of the whole problem).

Leader: Please think of an Example of a closure from the world of biology.

He asks for an Example from the organic world because the problem is a technical one.

Tom: How about a clam? (Leader writes: Clam. He asks Tom): Could you tell us more?
Tom: Well, I always think of a clam as being closed up tighter

Although the Example response may seem obvious to the leader, he still must ask for Tom's explanation. Tom may have in mind a connection than almost anything else I know. It's just about impossible to get through without breaking his shell.

Leader: Do you mean it's a very effective closure that you can get through only with a great deal of difficulty?

Tom: Yes.

Leader: Are there any other examples of closure from biology?

Dick: Natural selection.

(Leader writes it down and says): Yes?

Dick: Natural selection is the gradual closing out of certain physical traits or characteristics, like man's losing his tail or certain ducks losing their ability to fly.

Leader: If I get you, in natural selection a person or animal gradually loses certain physical attributes or capabilities and so in a sense they are closed out of that particular species.

Dick: Exactly: those things are obsolete and are left out of future generations.

Leader: Great! Can anyone think of any other Examples.

James: How about an iris?

Leader writes: Iris. He asks James to explain his thoughts.

which would never occur to the leader. In any case, the leader never makes the assumption that he knows what a member is thinking.

The leader, by restating the member's idea in the leader's own words, proves he has heard and understands.

You will note that during the Example stage, the leader writes very little and listens very hard.

James: I was thinking about the iris in your eye. I don't know too much about this, but it seems to me that iris closes out light and images and things like that.

Leader: Do you mean that, as part of the eye, the iris helps to close out some things you might see?

James: That's right.

Choice of Example and Examination

Leader: That idea intrigues me. Let's examine it.

He chooses it (1) because the concept of an iris interests him; (2) he can see no practical connection between eyes and the thermos; and (3) he believe the group knows enough about the iris to examine it.

Leader: What's with this iris?

Leader gets ready to write fast, abbreviating where possible, leaving out nonessential words but always using member's own words.

James: Well, I'm not even sure it's the iris that does this. It's more sort of a vague image I have, and I don't really have any more details about it. Except that it's the colored part.

This Examination is a good example of where an intuition is often more valuable than precise factual knowledge.

Dick: One thing about the iris that I remember is that it contracts and expands—sort of stretchable stuff that makes it possible to open and close.

In this Examination, no one has much precise factual knowledge, but everyone is familiar with the subject and can speculate about it. In this step it is more important to say something interesting than to say something that is correct. There is room here for contradictory views.

Tom: It's funny, but when James said the iris the first time, I thought he meant the iris of a camera, the part that's made of lots of metal leaves that fold over one another to let the light in and expose the film.

James: Also they fold over each other the most on the outside part of the leaves.

This is the sort of associatory material which can be especially valuable in leading to new areas of speculation. Remember also that each new step in the Flow Chart closes the door on the previous one, so Tom's thoughts about an iris are not restricted to James' idea from the world of biology.

Dick: There's also the flower, iris, but I don't know much about it.

Tom: I keep thinking of the eyeball. It's a funny, squishy substance.

Leader writes: Force Fit. He says: Let's go into Force Fit. How can we use these ideas about the iris to help us solve the problem of devising a thermos with an integral closure? (He chooses in this case to focus on the original problem rather than the goal.)

(Silence.)

Leader gives the group time to speculate and try to attempt a Force Fit.

Leader: Let's take this idea of the leaves. They remind me of the petals of a flower which seem to slide up and close together. Can we get anything from that?

When a group cannot make a connection after thirty or forty seconds, the leader tries to stimulate them.

Dick (excitedly): You mean sort of like the sections of a dome of the bowl of a collapsible flash attachment . . .?

Tom: I like that idea. I like the way those sections slide back and

Good building by Tom. Notice how he uses the Spectrum Policy: he points out what he likes about Dick's idea, then introduced the mechanical complication but

Excursion

disappear. How can we keep it from having so many mechanical parts?

James: Dick, you said something about the material of the human eye, that it was stretchable. Is there some way we can make an iris closure out of a stretchable material?

Tom: Hey, you get that kind of a closure when you twist a long balloon in the middle. You get two separate halves.

Dick: Yeah, and that is an air-tight closure.

Tom jumps up and draws a diagram (see Figure 4–4).

You could do it like this: have some rubbery material attached at the top and bottom, but be able to turn the top part, so when you do, it closes in the middle like a twisted balloon.

Comments

emphasizes that it is the group's problem, not Dick's alone.

Good listening and building by James. He is still speculating. Notice that he freely credits Dick with starting his thought. This recognition, small as it seems, is important in building mutually enjoyable interdependence. Without this you do not get whole-hearted teamwork.

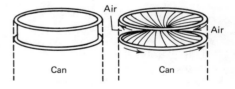

Figure 4-4

The group considered this idea to be a worthwhile viewpoint. Subsequent experiments proved that the closure met all the specification. Figure 4–5 illustrates its operation, fully open, half-open, and closed. It is now also being marketed as a closure for lipstick cases.

But now you have observed a couple of things. At the moment the group was stuck, the leader chose a strategy that allowed a little relaxation from the intensity of the problem, and a chance to look at the problem from a new light. Once he had a number of looks at the problem, he chose one and forced the group to apply it to the specific

Figure 4-5

situation. This may look tricky at first, but it really isn't and with just a bit of practice, you won't have much trouble doing it.

It might improve your feeling for this technique if we take a vacation from the cereal project for a moment, and examine another example of an excursion technique, Personal Analogy. In Personal Analogy, one places himself in a problem, and actually becomes part of the situation—but, from a point of view that is new. For example, you might imagine yourself to be a molocule floating around in a solution. Or, you could imagine yourself to be a hair shaft on a person's head; or, you can imagine yourself to be a propeller on a boat. It doesn't matter if it's relevant, or even seems vaguely relevant to the problem. . . . you can place yourself in the situation. Here's one way we have used this technique.

We were working on a new product concept generation project for a firm that asked us to limit ourselves to products to be used around the mouth. This firm already manufactured and marketed a number of these products, and the manufacturers had defined this particular concept project as one in which they would like to broaden their product line with similar products.

When we began the project, those of us in the brainstorming group soon ran into problems. Really, there weren't any unsolved problems that we had with our mouths. The products that we were using seemed to be relatively satisfactory, and the ideas being generated were more variations on standard themes (for example, a bourbon-flavored toothpaste) than serious new product concepts. To put the group in a different frame of mind, I suggested that we play a bit and use the Personal Analogy technique to take us to a somewhat different view. I suggested that we view the mouth as an office building, and we were the maintenance crew. Each evening they had to come in and clean up the office. This meant cleaning the floor, the walls and ceiling, removing the dirt and trash, and everything else. I didn't tape-record the work with the group, but as I recall, it went something as follows:

As we began talking about entering the building with our maintenance equipment and doing things like mopping the floor (actually bottom of the mouth), cleaning the walls, quickly we realized that the construction of this office building was unique. It was constructed so that there were a lot of little holes where the walls and the ceiling met (actually the spaces between the teeth near the gum line), and that dirt and trash could settle in these holes. One person said that it would be necessary for him to carry a stepping stool or small step ladder with him, and he would go from one space to another to clean it out. Another person replied that this was highly inefficient and that it would be easier to carry a long pole with him with a little point on the end so that he could dislodge the dirt (food particles). At this point, one member of the group mentioned that if the point punctured the ceiling, then liquid (blood) would flow all over the wall and floor and we would be forced to mop up, and thus increase the amount of work to be done. At this point, another member of the group said that using a pointed stick would not clean terribly well anyway. Why not use suction (in other words, a vacuum cleaner)? As we began to discuss this area, someone suggested that the really interesting thing about the vacuum cleaner was that one end of it is sticky, meaning things stick there or get sucked into the tube. This brought the conversation into sticky substances, and someone suggested that a sticky substance at the end of a long pole might be the most convenient way, since the maintenance man could move into the room, operate quickly and efficiently, and move out again without having to carry machinery with him, plug things in, and the like. While we were talking about putting a sticky substance on the end of a pole, someone came up with the following idea:

Brushing Gum. Brushing Gum is a chewing gum specially designed to stick to food particles. It allows you to brush your teeth at times when it is difficult. For example, you could have lunch and, on your way back from lunch, chew a piece of Brushing Gum. When you got back to work or home, discard the gum. You would discard a lot of the food particles that were lodged in your mouth. It might be that Brushing Gum could also freshen your breath or even polish your teeth in some nonabrasive way.

However, Brushing Gum was not submitted to this client, because a gum product, we discovered, was not acceptable to them. The point is this, by putting yourselves in a situation, and by becoming a part of it in a way we had never done before, we were able to see the problem from a new vantage point. This creative technique then gave birth to a new product idea.

Let me finish this synectics section by reminding you about something I said when I started this area. *Synectics is a system for solving problems.* This system can be learned from books, but if you're serious about this area, it would be worthwhile to speak with Synectics, Inc. However, even if you do not choose this, I think you will find the excursion techniques very useful, either when working by yourself or working in a brainstorming group. I know . . . . these techniques form some of my most favorite tools when I'm doing concept generation projects.

You have now been exposed to a number of what I like to call idea tools—sometimes referred to as creativity techniques. The three examples we have covered are adequate for you to get a feel of what these tools are and how they are used. Although there are many others— Concept Ladders and End/Means Analysis, to name two more, I won't delve into them here. Should you want to know more about them, the public library is a good place to look, since there are innumerable books on the creative process.

FLESHING OUT CORE (SKELETAL) CONCEPTS

After you have used these tools and generated a number of skeletal concepts (or core ideas) you need to flesh them out before you go on to prepare concept statements (which we will discuss in Chapter 6), and ultimately research them with consumers.

Obviously, if you were able to express the idea in one or two sentences during your idea phase, you will have no big problem expanding the initial idea into a full-blown concept. The problem is, that's not the optimum way to do it. What you need to do is examine each of the core ideas in a rigorous manner to make sure that, at least on an initial judgment, you are stating it as strongly as possible, and you are stating it in as many ways as possible. I would recommend the following checklist (my impression is that this idea of a checklist, indeed, many of the following items on a checklist, were originated by Alex Osborne, but I have no proof of this.)

CONCEPT PREPARATION CHECKLIST

- ► Combine
- ► Eliminate
- ► Adapt
- ► Modify
- ► Other Uses
- ► Substitute
- ► Rearrange
- ► Magnify
- ► Minify
- ► Reverse

What this means is that you should take each of your core ideas and expose it in a disciplined manner to a checklist like the above. Of course, it may be that when you are done, you have not been able to improve a concept at all. But that is the exception rather than the rule. Usually the outcome is that you will get several other thoughts and that you will manage to improve upon the basic idea. To demonstrate how this works let's take an example and apply the lesson. You'll note that some of the items on the checklist will seem to work better for this particular example than others. This is always the case, and you should not be concerned if there seems to be unevenness of quality in the items that finally come out. This is merely a function of the basic idea and its expandability in various directions.

As an example, let's take the home hair dryer. This is a small appliance that burst onto the scene in the last decade. Before that, hair dryers were found, primarily, in professional beauty establishments. Even the hand-held ones were expensive items that were rarely owned by consumers. Obviously, all that has changed. However, if you would have been looking for new product ideas when the hair dryer revolution started, you might have done the following:

1 *Combine.* You might have combined a hair misting device with the hair dryer to apply a conditioner, or a holding fluid to your hair and then quickly dry it into shape. Or, you may have combined it with another bathroom appliance—for example, the electric toothbrush, and used one basic motor to run several appliances.

2 *Eliminate.* It might have been possible to eliminate the handle or all the controls and have a small drying wand. Or, one could have eliminated the heat function and have a natural hair dryer.

3 *Adapt.* You might want to adapt the basic mechanism to be a tire-inflator which plugs into the automatic cigarette lighter for emergency use and which can be carried in your automobile. Or, you might want to use it as a "drain de-clogger," by forcing air into a clogged drain. You might want to make it into a toy game which uses a column of heated air to keep balls in the air.

4 *Modify.* You can modify it so that it can be readjusted for oily hair or dry hair or for use on baby as well as adults (the first all-family hair dryer).

5 *Other Uses.* One other use you might come up with is a window deicer (or defroster) for your automobile. You could promote its use as a dust remover for electrical appliances (such as T.V., radios, etc.), or, you might use it with a special kind of cleaning fluid which requires a heat application, and make it into an upholstery or carpet-cleaning kit.

6 *Substitute.* You could substitute a whirling nozzle (sort of like a pin wheel device) instead of a straight nozzle and get a more even flow on the hair. You could substitute batteries for the electrical input.

7 *Rearrange.* You could rearrange the action so that instead of blowing hot air onto the hair, it sucks air into it, thereby not exposing the hair to anything but ambient air temperatures as it sucks the moisture from your hair. Or, you could rearrange the handle-nozzle arrangement to create a left-handed and right-handed hair dryer. Or, you might rearrange the automaticity so that the dryer has some kind of moisture-sensing device. As the hair became dryer, the temperature would change and would not scorch the hair.

8 *Magnify.* First of all, you can increase the heat output and make a quick dry model. You might be able to increase the size and sturdiness of the item and market a professional model.

9 *Minify.* You might want to reduce the size of the model to make it into a travel unit (perhaps with a folding handle). Or, you might want

to make a small model for children to use after their hair has been washed.

10 *Reverse.* You might want to draw the water out of the hair, instead of causing it to evaporate through hot air.

Obviously you have noticed that some of these ideas are already in the marketplace. You have also noticed that some of the ideas seem to have no merit at all. This is normally the case. However, these examples represent about half an hour of work. Given more time, the help of one or two other creative thinkers, the list could have been expanded dramatically. However, I think you will agree that given that core idea, we managed to construct a number of other interesting things. That is the purpose of the checklist. It allows you to build on the core idea and to improve it and make additional ones.

Our investigation of new product concept generation is complete. Now, we will assume that you own a portfolio of new product concepts. Obviously, it makes sense to pursue only those that would seem to be the best investment alternatives. Chapter 5 explains the next step in our system. This step continues the risk reduction sequence by attempting to identify those concepts that make the most business sense for the firm.

5 The Business Evaluation System

Let's put aside concepts for the moment and return to the business aspects of new product development. We may have a group of concepts that seem to meet our guidelines and which seem to be acceptable—and in many cases—really good ideas. But we have a problem that can be stated as follows:

1 Our firm has limited resources.
2 Our R&R Department can handle only a few projects at any one time (including guiding the efforts of outside consultants)..
3 Our market research resources are limited.

But we have a great many ideas in our bank. Which of these ideas do we work on? How do we set priorities for these ideas? On what basis do we make these judgments?

What is needed is an accepted procedure for evaluating the potential worth of new product ideas while they are still in the concept stage. Such a procedure should provide as objective an analysis as possible for the proposed new product, and should direct itself to all of the key variables that comprise the marketing of a product: the potential volume and profit, an analysis of competition and the marketplace, the expected cost of entry, the cost and involvement of production, and the fit of the product into your company's way of operating. This procedure should result in the concepts being sorted into groups with specific characteristics—such as development time and cost, ROI, and the like.

This requires a procedure that combines "hard data" (such as market size) with a number of subjective determinations (such as market vulnerability). This procedure cannot be avoided if you are to fully evaluate the opportunity (indeed, the combination of hard data with subjective judgments is the basis for Baysian statistics). The key point, however, is to make these subjective determinations explicit, and to quantify them so that they do not assume a disproportionately important role in evaluating new product ideas.

Once you have developed this procedure (it is important that it be agreed to by the entire firm so that the results are accepted by all departments), it is possible to assign priorities to products, and even discard those with unacceptable prospects. If it is properly handled, you will always have a bank of ideas that you can plug into your development system as opportunities arise.

The following New Product Concept Evaluation System was developed for use by a packaged food products firm. It is not appropriate for all industries but can serve as a model for the development of one appropriate to your firm. You'll note that points are assigned to reflect the company's attitude toward each factor, so that some factors are worth a maximum of +5, others less; conversely, some can only contribute negative points (−5). In any event, these points are eventually added for each concept so that one summary number can provide the basis for assigning priorities among concepts.

CRITERIA

New Product Concept Evaluation System

1 *Market Factors*
   (This section includes: the size of market; growth trend of market; a determination of competitive strength and vulnerability; and, an evaluation of the strength of the proposed new product concept.)
   a. *Size of Market*   *Criterion Value*
         Translated to manufacturing dollars, the size
      of the market under consideration is rated posi-
      tively—relative to its increasing size:
      Market size over $150 mm   +4
      Market size $50− 150 mm   +3
      Market size $25− 50 mm   +2
      Market size less than $25 mm   0

b. *Trend of Market*

The marketing assumption on trend is that business is more easily gained by a product if a market is growing than if a market is static or contracting:

Excellent annual growth rate (10% or over) +4
Good growth rate (5-9%) +3
Growth rate about equal to population (2-4%) +2
Static market (± growth over past 2 years) +1
Contracting market (declining over past 2 years) 0
Severely declining market (-10% or more annually) −2

2. *Brand Potential*

The potential of a particular product is determined basically by two factors: the strength or vulnerability of the anticipated competition, and the soundness/strength of the new product concept.

(1) *Market Vulnerability*

Although often subjective in nature, an attempt must be made to evaluate the proposed market and the anticipated competition. Specific criteria, such as very heavy advertising and promotion expenditures for brands in the category, long-term domination, recent failures by other companies attempting to enter the market, all provide background for determining vulnerability. The assignment of points in this section will nearly always be the result of consolidation of various judgments:

Competition/market appears very vulnerable, based on evaluation of existing product performances, product positionings, or advertising/promotion support levels. +5

Mixed consensus by Marketing as to entrenchment of anticipated competitive products. (This "no-man's land" will be scaled anywhere from +3 to −3 based on combined judgment.) +3 to −3

General agreement that competition is heavily entrenched and/or has been unmoved by recent attacks by other companies. −5

(2) *Strength of Product Concept*

The strength of the proposed product concept is probably the most judgmental in nature of all the proposed criteria. Because it is at least equal in importance to any other single element in marketing a new product, every attempt should be made to judgmentally rate this quality as high as practical, giving the concept the benefit of any doubt or disagreement:

General agreement that proposed product is a strong product concept	+5
General agreement that it is a good concept	+3 or +4
Mixed agreement that it is a good concept	0
Concept represents no unique advantage in the proposed category	−5

2 Product Formulation/Performance

The proposed product, as conceived, should be evaluated as well as possible versus existing products performing the same primary consumer function. This criterion will be reevaluated after the product is actually formulated and, of course, again after it is consumer-tested.

Proposed formulation versus existing products:

Product represents a true breakthrough in technology and/or consumer benefits	+5
Product is somewhat above parity	+2
Product at parity with products already on the market	0
Below parity product	−1

3 Cost of Goods

Initially cost of goods per cent should be projected on the assumption that retail and trade pricing will be directly competitive, *unless* purposely designed to be higher or lower as an integral part of the brand's strategy. The cost of goods percentage dictates the eventual potential income which can be made available for profit and/or advertising and promotion support. A high cost of goods percentage puts a product at a definite disadvantage in the marketplace, and, if such exists, should dictate an automatic reevaluation of the proposed retail pricing structure.

Based on approximately competitive retail-pricing, cost of goods percentages should be weighed accordingly:*

---

*Calculated as a percent of *gross* sales (before selling expenses, etc.).

Cost of Goods	Generic Food Categories	Special Foods Categories
Under 15%	—	+5
15–20%	+5	+3
21–25%	+3	0
26–30%	+1	−1
31–35%	0	−3
36–45%	−3	−5
46% or over	−5	—

4 *Company Distribution/Marketing Ability*

This criterion should be an objective evaluation of whether or not the proposed product fits within the company's current or planned sales abilities and distribution patterns, or whether extensive restructuring would be needed. Rating would depend upon combined judgment, scaled from . . . +5 to −5.

5 *Profitability/Marketing Investment/Volume*

It is an important, practical consideration not to project a product's volume and profitability further into the future than marketing awareness will normally permit. On this basis, a proposed product should be evaluated in terms of profitability, marketing investment, and volume on a short term projection of the first 12 months in national distribution and a long-range objective of Year 3, following national introduction (the third year of a package goods brand in today's changing marketplace should represent a mature level of sales and profits).

a. **Profitability/Marketing Investment**

The same relative scale is applicable when projecting profitability (gross profit) and marketing investment (advertising, promotion and market research):

	Marketing Investment per each $1.0 million net invest. in marketing exp.	Break Even marketing investment =profit	Gross Profit (Pre-Tax) per each $1.0 million gross variable margin after direct expenses
1. Short-Term (first 12 mos.)	−1 additional	+2	+1 (additional to +2 for breaking even)
2. Long-Term (Year 3 National)	−5 additional	0	+2 additional

b. **Volume** Criterion Value

Aside from basic minimum volume requirements which may arbitrarily be set on new products by the company, there should be an independent projection of the proposed dollar and share of market objective based on known established trade policies on accepting new products. In the case of the food store trade, the ground rule for maintaining shelf position for a generic-category food product is a turn rate (velocity) of approximately one case (dozen) per month per major store.

Any projected new product sales rate which, when divided by the correct number of anticipated outlets, results in a velocity of less than these minimum should be penalized in this evaluation.[2]   −5

Using the Accumulated Criteria Points to Develop Standards

Based on the accumulation of the preceding Criteria Value points, approximate standards can be established for use in determining priority for a proposed product:

	Top Priority Product Range	Average to Good Product Range	Low Priority Product Range
		Ave. (+9 to +15) Good (+16 to +23)	
Preprofitability Section Points [3]	+24—+33	+9—+23	+8—−17
		Ave. (+11 to +17) Good (+18 to +25)	
Total Points	+26 or better	+11—+25	+10—−17

[2] If above average turn carries special benefits (to the marketer) with it, plus points can be assigned to this area also; generally this is not the case.

[3] In cases where sales volume estimates are particularly arbitrary (e.g., where you are dealing with positioning concepts) or where they are difficult to estimate, you can utilize preprofitability scores for setting priorities; later, when you have potential volumes, you can finish this evaluation.

Additional Checkpoints

There are several additional checkpoints that, although not designated with specific Criterion Points should represent caution flags and should cause a proposed product to be reevaluated:

1 Extreme seasonality, which could pull sales forces completely out of call pattern and develop an unprofitable return goods operation.
2 Extreme skews in demographic characteristics of potential consumers (extremely low income, "D" country profile, etc.).
3 Unusually heavy expenditures in time, energy and dollars in developing product—such as NDA requirement, or development by and purchase from outside supplier.
4 Potential problems with sources of raw materials.

The next step is to use the scores to set priorities.

SETTING PRIORITIES

This process, in effect, accomplishes 90% of the establishment of priorities. Those products with high potential scores (or potentially good investments) usually become high priority and so on.

The additional factors to add into the establishment of priorities are, of course, (a) development and proposed marketing timing, and (b) potential development investment.

All new products with high priority cannot obviously go into test, or expand nationally, simultaneously. Also, heavy R&D costs must be programmed to meet the resources of the firm. Timing, therefore, should be factored with potential.

The result should be this kind of priority ranking:

Action Categories

Group A-I. Products assigned to this priority group represent the highest possible marketing interest. There is immediate activity necessary on all areas on behalf of these products. These products can also be developed within normal product development lead time. Products in this group should be reported on at least every two weeks.

Group A-II.   Products in this group also represent highest marketing interest, but are anticipated to require longer development times due to areas of unknown information, manufacturing complexities, and so forth.

Group B-I.   Products in this group represent high potential but also represent eventual high investment. These projects will be pursued on a regular basis, but not with immediate urgency (the intent is to reduce the level of risk by further development so that the probability of success warrants the large investment).

Group B-II.   This priority grouping includes products that are not of high priority but that merit being carried in the program because of possible eventual marketing.

Group S.   All products dropped or suspended at any stage of development will be kept in this grouping, for the record.

Of course, the number of concepts that you pursue is dependent on how ambitious your program is, the resources of your firm, and the like. However, once you have categorized your concepts, you should be able to move to the next step with some assurance.

An operational hint . . . When you are dealing with a large bank of concepts (as we are in our example), it is sometimes easier to stop the evaluation of each concept at the Preprofitability level. This allows you to speed up the evaluation process, and usually does not represent a large risk—since, more often than not, you are dealing with concepts that fall in the same or similar product categories.

However, the Profitability section should not be dropped when you are dealing with a bank of concepts that exhibit strong differences. Invariably you will find:

► different investment levels
► different pay-back potentials
► different sales volume estimates

In this case, the Profitability section becomes important in the evaluation process, and cannot be avoided.

Regardless of your decisions, after your concept refinement research (the subject of the next chapter), you will be able to produce a sales potential estimate. At this point, you need to reevaluate all the concepts still under consideration. This will be your final priority setting before submitting concepts to the R&D process, and the advertising development process.

ADJUSTING THE EVALUATION SYSTEM FOR YOUR INDUSTRY

At this point, you may feel the need to modify the system to reflect the peculiarities of your own industry. Although you must make some modifications to adapt it to your specific needs, let me suggest caution —your industry is probably not that much different, in the sense of key market or product variables than the example we are using in this book. Items like market size, market growth trend, vulnerability of competition, and the like are germane to all markets. You should be careful in attributing uniqueness to your business—we all have a tendency to do so. However, some changes may be necessary, and let me suggest some factors in the evaluation system that you should review.

1 *Market Size (# 1a).* This is often changed. A manufacturer of home electronic equipment (e.g., televisions) would find the values in our example too low; a cosmetics marketer would be in the opposite position. Adjust the values for your industry.

2 *Cost of Goods (# 3).* Again, an obvious area for adjustment. The "0" rating should be for the cost-of-goods *your* firm would face (not the industry average).

3 *Profitability (# 5a).* Investment level, break-even period, and profit levels vary by industry (there is usually, however, general agreement on them), and, therefore, this adjustment should be a fairly simple one to make. Remember that there is some evidence that product life cycles are continuing to grow shorter. Therefore, make sure your system penalizes concepts that call for a longer-than-average break-even point.

4 *Volume (# 5b).* If your industry has a minimum sales level criterion (for maintaining distribution), it should be applied here.

Once you have developed your own business evaluation system, you have acquired a key part of your new product development system. By applying it at the end of each step, you will be able to view your alternatives (the "active" concepts) as potential businesses—investment alternatives with an increasing degree of certainty. Ultimately, of course, it will help select the best opportunity.

Note that in constructing your evaluation system, you should make sure you involve all members of the project team (or the key people involved in the new product development process) and gain their agreement to the system. I must emphasize that this is the only way this system will be able to perform its true function—that of setting priorities for all departments involved in new product development and gaining their agreement and enthusiasm for the project(s).

CASE: THE MIDDLE SOUTH MILLING COMPANY— SELECTING THE CONCEPTS WITH THE BEST POTENTIAL

At this point, let's return to our case. You have a "portfolio" of 82 concepts. Which of them do you put market research (and ultimately research and development) funds against? The answer will evolve through the new product concept evaluation system you have developed for your firm. (Let's pick four concepts from the portfolio and put them through the system just discussed. It will give you a feel for the process.)

You probably remember that the concepts had been divided into four groups on the basis of the product category they fell into: cookies; powdered beverages; cereals; and snacks. Taking one from each . . .

1 *Cheesecake Puffs.* This is a puffed cookie. The shape is like a small cream puff. The crust tastes like graham crackers. The filling is a creamy filling that tastes like cheesecake. These could come in several flavors: Creamy Cheesecake; Cherry Cheesecake; and so forth.

2 *Profruit.* This is a powdered beverage. It is made of natural fruit crystals, fructose, and powdered protein. It can be mixed with milk or water. It comes in three flavors, orange, grape, and cherry.

3 *Puffed Granola Cereal.* This would be a granola like cereal that would be "puffed" much like some wheat or rice cereals currently on the market. It would be positioned as a "natural" (sweetened with honey and molasses). It could be marketed as a single-flavor

brand, or it might come in a variety of "flavors" (e.g., cinnamon; vanilla and almonds; etc.).

4 *Puffed 'n Stuffed Snacks.* These would be similar (in shape) to the Cheesecake Puffs, just described, but the crusts would have the taste of snacks like corn chips, potato chips, and the like, and the creamy insides would taste like dips; e.g., sour cream and onion. They could be packaged in a variety pack, or as a line of products.

Let's make a preliminary business judgment on these ideas by putting them through our evaluation system.

CHEESECAKE PUFFS
  Market Factors
    Size of Market
      Market over $150 million .... +4
    Trend of Market
      The previous year had a 16% growth .... +4
    Brand Potential
      (1) Market Vulnerability
        General agreement that market is enterable by new
        brands/flavor.. +2
      (2) Strength of Product Concept
        General agreement that this is a good concept .... +3
  Product Formulation/Performance
    Agreement that, with our technical/manufacturing
    facilities, we could produce a product that is somewhat
    above parity .... +2
  Cost of Goods
    With the decisions that (a) we want to be in the regular
    cookie section (not the specialty food section), and
    (b) we want to be competitively priced, it was
    estimated that our cost-of-goods would be 25%........................ +3
  Company Distribution/Marketing Ability
    The company has a system of good food brokers, 20% of
    whom already have a cookie client and thus we would have to
    add some brokers if we marketed a line of cookies—
    therefore, our distribution system is not perfect for this
    proposed product (but the correction does not constitute
    an insurmountable problem) .... +2

Profitability/Investment/Volume
According to our best guesstimates, we will break even at
the end of Year 1 (national) (+2), and will be generating
a $2.0M gross profit by the end of Year 3 (+4)............................. +6
Volume—Sales estimate indicates no velocity problem............ +0
Total Points—Cheesecake Puffs.. +26

PROFRUIT POWDERED FRUIT AND PROTEIN DRINKS
Market Factors
  Size of Market
    Market over $150 million .... +4
  Trend of Market
    The growth is established to average 15% a year..................... +4
  Brand Potential
    (1) Market Vulnerability
        Agreement that segments of market can be
        entered although market is competitive .... +2
    (2) Strength of Product Concept
        General agreement that this is an extremely
        strong concept .... +5
Cost of Goods
  The product will be premium priced.
  The cost of goods should be 20%... +3
Company Distribution/Marketing Ability
  The channels would be the same as our regular
  products, although this is a new section of the store,
  and this might present us with a few initial problems............... +4
Profitability/Investment/Volume
  Break-even should be reached by the end of year 2. By the
  end of Year 3, we anticipate that we will be generating
  $3.5 million in increased profit... +7
  Volume—sales estimate indicates no velocity problem............. +0
  Total Points—Profruit Powdered Drinks.................................. +34

PUFFED GRANOLA CEREAL
Market Factors
  Size of Market
    Market over $150 million .... +4
  Trend of Market

The growth rate of the most recent year was 11%.................. +4

Brand Potential
   (1) Market Vulnerability
     General agreement that the
     cereal market can be entered by a new brand................... +3
   (2) Strength of Product Concept
     General agreement that product concept is strong,
     because (a) granola cereals have experienced an
     above-average (for the cereal category) growth, and
     (b) puffed cereals have been established sellers for
     some time... +5

Product Formulation/Performance
   Agreement that we can produce a product that is above
   parity—but which would not represent a true
   breakthrough .... +2

Cost of Goods
   The cost of goods is estimated at 18–20%............................. +3

Company Distribution/Marketing Ability
   Since our firm already markets a cereal product, we would
   not anticipate any problems in introducing a new one .... +5

Profitability/Investment/Volume
   We estimate that we will not break even until Year 2
   and will be generating a $2.0 million gross profit at
   the end of Year 3 .... +4
   Volume—estimate indicates no velocity problem.................. 0
   Total Points—Puffed Granola Cereal .... +30

PUFFED 'N STUFFED SNACKS
  Market Factors
   Size of Market
    Market over $150 million .... +4
   Trend of Market
    Sales growth was 3% .... +2
  Brand Potential
   (1) Market Vulnerability
     General agreement that market is somewhat
     vulnerable to new entries .... +3
   (2) Strength of Product Concept
     General agreement that this is a fairly strong

product concept .... +4

Product Formulation/Performance
Product represented a true breakthrough in consumer
benefits .... +5

Cost of Goods
The decision was reaffirmed that we do not want to be
in the specialty food category. This means that we must
be priced near the market, which leads us to a relatively
high cost of goods (30–35%) 0

Company Distribution/Marketing Ability
Snack foods get to retailers (e.g. supermarkets) one of
two ways: (a) through local trucks whose driver then
stocks the shelf, and (b) through the standard channel
(manufacturer to warehouse to retailer). We would be
forced to use the second channel which is less desirable;
therefore, we would rate ourselves as having only
average abilities in this area .... +2

Profitability/Marketing Investment/Volume
A preliminary estimate indicates that we will be "out"
$1M at the end of Year 1 (-1), and, at the end of Year 3
will be generating $3.0M in gross profit (+6) .... +5
Volume—sales estimate indicates no velocity problem 0
Total Points—Puffed 'n Stuffed Snacks .... +25

If we proceed like this through all 82 of the concepts in the portfolio, we wind up with the following scorecard.

	Cereal-Related Concepts	Powdered Beverage Related Concepts	Cookie/Dessert-Related Concepts	Snack-Related Concepts	Remaining Concepts
No. of concepts in group	24	17	19	18	4
Points Range	+35—18	+39—24	+33—+9	+30—−2	+21—+8
Average	+24	+29	+23	+18	+16

You now have come to a decision point. Which of the groups of concepts do we take to the next step? Further, within the selected group, do we include all the concepts, or just some? If some, which ones?

The answer to the first question you feel is that it is generally easier to handle a group of concepts that are similar (the reason for this will become obvious in the next chapter). In this case, the businesses posed by the powdered beverage products seemed to be the most attractive, and, after a discussion with Jerome, that category was selected for the next step in the process.

The answer to the second question(s) is in the priority system just described. For the beverage products, the concepts would look like this:

Status—Powdered Beverage—Type Concepts

Category		No. of Concepts
A-I	(highest priority; immediate activity indicated)	6
A-II	(high marketing interest; anticipated long development period)	3
B-I	(high potential; but high investment)	1
B-II	(low interest at present, but possible future interest)	2
S	(no marketing interest)	5

Thus, it would appear that 10 concepts are attractive (**A-I, A-II** and **B-I**), and merit further work. Your experience tells you that this is a manageable number (you prefer to work with 6–15 concepts at a time). The beverage concepts are now ready for the next step in your system.

6 Refining the Concept

Let's step back a moment and evaluate the situation as you work your way through this system. At this point, you have developed a number of new product concepts that (a) meet your general objectives/parameters and (b) appear to have the potential of being interesting business propositions. But there is a great deal that you still do not know. For example:

- ► How much appeal does each concept have to your potential customer? (What is the sales potential?)
- ► Who among your customers finds this concept especially appealing?
- ► What is it that you can say about the concept that is most attractive to the customer?
- ► What physical action must this product deliver to satisfy the expectations of your customer?
- ► What is the final satisfaction (hereafter called "End Benefit") that a customer will get from it?

The purpose of this chapter is to answer these questions, and to prepare and take the concepts through the quantification stage. Although steps *D* and *E* in the chart on page 109 are of great importance in the system, note that they represent relatively small expenditures in time and usually money.

The steps shown can handle a number of concepts at one time—perhaps your entire needs for one to two years of new product work. You should also note that, in a crash program—a program in which it will be necessary for you to skip some of the steps in the sequence—that this is one step that is extremely risky to skip. It may be possible for you to successfully use judgment to ascertain whether the proposed advertising communicates the correct positioning, and whether the

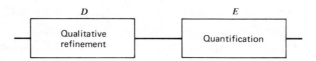

D   E

| Qualitative refinement | Quantification |

- ▶ Identify good ideas (those with sufficient interest to merit further consumer research).
- ▶ Develop consumer perceptual framework for each concept and for each category (attitudes, attributes, and language), and strengthen the presentation of the concept.

- ▶ Define consumer targets (demographics and psychographics).
- ▶ Provide Sales Volume Potential for each concept for use in investment calculations.
- ▶ Prepare Positioning Blueprint and Product Blueprint for each concept.

actual product delivers what the customers say they want. But it is very risky to use judgment on new product concepts to guess exactly what the end benefits of the physical product should be, and what the best way to position it is. It is my opinion that most new product failures result from taking this step haphazardly or skipping it entirely.

WHAT IS A PRODUCT?

At this point, it is necessary to have a common definition of what a product is. Let me suggest that a product is really a combination of physical and communications attributes that are intertwined into a complicated package. For example, compare these two products: a Volkswagen Rabbit, and a Mercedes Benz sedan. The end benefits of each of these is partly the same (it transports you and other people and luggage), but the similarity stops there. The Volkswagen says (communication attributes, or values) a lot different things about its driver than does the Mercedes. The VW says "practical" . . . "not concerned with what other people think" . . . "uses money wisely," while the Mercedes says "has arrived" . . . "has flair" . . . "solid citizen" . . . In other words, the total end benefit of each of these is different, and certainly the product attributes and communications attributes are extremely different. They are both automobiles, but they are quite different products.

Using the automobile, which has such a strong place in our culture, is an easy example. But all products are complex in their mix of end benefits and supporting attributes. Think for a moment of the different positionings that you observe in such categories as cold remedies (Vick's vs. Contac), men's suits (Sear's vs. GGG), women's dresses (D. von Furstenburg vs. Johnathan Logan), cosmetics (Maybeline vs. Elizabeth Arden), furniture moving services (Ajax vs. Allied), and so forth. Obviously a product is indeed a complex thing—and in any one category, products usually compete in more than just name. They compete in positioning also. So a product is a complex combination of positioning and physical product. The purpose of this chapter is to use our refinement system to optimize both.

HOW TO WRITE A NEW PRODUCT CONCEPT

To test concepts you need to prepare them in a form that enables you to show them to your customers. My preference is a form that has a simple visual and a verbal statement that contains the following points:

1 A statement of the problem that the product is meant to solve.
2 A definition of the type of solution that your product provides.
3 The necessary supporting attributes (both physical and communications) that lend credibility to the product's ability to solve the problem.

By this I mean that when you write a concept statement, you should state what kind of problem the product is proposing to solve. This problem may be unaddressed by products currently in the marketplace. Or it may be that you feel that current products are not sufficiently solving this problem. Or, it may be that in your definition of the problem, you attempt to segment your market. Regardless, the first paragraph of the concept statement should set the stage for the subsequent solution by defining the customer's problem. In the subsequent paragraph, you need to tell the customer that your product will solve this problem, and then give the necessary attributes (whether they be part of the physical product or the communications), to support the fact that you can solve this problem. Some of these can be implicit. For example: if you are talking about a concentrated liquid, you don't have to state that it comes in a bottle, although in the visual, someone may be seen holding a bottle. The statement should cover a wide range of these attributes.

The visual is a much simpler situation. Basically, it should show the product at its point of use and, indeed, if possible in the processs of being used. It should show the product, further, in its correct packaging and in the correct scale (for example: if it is something that you might hold in your hand, the hand becomes a convenient scaling device). The art work need not be extremely detailed. And background details, details such as the way people look or dress, should be held to a minimum unless they are absolutely relevant to the situation. The artwork is only to support the written communication and to add a modicum of interest to the concept presentation.

There are a few other rules of thumb that you should follow in preparing concepts boards:

1 Use normal language. Often the concept board will be used when no one is around to explain what a word or term means. Also, make sure the sentences are short. You're not writing a traditional English composition. You are writing more in the style of advertising without attempting to interject creative twists (there are no slogans, etc.).

2 The verbal section of the concept board should have a number of paragraphs. Avoid long, involved paragraphs, particularly when you are referring to several kinds of supporting attributes. It is better to break them into paragraphs that contain one, or at most, a few kinds of supporting attributes.

3 It is best to avoid catchy names in concept statements, unless the name is an integral part of the product concept or aids in the communication of the concept. It is best if the name indicates the function of the product. For example: "A SAFE TRICYCLE" will be better than "HEAVY WHEELS" if you are talking to mothers who are prospective purchasors of a tricycle type toy that will not tip over. Ultimately, you might want to call it something like "HEAVY WHEELS." But that would be a result of what you learned in your positioning research. It almost never is a good idea to use names in concept statements. I must say, though, that like most statements, this may be tempered. In the area of cosmetics, the name often becomes a part of the total package. Therefore, in areas like cosmetics and toiletries sometimes a name has to be part of the concept statement. It is an area in which you need to use good judgment.

4 Finally, the concept should have a one- or two-sentence summary that puts the concept in perspective.

The following are two concept boards that demonstrate the kind of concepts that should be prepared for consumer research.

112

Sixteen-Hour Facial Lotion

Today's active woman demands a lot from her cosmetics because she is often on the go from morning till night. Unfortunately, in her busy day there's often not a chance to change make-up. And the kind of make-up that you like to use in the morning is not always right as the day goes on, or when you sit down for an evening meeting. For different times of the day, your needs are different, and there isn't one cosmetic that will do everything you want.

That's the reason a well-known cosmetics company developed *SIX-TEEN-HOUR FACIAL LOTION*. You can apply it in the morning and feel comfortable that you're doing the right thing for your face and making it look good all through the day and evening.

It has cleansers to remove dry skin early in the morning, a sun screen to protect your face throughout the day and an emolient to make your skin soft and attractive all day long. It is a clear lotion and acts as a perfect base for whatever cosmetics you want to put over it. You won't have to worry. You will look good all day and your face will be protected all day.

And *SIXTEEN-HOUR* cosmetics are safe too, because they're made of natural ingredients. In fact, these are the same ingredients you probably would use if you had the time and expertise to formulate a facial lotion that's just right for you.

SIXTEEN-HOUR FACIAL LOTION. An answer to a question today's woman has raised.

114

The Luxury Adventure Vacation

We all enjoy going somewhere new on our vacation. And for some of us, the ideal vacation is one that combines a little bit of adventure with a little bit of luxury. We don't want to go to the same old resorts. We want to see something new and put a little adventure in our lives. But we don't want to give up the nice food and accomodations that we like when we go on vacation. After all, a vacation is a time to relax. The problem is that most tours are either too much adventure and not enough luxury or, too much luxury and not enough adventure.

That's the reason behind *THE LUXURY ADVENTURE VACATION.* The vacations are made just for the adventurers who don't want to give up their luxury. *LUXURY ADVENTURE VACATIONS* give you a complete house trailer, with maid service, and a guide. This house trailer is placed right where the adventure is.

All you do is fly, by helicopter, right to the encampment of house trailers (never more than eight). You are met by your guide and given the house trailer that you will use as your home away from home. During the day, you can go on camera safaris, or scuba diving, or exploring and mountain climbing (whichever tour you select). You are guided by expert local guides who speak fluent English. During the evening you return to your very own trailer, with all the comforts of home. Of course, the food is as good as you would get in a luxury hotel in London or Paris, but you eat it in a spot where few travelers get to go. And you don't have the bother of packing and unpacking.

The trailers are moved during the day while you are adventuring. After your adventures, the helicopter will take you to the new trailer park. Each night you are back safe and sound and very comfortable in your trailer.

LUXURY ADVENTURE VACATIONS can be held in South America; Africa (both Morocco and the big game preserve in Kenya); Mexico and Central America. You will be able to select your kind of adventure.

LUXURY ADVENTURE VACATIONS. The best of both worlds in a world that's loaded with adventure.

THE REFINEMENT PROCESS

Generally, the refinement process consists of two steps. A qualitative step which allows us to state the concepts in the strongest way, and a quantitative step which allows us to define the concepts tightly for our future product and communication work and to assess them as business propositions.

The Qualitative Step

In the qualitative step, you must accomplish the following:

1 Identify those concepts that appear to be the strongest (have the most consumer interest). Further, you should strengthen these concepts by correcting any communications problems, emphasizing what appear to be their strong points, and so forth.

2 Those concepts that are obviously weak must be identified and discarded.

3 Those concepts that may have some merit but which, at the moment, are nowhere near being stated correctly (and would require more qualitative research) should be put aside. They can be reworked and researched again at a later time, or simply discarded if additional concepts become unnecessary.

4 You must determine how the consumer views the category with which you are dealing. This means you must understand their attitudes, the language they use to express their thoughts about the category, how they see the various products in the category, what they see as important product attributes in the category, and particularly important, what they see as the end benefit and the important attributes (both physical and communication) for the concept(s) that you are interested in pursuing. This data will be used in the next stage of the research.

Generally, the technique used for this type of qualitative research is what is called a Focus Group. A Focus Group is usually composed of nine to twelve people who are representative of the potential customer for the type of product that you are researching. When a Focus Group is dealing with new product concepts, it can usually handle six or seven concepts. Normally you would want two or three Focus Groups for each group of concepts.

Focus Groups take many forms, but generally the scenario involves the leader introducing the consumers to the idea of sitting around and talking about new product concepts. In addition, they explain what a concept board is (this is called warming up the group). Then, one by one, they discuss each of the concepts. For each concept, all members of the group are allowed to indicate their likes, dislikes, thoughts, feelings, whatever. When all concepts have been discussed, it is usual for the leader to refocus on all the concepts and to make comparisons, determine preferences, and the like. As part of this, the Group often is given a copy of each concept statement, asked to underline the important points and to cross out the things they dislike. The reader must be cautioned that a Focus Group must be run by someone who is skilled in this technique, because a Focus Group involves the application of clinical therapy techniques. The leader must moderate the Group in such a way that it is at once nondirective, and at the same time, focused on a given subject. The example at the end of this chapter will give you insight into this process.

The Quantitative Step

Once the concepts have been culled and refined through a qualitative technique, it is time to move to the next level of sophistication in the refinement process—quantitative concept evaluation. The objectives of this critical step in the process are as follows:

1 To allow you to make some preliminary sales volume estimates (or some ranking of relative consumer interest).
2 To identify the demographic and psychographic characteristics of the potential consumer for each concept.
3 To provide you with a Positioning Blueprint that will help to direct the development of communications.
4 To provide you with a Product Blueprint that will help to direct product development.

In quantification, a sample of prospective customers are exposed to the concept. Generally, this means that each concept will be exposed to between 200 and 400 prospective customers. The nature of the research can take a number of forms. For a concept that is meant to appeal over a broad range of the population, a nationally representative mail panel might be used (for example, for credit card services). When highly personal use is envisioned, personal in-home interviews may be called for. Commonly, shopping mall intercepts are used, since they are reasonably cost efficient.

Regardless of the specific method recommended by your research department, a general procedure should be followed. The respondent is exposed to the concept board and then asked to give his or her assessment of its positives, negatives, and benefits. This is an open-ended area (that is, there is no predetermined group of possible answers), and the interviewer will probe all the responses possible from a respondent. After getting these top-of-mind reactions to the concepts, the respondent is presented with an attribute list and asked to rate their significance. Next, a measurement of interest in actually trying the product is taken, and further, potential frequency-of-use questions are asked (sometimes called substitution analysis). At the conclusion of the research, the respondent is asked various demographic and psychographic questions. These interviews are then tabulated and subjected to various statistical techniques.

The result of this is that for each concept you can construct the relative sales potentials, determine the form the product must take, and establish the key elements of your communications. Once you put this new data through your business analysis system, you will be able to judge which concept(s) you should proceed with.

THE POSITIONING BLUEPRINT

Figure 6-1 is a Positioning Blueprint for a liquid dishwashing product. A very specific end benefit has been derived from the research, and the communication attributes that support this end benefit (in a sense make it believable to the customers) have been clearly defined. It is very important to note that each of these supporting attributes has a numerical value attached to it. These numerical values (they add up to 100%) show the relative weight that each attribute deserves, based on the research. These relative weights are important because they show what kind of trade-offs can be made without weakening the positioning unnecessarily. Although this area will be discussed further in Chapter 8, suffice it to say that if you are looking at three supporting attributes, with relative weights of 70%, 20% and 10%, then in any kind of trade-off situation, the attribute worth 70% takes precedence. The whole purpose behind this kind of blueprint is to help manage

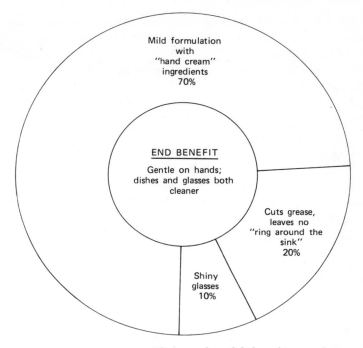

Figure 6-1 Positioning Blueprint, liquid dishwashing product.

these kind of communications trade-offs. It's one thing to know that there are three key attributes to a product; it's quite another thing to know their relative weights. The latter is a powerful decision tool.

THE PRODUCT BLUEPRINT

Figure 6-2 is an example of a Product Blueprint. The Product Blueprint is to the R&D people what the Positioning Blueprint is to the advertising agency or packaging firm. It tells them what end benefit(s) this product must deliver. It also tells them what the product characteristics (product attributes) must be and their relative value to the whole product. In fact the trade-offs in R&D are often much more acute than in the communications process. I have found the Product Blueprint to be of inestimable value.

Figure 6-2 shows that the effect on the hands is the most important supporting attribute for the end benefit. Should a trade-off be neces-

After washing, hands
are soft and smooth and
have no "dishwashing redness"
55%

END BENEFIT

Formulation is
beneficial to hands
and simultaneously
efficacious for dishwashing

Product looks
and smells
gentle: made
of "natural" soaps
25%

No spots
on
glasses
20%

Figure 6-2   Product blueprint, liquid dishwashing product.

sary between this attribute and "spotless glasses," the answer is obvious. A great deal of R&D time is thus saved.

Let's consider another example. Visualize a cosmetic that has three key supporting attributes:

1 Made of all natural ingredients—65%.
2 Maintains its effect on the face for up to 24 hours—25%.
3 Easy to apply; not messy—10%.

Now, R&D has a number of trade-offs that it is going to face. It may be that it is not possible to formulate a product that can stay on the face for up to 24 hours and still be made of all-natural ingredients. If this is the case, then the R&D people have a clear idea of what trade-offs to make. It would be better at this stage to have something less than 24-hour effectiveness if the all-natural ingredients attribute could be maintained. And, of course, the easy-to-use attribute always takes second place to trade-offs involving one of the others. This may appear to be an over-simplification, but it really isn't. You must remember that in this example in which we had three key attributes these were the three most important from the whole list of other physical attributes. Any trade-off involving one of the three most important ones and others that were shown as relatively unimportant is an easy decision to make. It's when you begin trading off among important attributes that the situation tends to involve judgment, and the Product Blueprint becomes especially helpful.

At this point, you are ready to seriously consider allocating your company's resources (R&D and Advertising resources) to pursue one or several products. All you need to do is put the concepts that appear most interesting to the consumer through the Business Evaluation System. You can now see them as business propositions and potential investments. The ones that are most attractive to you can be turned over to R&D (via the Product Blueprint) and to the advertising agency (via the Positioning Blueprint).

CASE: THE MIDDLE SOUTH MILLING COMPANY CASE— DEFINING THE BEST POWDERED BEVERAGE PRODUCT INVESTMENT ALTERNATIVE

As you discussed the situation with Jerome, it became obvious to you both that, given the resources of Middle South, what the system needed to produce was one well defined investment opportunity that Middle South could take advantage of in the next two years. After that, Middle South would seek to test market about one product per year. Given this constraint, it was decided to pursue the six concepts that formed the highest priority (A-1) group. It was decided that these would be prepared in the approved concept board format and that they would be put into Focus Groups in Boston, St. Louis, and Phoenix immediately. You authorized R&R to organize the Focus Groups and to begin briefing the moderator, and decided you would attend to make some first-hand observations.

The results of the groups provided sharply-defined direction. Your observations, which were supported by the findings and recommendations of the research firm, were as follows: One concept, PROFRUIT,

122

PROFRUIT

There are lots of times when children like to have a nice fruity drink—for example when they've been out playing, when they come home from school, or even as a snack. Adults, too, often find themselves thirsty for a good fruit beverage. But the problem is that a lot of the fruit beverages, whether they are in powder or cans, contain a lot of sugar, and really don't have much nutritional value.

That's the reason a major food company developed PROFRUIT. PROFRUIT is a powdered beverage (you can mix it with water or milk) that is unlike anything in the marketplace. PROFRUIT is made of dried, fresh fruit powder, and powdered protein. It is sweetened by fructose, a natural fruit sugar. PROFRUIT contains absolutely no table sugar. In fact, all the ingredients are natural, healthful ingredients—there aren't any additives.

The protein allows you to serve your children a body-building drink any time they are thirsty. In fact, an eight-ounce glass contains about the same amount of protein as a peanut butter sandwich.

But the best part is the taste. Mix it with water for a clear, delicious fruit drink. Mixed with milk, it tastes like a milkshake. It's sweet, but not too sweet. And, it comes in three delicious flavors: Orange, Cherry and Mixed Fruit.

PROFRUIT. A new natural fruit drink that gives you protein in a delicious, thirst-quenching beverage. Now your family can have a fruity drink anytime they want, and you don't have to worry about your family drinking things that aren't good for them.

was clearly superior to the other five; three of the concepts had some merit but were of lesser quality than PROFRUIT. Two concepts seemed to have no consumer merits whatsoever.

You discussed the situation with Jerome. Putting PROFRUIT, together with the other three relatively good concepts, through your Business Evaluation System yielded no reason to disregard the conclusion that you and Jerome had already come to: to put PROFRUIT into the quantification stage by itself and not incur any research expenditures for concepts that you probably would not pursue.

You then contacted R&R and said that you were ready to go into the quantification step with PROFRUIT. As a next step, it was necessary to relisten to the tapes so that a listing of the relevant attributes for the PROFRUIT concept could be constructed for use in researching the Positioning and Product Blueprints. Since Jerome was interested in participating in this process with you, you made transcripts of the two groups that were most interesting.

PARTIAL TRANSCRIPT

(M = moderator; R = a single respondent)
Boston
M Here we have PROFRUIT (Proceeds to read copy). PROFRUIT—what do you think? Sandy?
R It really appeals to me.
M What was there about it?
R Well, the natural fruit part of it . . . no preservatives, and my children love any of those drinks, and I make a lot of different fruit drinks, and that sounds better than any I've ever heard of.
M Okay . . . how about you? To whom would you serve this?
R My 18-year old.
M Okay . . . and you?
R My teenager doesn't know what it is to drink water, so I'd give him this . . . it would be better for him. Protein is important.
R My children are always thirsty, and I never buy junk drinks for them.
M How about this?
R Oh . . . I think it would be great, depending on how expensive it is.

M Jan?

R My children are always thirsty, too, and one thing I've noticed is things like the canned peach nectar are so expensive that I use it sparingly. I feel badly that I do, because it is pure, natural . . . I honestly like the idea of protein . . . and somehow it seems more natural.

M What are you serving to your kids now?

R Well, I usually buy two cans of apricot or peach nectar when I go shopping, or just frozen juices.

R Well, it sounds like a very good drink for all ages, and the fact that it doesn't have sugar added makes it very good for those of us concerned about nutrition.

M How about you?

R I would buy that for my husband and myself, and our grandchildren. It wouldn't be bad for their teeth.

M And you?

R Yes, I would buy it myself. I would serve it to my husband, and I would also serve it to my grandchildren. They need body-building protein.

R I would like something that would be in a jar and that you could mix up in a glass, rather than a quart or half-gallon, because my refrigerator is usually so loaded that when I mix up a package of Kool-Aid, it takes up too much room. It doesn't say one way or another, but I guess they can jar it.

M So, you would like it by the glass rather than the pitcher?

R By the glass, it sounds very worthwhile.

M What are you serving now?

R Well, my husband and my young one will drink soda, if I have it available. If not, they drink water or milk.

M Yes?

R Well . . . I was just going to say that I could picture that on a hot summer day when you have ladies over, and you want to serve something cold . . . take an orange slice and put it on the glass and it would really be delicious.

M Do you see this as an additional product in your home or as a replacement for something that you are now using?

R Additional.

R Additional.

R Additional.

M You still would serve whatever you're serving. How many additionals do we have? Four additionals and four replacements.

M What would it replace?

R Probably the fruit nectars.

R Well, the Hi-C and the Wyler powdered drinks.

M Would you be serving it for purposes of thirst, or are you looking for additional nutrition?

R It would be thirst at our house.

R Thirst, but nutrition would probably be a good thing.

R When kids are drinking in such large quantities, especially in the summertime, you should be concerned about what they are drinking . . . that it is nutritious as well as wet.

M Okay . . . we'll use the same procedure. I'd like you to read through . . . (concept reread).

R I like the thought of it sprinkled on toast.

M Why not . . . I like to think of it as a jelly replacement.

Okay . . . what other things jump out at you about PROFRUIT? Anyone?

Okay, based on what you know about PROFRUIT, how many of you would be likely to try it at your supermarket the next time you shop? Full house!

PARTIAL TRANSCRIPT

St. Louis

M PROFRUIT—What do you think about PROFRUIT?

R I think it sounds pretty good.

M Sounds pretty good . . . Why? Why Sue . . . does it appeal to you?

R Well, I like the natural bit, instead of using all the sugar. One thing that would be instrumental about whether I buy it or not would be the cost.

M What are you comparing it to?

R I think orange juices, fruit punches . . . I go from one thing to another so that I'm not continually giving them one thing.

M What would a packet compare to . . . when you talk about orange juice, are you talking about concentrated?

R Yes . . . that I mix with my Kool-Aid.

M You make a combination.

R Right . . . I make a combination, or whatever, but I will use the powdered form and then mix my frozen orange juice with it.

M What's the price on it . . . roughly?

R Well, if I put a can of 40¢ orange juice into my 20¢ Kool-Aid, then I can come up with a half-gallon, or almost a gallon.

M Okay, so there's a 60¢ value . . . Okay, what about the rest of you.

R My kids would love it . . . I think children would like it. I use apple juice or frozen grape juice for my kids, so if I thought it was something that contained no sugar and wasn't outrageously expensive, I would buy it . . . because it has natural sugar. And, if it has protein in it, I won't have to serve all those sticky peanut butter sandwiches.

M What does it have to be to be comparable in price . . . is it outrageous like apple juice?

R No, apple juice is 55¢ a can and let's see . . .

M Does it reconstitute to . . . how many ounces?

R Yes . . . that's less than a quart so you're spending a lot on juice . . . at least I know I do, and I dilute mine some.

R I'm doing the same thing at home . . . I find myself with something like 14 playmates with my children.

M What about the rest of you?

R I really wouldn't be interested . . . I don't think.

M Why not?

R Well, we use frozen orange juice for breakfast, and when it comes to drinks . . . it's a diet drink, or coffee, or iced tea. We don't have any kids at home, so I don't think we'd use it.

M Well . . . how about adults?

R I think sprinkling it on toast, like cinnamon . . . I don't like all the sugar, and if the children could have something that they could see going on, that would be of interest to me.

M I don't understand why, if you don't like sugar, you like the fructose. That's sugar.

R The taste . . .

M Taste . . . but it's still sugar.

R Yes, but it's natural.

M But what difference does that make?

R A lot of difference. White sugar is a chemical.

R But so is fructose. I'm a chemist, and I'm an organic chemist, and I don't think there's any difference.

R Isn't there a lot of difference?

R Well . . . it's a more complex sugar, but it breaks down in your body the same . . . I don't see that it makes that much difference. One is complex, and the other is what I would call a simple sugar.

R Well, a diabetic can't eat sugar, but he can eat fruit.

R In a book I've been reading, it goes into a great deal of the effect of sugar in your digestive system. Sugar has caused me a great deal of pain for years, and I didn't know it. We had a doctor tell us that there's so much evidence against sugar, that were it any other product, it would be banned.

M Let's not argue the effects of sugar . . . Okay . . . let's get back to my product.

R I'm interested in knowing about the flavoring that's added. For instance, to the cherry. Is this artificial flavoring?

M I don't know . . . do you think it would be?

R Well, if it's all natural (like it says on the outside) and not prohibitive, you'd find a great place to sell it at my house . . . probably by the case.

R It would go over in my home . . . especially with kids who can mix it themselves. There would be no limit to how much they could drink of it. We're really trying to get away from soft drinks. They tend to drink tea, milk or fruit drinks . . . . something like that . . . and they would probably enjoy it. And I like the idea of a drinkable protein that is not milk.

M Okay.

R This might be nice to take camping. It's very cumbersome if you have to haul along juice. And, with our antisugar campaign at home, this has eliminated an awful lot of drinks. And the canned fruit drinks . . . I've completely given up on because the fact that you're paying a good price for water and sugar and, frankly, no fruit . . . I think they even label them fruit-flavored now. They really aren't fruit, so this would be real nice.

M Okay.

R It would be a good space-saver too. I buy the apple juice, or V-8 juice, or tomato juice, and they are very bulky.

M Do you think you would try this?

R Oh, I definitely will. My children drink too much milk, but I hate to stop them. Now there is another way to give them protein.

M What about the beverages your children have at meal time. Are you concerned about the nutritional values of those items, or thirst?

R Nutrition.

M Even when the neighborhood kids come in?

R Well, we can use water too.

M But I mean, are you really concerned from a nutritional standpoint, or are you merely trying to satisfy their thirst?

R Well . . . thirst.

M What about you Gail?

R I think when my kids just have to have a drink, it's thirst. But I'd also like to combine the two. I want to give them something to drink that is not going to harm them. Sometimes I'll give them a pitcher of ice water, but that doesn't always work, you know. And, there are times when I don't want them to eat, and a glass of juice will give them a little extra they need to make it until meal time.

M And what are you looking for then?

R Nutrition.

R You would be surprised how many teenagers are interested in natural foods . . . even my own son is learning to take his iced tea without sugar.

(Respondents are asked to read statement.)

R I've changed my mind about one point. That frothy fruit shake with milk sounds interesting.

M It does say, either mix it with a glass of water, or milk.

R Yes . . ... that sounds interesting.

R Something else . . . the coloring of this. It may have artificial coloring in it . . . that's something that bothers me. Some of the so-called natural things on the shelf are anything but natural . . . it really is a misnomer.

M Okay.

R What about the powder? Is it easy to dissolve?
(tape unclear regarding crystals . . . too many voices talking)

M Okay . . . for those of you who are thinking about buying it, would this be an additional product in your household, or would it replace something that you have now?

R In mine . . . I'm sure it would be additional.

R Additional.

R It would replace it in mine.

M What would it replace?

R The apple juice.

R I would try it, and if I like it, it would replace.

M What would it replace?

R The Kool-Aid.

M Is there anything else like it on the market?

R No nothing. (This is generally the response from the group.)

M Okay . . . based on what you know about this idea, how many of you would be likely to try it? Okay . . . all but Alice.

In rereading the transcripts and typing up the notes from all three groups, you put together the following list of end benefits and attributes that you discussed with Jerome.

Good for kid's health
Doesn't taste artificial
Good for all occasions
Not harmful to teeth or complexion
Not filling
Easy to serve
Made from dried fresh fruit
Can be stored indefinitely
Good mixed with water or milk

No harmful additives
Children can fix
No aftertaste
Quenches thirst quickly
Made from dried fresh fruit
Adults like to drink
Low in calories
Easy to prepare
Children love to drink it
Made of natural ingredients
Good for kid's snacking
Has fruity taste
Contains body-building protein
Contains no table sugar
Sweet, but not too sweet
Eight-oz. glass contains m.d.r. of vitamins

As you and Jerome studied the list, you began to understand that, in reality, the list was a mixed bag. It contained end benefits that were communications-oriented ("children love to drink it"), and physical ("quenches thirst") end benefits; and also attributes that were both communications attributes (for example, "fruity taste") and physical (for example, "made from dried fresh fruit"). Also, you were not certain if the list that you had was really comprehensive. However, it did begin to give you an idea of how people felt about products of this type.

The next step was taken by the Research Department at R&R. One of their social scientists stripped the tape of all consumer perceptions by relistening to the tapes and constructing a list as she listened to the groups discuss all the concepts. Combining her list with yours and reducing it to a manageable number, you were now ready for the quantitative phase of the research.

The concept had been revised slightly (Figure 6-3). It was decided to use the concept board in a supermarket mall intercept research design. R&R said that it would be valuable to use one of their control concepts appealing to this same target. You agreed. The research results, available six weeks later, indicated the following data:

1 Positioning Blueprint
End benefit = kids like to drink

Key Communications Attributes
- ► No harmful additives/natural ingredients—55%
- ► Protein/body-building protein—20%
- ► Fruity taste—25%

2 Product Blueprint
End benefit = quenches thirst quickly

Key Product Attributes
- ► Fruit Sugar—50%
- ► Made from dried fresh fruits—30%
- ► Not filling—10%
- ► Eight-oz. glass = 10% of protein growing child needs—10%

3 **The Demographics** showed that the product appealed to two distinctly different groups—although one group had a much higher interest level. The most interested group was mothers with children (over 3 and under 16). Making a mental calculation, you suspected that this had to be about 40% of all U.S. households. The frequency-of-use data for these families, according to the research, was three-plus times weekly— although you knew from past experience the use of this kind of product varied by season. The second group was somewhat younger, mainly single- and two-family households. They saw it as an occasional use product—less than once a week. Still, you knew that approximately one-half of the households in the U.S. would qualify as one- or two-people households and that this market still might be significant.

4 **The Psychographics** did not yield anything unexpected. People who generally were interested in health, body care, self-improvement, self-actualization, responded more positively to the product. However, the differences were not significant, partially because the product did well across most of the groups. It did seem, however, that PROFRUIT had healthful overtones.

Using anticipated trial and expected repeat rates for satisfied customers (from curves they had compiled over the years) and usage (which was double-checked by comparing the research results with other usage data), R&R projected a national volume of 3.5 million cases. These would be 24-pack cases in which each item retailed for $1.99. The $1.99 price was the current price for containers of powdered beverages, but in the case of PROFRUIT you visualized that the quantity would be about 25% less—thus making it a premium price product on a per-ounce-served basis. Assuming a 25% trade margin, this resulted in factory sales in the area of $75 million. Even with high promotional expenditures, you felt that it would be possible to return 8–10% in after-tax profits. Given the new data, you put PROFRUIT through your Business Evaluation System again and found that it still, in your opinion, represented an attractive investment alternative.

You discussed the result with Jerome. He agreed that positioning the product as a healthy food (but not a health food) and advertising it to adults as something that children particularly liked, would allow you to straddle both markets simultaneously. He further agreed with you that, in attempting to straddle the markets, you well might not maximize sales in either segment but that the net result probably would be your best alternative.

Since Middle South was a privately held company, you were not privy to the total sales and profits per year. But, it was your guess that factory sales were in the area of $125 million per year, and net profits must be somewhere in the area of 5% after tax. Clearly, this was a staggering opportunity for Middle South Milling Company. Jerome stated, "Even if the sales forecast is wrong by 50%, this product has the potential of transforming Middle South into an entirely different kind of company."

The magnitude of the opportunity obviously posed some problems. Any product that was so successful undoubtedly would attract the attention and the competitive activity of other powdered beverage manufacturers—many of whom were large, powerful companies in the food business. An outside legal opinion showed that Professor Hartman's process could not be made into a fool-proof patent. Further, both you and Jerome recognized that the category was one in which heavy promotional expenditures were common. Obviously, there was a big opportunity that carried some risks with it. It was agreed that you would meet the following Friday and discuss the matter further.

Before the meeting, you decided that there were four basic questions on which this, or any opportunity, turned. They were:

1 Is there a demand for this product?

2 Can we produce the product?

3 Can we obtain retail distribution for the product and hold this distribution through some introductory period?

4 Do the economics of the business proposition look attractive?

At the meeting Jerome agreed that these were key questions. You both agreed that the preliminary evidence was that the answer to all four was affirmative. You indicated that to take the next step—developing the actual product—would probably cost about $30,000 in development costs and about an additional $10,000 in market research funds. If the advertising were to be developed and tested simultaneously, the figure would be somewhat less than twice this amount. Jerome likened it to a poker game. In this case, it would cost $40,000 to see the next card. He also stated that, given the other investment alternatives facing the firm in the next few years, there was nothing that had the allure (or for that matter, the return on investment or present value of this opportunity). On that basis, it was decided to proceed to the product development stage but not to produce the advertising until Professor Hartman could deliver a product that matched the concept.

7 Developing and Testing the Product

At this point, you have decided on the new product or new products to develop. You have put them through the Business Evaluation System and have received management approval and agreement that these appear to be worthwhile potential investments.

The objective of this chapter is to dwell on your work with the Research & Development department of your firm (R&D) in developing products that match the concepts. This can cover many different kinds of scientific and engineering work—depending on the firm you are in. For example, if you are developing a new electronic wristwatch, your work with the R&D people (and the number and kinds of alternatives they are able to turn out) will be much different than if you are working for a cosmetics firm or one that produces temperature controls for industry. The principles will remain the same, but the details of your work can change considerably. Therefore, in this chapter, we will try to spend most of the time on principles and not worry too much about the details.

THE NEED TO USE A PRODUCT BLUEPRINT

The key to your work with the R&D people is the Product Blueprint. At the quantitative research stage be certain you involve the R&D personnel in isolating the physical attributes that are potentially important for a product of the type you are considering. They also must have complete access to the final research results. By that point, they already have some idea of what it is you are talking about. Your job at this point

135

is to make sure that this is communicated to them in the most useable form. I would assume your company has some document that is used to request the start of a new assignment for R&D. Let me suggest that, whether or not such a document exists, you should submit at least the following data:

1 A copy of the concept statement.

2 The Product Blueprint from research. It is important that this Blueprint be elaborated on in detail. You need to spell out in two or three sentences exactly how the customer sees the End Benefits. You also need to state the attributes in their correct numerical weights and the various kinds of language that the consumer uses for each of these attributes (after the Qualitative Stage but before the Quantitative Stage, you summarized these attributes in a single sentence, or phrase, for the sake of the research questionnaire. At this point it is necessary to expand each of these attributes so that you communicate to the R&D people enough of the language for each of these attributes. They then get a wider view of what the customer is talking about).

3 You need to indicate some preliminary thinking about packaging. This certainly is not final packaging, and we are certainly not talking about graphics or any kinds or refinements. But they do need to know if the product will be shipped in a drum, in a small bottle, or whatever. Therefore, it is necessary for you to help them understand the situations in which the product will tend to be used. For example, if the product is to be taken out of the home in a woman's handbag, this should be stated. If it is industrial cleaning equipment, then it will be stored over a wide range of temperatures and used by nonengineering workers to perform certain kinds of cleaning tasks.

4 You should describe the customer so that they have some mental picture to whom the product is aimed. This can take the form of demographics, psychographics, degree of experience with this kind of product, place in life-cycle, and so forth. It is essential that the R&D people be able to visualize who it is that they are designing this product for.

5 You should also show such things as channels of distribution, how you intend to ship this product, and the like.

6 A target cost of goods.

7 If you see it coming in many sizes, or flavors, or variations.

Some of this may seem to be properly the work of R&D, and you may say it should not be specific at this point. To a point that's true, but it is necessary for you to outline your preliminary thinking for the R&D Department. Certainly they know that methods of packaging are almost always variable, and from what you say about the usage situation, they might come up with new packaging forms. This is to be hoped for; indeed, sound thinking on their part is to be expected.

It is important to remind you that in your meetings with the R&D people, you should stress the use of the numerical weights of the product attributes and further, remind them of the product attributes that were tested and found unimportant by the customer. You cannot assume that R&D will remember all the trade-offs because, for much of the time, they were working on other projects.

TESTING THE PRODUCT

After some time, R&D will have a number of prototypes that appear to meet the requirements of the Product Blueprint. At this point, the question of testing the product will arise. Although product testing varies quite a bit by industry, let me give you some thoughts that you should consider.

First, it is necessary to do some internal testing. You should be able to look at a number of prototypes and decide on one or two that look best after testing several in your lab. This can be done with customers who are available locally. The point here is that you want to winnow the number of prototypes to one or two that in your combined judgment best meet the product concept and the Product Blueprint.

Once you have identified one or two prototypes, it is necessary to expose these prototypes to a large enough sample of potential customers to enable you to make projections from the results. Your firm may have an established way of doing this. You may choose, however, to use an outside firm to perform this. Should you go outside, you will discover that the number of firms that do this type of testing is large. These are some:

1 Battelle Institute
2 Arthur D. Little
3 Home Testing Institute
4 United States Testing Company

Obviously, there are many others. The decision to test it yourself or use an outside firm is up to you and your Research Director.

However, in testing products, please keep in mind the following:

1 You must always test using the concept. It is important that the respondent react to the concept so that you are able to differentiate their reaction to the product by "concept acceptors" and "concept rejectors." This is a rule that you cannot avoid because it would be very difficult to interpret the product test results if you do not know this. Of course, the results must be reported on this base (concept acceptors). Also, the degree of concept acceptance should be compared with your previous research (the Quantitative phase) to see if the kinds of trials that you predicted at that stage still seem to be appropriate.

2 You should always look on a product test as a chance to improve the product, not merely to decide if it's acceptable or which of two prototypes is best. Therefore, the test should contain a number of opportunities for the customer, after they have used the product, to state likes, dislikes, ways of product improvement, and the like. It is almost always the case that minor, but important to the consumer, improvements can be made without altering the basic prototypes.

3 It is important that the test results be interpreted on a number of bases. For example, the data should be interpreted by heavy user versus light user; by different types of usage; and by special types of consumer (for example, on the basis of demographics, psychographics, or on any other base that it would seem useful to look at). This means the same kind of usage questions, demographic questions, and, if you included them, psychographic questions, that were used in the Quantitative questionnaire should be included in this phase of the research. This will allow you to connect the data from the various research stages to get additional confirmation that you are on target.

4 In product testing it is usually a good idea to avoid fancy names or fancy packaging unless they are an absolute necessity to communicate the total product idea. Keep in mind that when you are doing the product test, *you are really trying to see whether you have developed the kind of product that will generate repeat purchases.* You want to know that the actual product will perform in a way that the customer finds desirable over a period of time. You are forcing trial in this type of research and trial is the baliwick of the Positioning Blueprint and the advertising that comes from it. Therefore, since it's my opinion that names and packaging have the greatest impact at the time of trial and not for repeat purchases (and I know that I am making a broad general-

ization here). Therefore, I feel that it is best to avoid unnecessary packaging and names at this point.

5 Of course, you want to ask respondents whether they would buy the product if it were available in the marketplace. This should be done before mentioning price. Then it should be asked at an indicated price(s). I will discuss this in the next section of this chapter.

6 Also, the respondent should be asked to rate the product on the same product attributes list that you used in Quantitative research with this concept. Ideally, you should get back the same kind of Product Blueprint that you sent to R&D to start the process.

From the results of the product test, you will be able to judge whether your prototype is acceptable to the consumer; that is, whether it would be the kind of product for which you could expect repeat purchases. You should be able to compare the results of this research with some type of normative data. Also, this normative data should include products that actually were marketed and thus you will have some idea about the validity of the sales projections. If you do not have this kind of data, then it may be worthwhile to use an outside firm with normative data for your category.

TESTING AT MORE THAN ONE PRICE

In a product test you ultimately have to investigate price. My feeling is that this should be the last area covered, because what you are really trying to measure in this test is satisfaction with the physical product itself. However, you can't avoid the price issue, and my preference is to split the sample on the basis of more than one price. I say this because testing at more than one price allows you to infer a demand curve for the product. Granted, there is often a large gap between what someone says they will do and what they actually will do. Testing at more than one price does not eliminate the need for you to view these kinds of responses judiciously. What it does do, though, is that it allows you to think more intelligently about the pricing options.

For example, consider the thought processes you might go through if you were faced with a situation where 90% of the concept acceptors said they would like to try the product before they heard the price, and 70% of them said they would like to buy the product after they heard the price. On the other hand, consider the decision situation if you knew that 90% of the concept acceptors would buy before they heard the price; 70% of them would buy it at Price "A" (lower price) and 60% would buy it at Price "B" (the higher price). This is a lot more data. It indicates that you might be better off charging the higher price. It allows you (as you will see in the pricing chapter) to think of pricing on the basis of demand rather than cost-plus pricing. Of course, none of these numbers can be taken in the absolute sense. But in the relative sense, they become very valuable decision tools.

A Cautionary Note

When testing a prototype, make sure that it is as close to production quality as possible. Often prototypes are to a great extent hand-built and are far superior to the product that would actually be produced. This can lead to misleading results. Make sure you avoid this error. It is too common and can be avoided if you are alert to the problem.

WHEN THE PRODUCT SEEMS TO TURN OUT BETTER THAN THE CONCEPT

It sometimes happens that reaction to a product is so good that you begin to question the trial assumption of the Quantitative Stage. This is a highly desirable position. What the prospective consumers are saying is that the product performs much better than your concept indicated. This is not that unusual because many people have trouble believing something could work so faultlessly, taste so good, or just perform so well that they are unwilling to accept that this will happen. It also means that, if you can get them to try it, you should be able to obtain a better than average repeat rate. I would caution you, though, about changing your initial trial figures. They still are in the baliwick of the advertising. It may be possible from the results of the product test to make stronger claims in the advertising than you would have thought possible from the results of the concept refinement work. This indeed may affect your initial trial calculation, but you can readjust this in the test market simulation phase. Adjusting your trial upwards on the basis of hands-on experience of customers, however, is dangerous. That's not what this piece of research is meant to do.

At this point, if you are happy with the results of the product test, and if the cost of goods and other business factors appear to be in line, you can move to finishing the advertising that you may have already started or that you should start at this point.

CASE: THE MIDDLE SOUTH MILLING COMPANY— DEVELOPING PROFRUIT

As a first step toward developing PROFRUIT, you decided that you needed a complete presentation of the facts-to-date for Professor Hartman. You knew that Professor Hartman was preparing to begin the development in the next two weeks and was to be assisted by a colleague who had done some work in dried fruit juices.

As a first step for your presentation, you prepared the Product Blueprint. This came directly from the research:

End Benefit = Quenches Thirst Quickly

Supporting Product Attributes

Attribute	Value
Fruit sugar	50%
Made from dried fresh fruit	30%
Eight-oz. glass equals 10% of protein required for children	10%
Not filling	10%

Also, you knew that it would be essential to have Professor Hartman and his colleague understand the consumer language that you found to be important. To accomplish this, you provided him with the Positioning Blueprint and the additional consumer language for each of the four attributes.

When it came to the target, you and Jerome made a decision. The primary consumer target would be Households with children ages 3–16. All product testing would be done with this audience. You told Professor Hartman that there was a secondary target, and identified this target for him, but cautioned him that he should not consider this in his formulation work.

With respect to the cost of goods and packaging, you said that for a cannister holding enough powder to make six quarts of drinkable fluid, he should aim at about a 40¢ for cost of goods (and in making his calculations, should be thinking in terms of about 2 million cases, each holding 24 of these canisters). As a further step, you said that the flavors—cherry, orange and mixed fruit—should be the primary flavors, although some changes might be made in the future. Also, you said that you were thinking of cardboard canisters with metals ends and a plastic cap.

To help Professor Hartman and his colleague understand the problem, you arranged for the Research Director from R&R to be part of the presentation. The objective was that she give some insight into the psychographics and behavior patterns of the consumer target.

The presentation with Professor Hartman went well. He had worked closely with you and the agency throughout the research and seemed generally in command of the situation. After telling this to Jerome, you both agreed that Professor Hartman, although primarily a technologist, had a consumer-oriented mind and was able to put himself in the position of using the product, not just making it.

Three months later Professor Hartman came to you in an interesting quandary. He had developed two different products. Both of them seemed to meet the Product Blueprint for PROFRUIT, although there were several differences between the products. Both of them had achieved about equal ratings by students who had been called in to taste the product. Professor Hartman said that he had held over 500 tastings on campus, until he arrived at the two formulations. As you discussed this further with him, you realized that many of these tastings had been with students—the population most easy for Professor Hartman to tap. Although some of the tasters had been mothers with children in the target age range, most were not. It seemed that this was a problem.

You decided the next step was to look at the formulas. Formula "A" produced a clear liquid, contained about 10% of the recommended protein for children, was not particularly filling, and produced a drink that, when mixed with water, looked like Kool-Aid. Formula "B" produced a cloudy drink when mixed with water, contained about 15% of the recommended amount of protein, was a little more filling, and had more "mouth feel" because of its suspended particles. It also tended to make a little better "milkshaky" drink when mixed with milk than Formula "A" did. As you and Jerome looked over the situation, you realized the following:

1 One formulation—Formula "A"—was much closer to the Product Blueprint than the other;

2 Both formulations tasted good and seemed to have consumer merit;

3 The "cloudy versus clear" issue, and indeed, the difference in protein, were probably not significant, given the kind of research that had preceeded Professor Hartman's work. In one case, the issue (cloudy versus clear) had really not been researched, and in the other case (the amount of protein) it had been stated only one way in the concept, and a higher value for protein had not been tested—however, given the low value of protein in the Product Blueprint, it would seem that the higher value would not be particularly important.

You decided that it would be best to test both products. The issue became more complex when you realized that you both wanted to test it at more than one price. Based on what you knew of the economics to date, and the other alternatives facing the consumer, you agreed to test at $1.99 and $1.69 for a six-quart container. This would make it a premium price product since the competition was selling at about $1.99 for an eight-quart container. This would be the range in which you ultimately would like the product to sell. Therefore, the testing should be at these points.

While discussing this with the Research Director of R&R, it became obvious that you were talking about a Latin Square design. This is a design in which there are four cells, and there are two variables being tested. At this point you agreed with the Research Director that the objective of the next piece of research should be as follows:

1 See which product is preferred by the primary target.

2 Obtain some inferences about the demand curve for both products.

3 See how the product compared with what the target consumer is already using.

4 Obtain the kind of data that would allow the refinement of the sales estimate. Also, it was agreed that the same kind of measurements that developed the Product Blueprint, and so forth would be used in this piece of research so that a comparison could be made.

5 See if the product could be improved.

About eight weeks after the research was initiated, you and Jerome were invited to attend the presentation of the results at R&R. The outcome of the research could be summarized as follows:

1 The concept acceptance was almost as you had seen it at the quantitative research phase (among target groups).
2 After using the product, the playback on the Product Blueprint was not significantly different between those who used Formula "A" and those who used Formula "B".
3 Formula "A" was preferred over Formula "B"—this was among mothers with children 3–16—no other type of population was in the sample. This preference was at a statistically significant level and, for "heavy users" Formula "A" had almost twice the preference than Formula "B" (as measured by the desire to buy at the price indicated).
4 There were some minor product problems. Most of them seemed insignificant except that "B" seemed to be "too sweet."
5 The sales estimate indicated interesting differences. Based on the response to the questions, R&R had calculated the following "going year" sales forecast:

	Formula "A" (million cases)	Formula "B" (million cases)
$1.99	1.9	1.5
$1.69	2.2	1.6

6 On a "how it compares to the product in current use," the Formula "A" received higher ratings than Formula "B".

It was obvious that the demand curve for Formula "B" was somewhat inelastic, while that for Formula "A" showed elasticity. In other words, if you lowered the price for Formula "A", you could expect to sell more, but lowering the price for Formula "B" did not result in many more cases sold. It was generally agreed by the people at the presentation that Formula "A" really seemed to perform better with families with children. This fact, plus the fact that heavy users showed a higher tendency to repeat for Formula "A," was substantiated by other parts of the research which showed that it had been substituted for powdered drinks at a much higher level than Formula "B" (which had received a good piece of its substitution from cans and frozen beverages).

The issue now seemed relatively clear. Formula "A" seemed to meet the needs of the target audience better than Formula "B". Also, as Jerome hypothesized, it seemed reasonable to think that Formula "B" might appeal to smaller households which were using more canned and frozen beverages. This would explain the result of Professor Hartman's campus tastings.

The sales projections also looked approximately right. It was premature to begin thinking of demand curves and optimum pricing. Indeed, as you and Jerome had agreed sometime before, it might be better to move with a penetration pricing strategy when the time came to introduce the product in order to secure as large a share of the market as possible, rather than attempting to optimize short-term profits regardless of the elasticity of demand. However, all that was in the future. The next question at this point was do we proceed with the project, and go to the next step—which was to develop the advertising?

The issue was complicated by the fact that Red Hartman felt that the powdered beverage market might be too competitive for Middle South, and that perhaps it made more sense to use a formulation similar to Formula "B" and attempt to develop a line of powdered drink mixes (for example, Piña Colada). He argued that this market was (a) expanding; and (b) less competitive. There was no dominant factor in the market. He agreed, however, that the market also was very small. But, after discussion, it seemed best to go forward with Formula "A". This was decided for the following reasons:

1 Moving into the mixed drink market would probably bring with it the need for some new channels of distribution (a time-consuming and costly task).
2 The powdered beverage market for children's drink was larger.
3 Formula "B" might not be optimum as a drink mix in its current formulation and probably would require reformulation and retesting.

As part of the decision, you and Jerome calculated that to begin work on the advertising would require a budget of about $50,000. This included preparation of rough advertising, testing rough advertising, preparation of final advertising, and some creative fees to the agency (the contract between Middle South and its advertising agency, James & James, stated that some creative time needed on the new product work would be considered part of the service normally provided by the agency; but you and Jerome felt that, since you wanted to be rigorous at this stage and look at a number of alternatives, more creative hours would have to be purchased). About one-half of this amount would be used for producing rough advertising and testing it, and the second half for producing a final piece of advertising ready for exposure in the marketplace.

As a final disciplined step you and Jerome put the business proposition (as it was forming) through the Business Evaluation System. At the end it still seemed to be the best immediate alternative facing Middle South. Also, it continued to meet the objectives of the new product development program and the corporation as a whole.

The next day, you and Jerome discussed the matter further. The wisest path seemed to be to proceed. If Middle South was to grow, much of the growth—as currently planned—would have to come from new products. PROFRUIT seemed to be a solid product. At the end of lunch, you and Jerome agreed that you would call Mel James the next day and begin creative work on PROFRUIT.

8 Developing (and Pretesting) the Advertising and Other Communications

In Chapter 6, we discussed one part of the output of the concept refinement system, the Positioning Blueprint. It is the Positioning Blueprint that provides the basis for the development of all the consumer communications (advertising, packaging, and point-of-sale being the three primary consumer communication media). Although the development process for the various communications media may take place in different ways, in the main they have the same basic objective—to communicate the product's positioning. Therefore, in this chapter we will use advertising as the most obvious of the three to illustrate our point. What holds for advertising will hold for packaging and point-of-sale.

This chapter is aimed at helping you understand how to start the development of the advertising for a new product. This objective, plus the constraints of space and time, pose some limitations for us. The chapter will not get involved in how advertising is developed (however, it will talk, briefly, about how to pretest the advertising), nor will it get involved in the area of post-testing, although we will allude to this in a later chapter. These areas are really quite large. Entire books have been written about them. We will concentrate on converting the Positioning Blueprint into the beginning of the advertising development process.

147

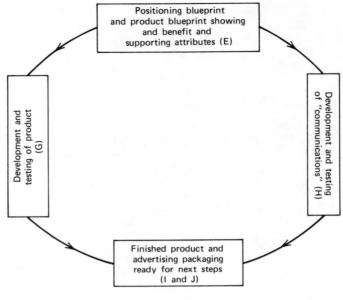

Figure 8-1

THE POSITIONING BLUEPRINT

Let's step back for a moment. In Chapter 6 (the concept refinement system), we developed a Positioning Blueprint and a Product Blueprint. In Chapter 7, we used the Product Blueprint to develop the actual product. Now we must use the Positioning Blueprint to develop the communications. But before we do that, it may be useful to reiterate our definitions of a product.

For our purposes here, it is useful to restate that a product is a bundle of satisfactions. Some of the satisfactions are physical, and some of these satisfactions are, for want of a better term, psychological. Although various people can see a product in quite different light, for most products there is a concensus about what the product represents, what physical action it has, and what psychological satisfaction it represents. In the previous chapters, we attempted to develop a product that met the physical requirements. In this chapter we are really aiming at developing the communications attributes that lead to the psychological satisfaction a product provides. For the sake of a definition, let's define communications attributes as those values that people understand and believe about a product.

Returning to the matter of the Positioning Blueprint, we now see that what we are trying to do is communicate the End Benefit with the proper supporting attributes (or proper communications attributes) so that the end result is that people understand and believe the correct (and most important) things about the product. At this point, I must remind you that what you want your potential customer to understand and believe about your new product is precisely what they told you is important about the product—in other words, what they want to believe about the product. WHAT WE HAVE DONE IN CHAPTER 7 AND WILL DO IN CHAPTER 8 IS TO COMPLETE THE DEVELOPMENT OF THE PRODUCT THAT PEOPLE TOLD US THEY WANT TO BUY.

We have taken the marketing concept to its logical last phase. In our new product work, the consumer actually has designed the product. We've given them exactly what they want. Granted there are some inevitable slippages. We cannot expect that R&D will develop a perfect product every time. It certainly is not possible to do that. But it is possible to come very close each time because, with the knowledge of the necessary trade-offs, the final compromises can be made with the consumer's references in mind. The same goes for the communications. It is unreasonable to think that an advertising agency can exactly match the Positioning Blueprint in its advertising every time. Sometimes they will; other times the best they can do is to come pretty close. This is not something that should bother you. What I am trying to say is that the Blueprints represent optimums, and your job is to fit the pieces together as close to the optimum as possible. Don't worry about maximizing everything. It probably will take too much time and effort, and indeed, may not be possible. Marketing certainly exists in a time continuum. Tastes change. Marketing factors change, and so forth, and the intelligent new product developer knows that he must seize opportunities quickly.

THE POSITIONING STATEMENT

The Positioning Statement is the basic document that you will turn over to your advertising agency. The Positioning Statement incorporates the Positioning Blueprint and any facets of the Product Blueprint that need to be communicated in the advertising. Although it is technically not part of the Positioning Statement, you also need to provide a target definition (who's going to buy, what the demographics of the people are, what the psychographics are, how they would use the product, etc.).

The Positioning Statement is an amalgamation of the Positioning Blueprint and those facets of the Product Blueprint, if any, that need to be communicated. Generally, these facets are the physical end benefit that becomes tied in with the end benefit of the Positioning Blueprint (the following example will make this clear), and perhaps one or two of the physical product attributes that lend support to the communications attributes. I must emphasize that even though the Positioning Statement is an amalgamation of the Positioning Blueprint and the Product Blueprint, it must differentiate between that information needed to be communicated to the ultimate customer, and that information included for the information of the user. Although the Positioning Statement is used by many people, and they need to know the complete product story, it must be made clear which is which. The advertising agency does not concern itself with communicating much about the physical product unless it is essential to incorporate some of the supporting attributes from the Product Blueprint in the advertising. In fact, there is sometimes a danger in a positioning statement that covers both the Positioning Blueprint and the Product Blueprint because people can get confused about what it is that must be communicated. However, there is also a danger in having a Positioning Statement that is too narrow. I think this is the greater of the two evils.

Continuing, the Positioning Statement must clearly state the end benefit. It must give the key communications attributes (and their relative importance). It should provide the reader with knowledge about how the product will be used (when, where, under what conditions, how often, etc.). Of course, it will have been proceeded by a hard Target Definition Statement. Further, the Positioning Statement should cover such areas as:

▶ Competition
▶ Packaging
▶ Other marketing details that will help readers understand the product.

In other words, the Positioning Statement should communicate what the product is, what it does, who is going to use it, how they are going to use it, where it is going to be sold, and what its competition looks like. THE KEY POINT HERE IS THAT THE MARKETING PROCESS (AND BY THAT I MEAN THE DEVELOPMENT OF THE ADVERTISING AND MARKETING PLAN) MUST FOLLOW, AND BE BASED UPON, THE POSITIONING STATEMENT.

CREATIVE OBJECTIVES AND STRATEGY

Once the Positioning Statement has been agreed upon, the next step in the development process with the advertising agency is to prepare creative objectives and a strategy statement. These will differ at each agency, and this is not the place to be rigid about format. Regardless of the format, however, the objective-strategy statement should contain the following information in relatively specific terms:

1 The *end benefit* (the *single* most important selling point is that the consumer must understand and believe in the advertising).

2 The supporting *communications and product attributes* that provide a rational basis for the end benefit.

Again, this probably is the Positioning Blueprint almost as it came from the concept refinement system. It is important that the numerical values of the supporting attributes be maintained for the Positioning Blueprint and that the communication device (e.g., print ad) should aim at putting relatively heavy emphasis on those carrying a higher numerical value. However, modifications in these weights may be necessary if there was some amalgamation of the Positioning Blueprint and the Product Blueprint. If the Positioning Blueprint has been modified by combining it with some aspects of the Product Blueprint, then new numerical values must be estimated, and this estimation must be reflected in the objectives-strategy statement. In a sense, you now have a modified Positioning Blueprint.

3 The *image of the product that is to be conveyed.* This goes beyond the communications attributes. It refers to the kind of overall image that you would like to leave in the person's mind about the product (Is this an economy product? Is this a luxury item? Is this a product to be used under rugged conditions?). What we are talking about here is, combined with #4, below, the feel or imagery that remains behind about a product and the company that makes it, imagery that goes

beyond the specifics that are communicated about the product. It is my impression that these areas are often omitted from the objectives-strategy statements. I think this is a big mistake. Members of the company's management team and the advertising agency usually have good instincts about the image that should be portrayed about the product and its company. But this should be made explicit so that everyone can agree beforehand and enter into the process of defining this image.

4 The *tone of the advertising*. This is related to #3, above, but is concerned more with how things are said, rather than what is said (or implied, as the case may be). For example, do you want to convey, through the way the advertising is prepared, that you are a space-age company with highly sophisticated technology? Or, do you want to convey the impression that you are a small, homey company with a lot of personal interest in the products you manufacture. Obviously, the first might be correct if you were introducing an electronics line. And the second might be perfect if you were introducing a new cooking sauce. However, if you reverse these, you would be running counter to what seemed to be the trend for these kinds of products. Perhaps that would be a good strategy, perhaps not. Regardless, it should be stated so that it becomes part of the strategy, and not an accident.

5 *Usage situations*. The statement should contain some mention of the situation in which the product will be used. It is not uncommon for a product to have a number of different situations in which it can be used. These situations often represent different areas of vulnerability of competition, and also different volume possibilities. The Positioning Statement should have contained the use situations that are most important to this product. The key one or two should be included in the objectives-strategy statement as an indication of what should be shown in the advertising.

CREATING THE ADVERTISING

Armed with an agreed-to creative objectives-strategy statement, you and the agency can now proceed to develop the advertising (you can use it to start the packaging work, although it is usually a good idea to find out what the advertising theme will be before you finish all the packaging—you may find it useful to tie it together). It is not the purpose of this chapter to delve into the world of creating advertising. Suffice it to say that you will want to meet with the agency often. You should take an involved and supporting, albeit objective, position.

And, most important, you should constantly check the progress against the objectives-strategy statement. This is key. Bad advertising that does not meet objectives or is not on strategy, must be stopped as soon as possible. It can become the approved campaign—through a process I have never been able to understand (although I think it has something to do with the "charm" of advertising executions).

TESTING THE ADVERTISING

About testing the advertising, I would like to give you three rules.

1 Always test the advertising.
2 Never test only one alternative.
3 When you test it, make sure that it meets the creative objectives.

Let me elaborate on each of these. First, you must test the advertising. It is impossible from looking at advertising to be sure that you will communicate what you intend. The communication process is much too complex. Granted, some ads are much more straight-forward than others; for example, the ad for a new copying machine to be used in the home probably would be a lot more straight-forward and factual than an ad for a new men's fragrance. Not testing the ad for the copier might involve a lower level of risk than not testing the ad for the men's fragrance. I would grant that. Regardless, for most products the advertising is the main way consumers will initially learn about the product. It is too important a variable to be left to judgment. Therefore, always test it.

About Rule #2, it is always necessary to test more than one alternative. Testing one alternative is merely a confirmation of your judgment and, perhaps in the most extreme, a "disaster-check" type of behavior. If you are only testing one alternative, it means that you are putting a program together and, unless the advertising turns out to be an absolute flop, it will be used—possibly with some modifications—and will not be retested.

Now I realize that testing advertising can be expensive, both in terms of money and time. It still has to be done. With print ads there can be a larger number of alternatives than with television, in which case two or three alternatives that have been well defined and improved through marketing judgment may be enough. The number is unimportant. The point is simply that you must test more than one alternative.

Rule #3 is important to keep in the back of your mind. When you are testing advertising, you are often testing it through some kind of syndicated service (we'll talk a bit about this later in the chapter). They will provide you with all sorts of measures that they have developed over a number of years. These can be useful. They are generally meant to help you improve the overall effectiveness of your advertising and to help you understand how effective it is. And, of course, the service will always have the normative data that will help you to make some comparisons. That's fine, but that's not enough. You must test it against your measurements—the creative objectives (taken from the Positioning Blueprint, or the Positioning Statement). The ideal situation for you to be in after testing your advertising is to find that the consumer played back to you your Positioning Blueprint. You will remember that it was this Positioning Blueprint that the consumers initially told you was what they wanted to hear about this product, and it was this same Positioning Blueprint that you used (possibly with some modifications) to start this advertising. Do not be misled by the conventional measures of excellence (provided by the services). *Your measurement of excellence is whether your communications reproduces the creative objectives as taken from the Positioning Blueprint.*

EXACTLY WHAT DO YOU TEST

There is the question in advertising testing that might be called "degree of finish." In other words, the question here is how close to a finished advertisement must the test advertisements be? Can they be rough artist's renditions, or must they be the finished photography?

Clearly this is a topic far beyond the scope of this book, but I mention it because it sometimes enters into discussions about testing advertising for new products. You should rely on your own judgment and the advice of experts when this issue comes up, because it can change by product category and also by the kind of testing that you have to do. Let me give you a few thoughts:

1 Generally, I don't mind testing advertising in rough form. In fact, this can be initiated with a large number of alternatives tested in

rough form (let's say, through some technique such as focus groups), and then the few alternatives that appear to have merit tested in a more finished form.

2 The more the product "sell" depends on an "emotional" appeal, the safer you are with testing alternatives in a more finished form. This is because the amount and type of emotional feelings evoked by a finished ad can be much different than that for a rough, and after all, it depends a lot on artistic techniques, and so forth.

3 One safety check that you have will be the communication of the advertising itself. If you are using the Positioning Blueprint as a standard against which the advertising will be compared, then at the very least you will know if it is communicating the correct material. There is much more to testing than this, but if the ad is not doing the bare basics, then I wouldn't depend on it doing anything more sophisticated.

WHAT SERVICES SHOULD I USE TO TEST THE ADVERTISING?

There are a number of services in existence for a long time that specialize in the testing of advertising. Some do what is called on-air testing. This really means that your commercial is actually broadcast in a standard environment, and then by telephone, people are questioned about it. Burke Research is one firm that is well known for this kind of advertising testing.

Continuing in the area of television commercials, some firms use what are called "theater" or "laboratory" techniques. A.S.I. and Yankolevich, Skelly & White are firms that do this kind of research. In this format respondents are gathered together and see the commercials in the context of a television show and other commercials, and the like. The respondents then are questioned rigorously on what the ads say.

Print advertising is usually tested with some attempt to fit into its normal environment. Some firms use what are called portfolio techniques (putting a sample of the ad in a type of photo portfolio book along with other ads). Others will attempt to bind it into samples of a magazine. Each of these has its proponents. Gallup-Robinson is well known for testing print advertising and is also active in the area of testing television advertising.

If your advertising is going to be outdoor, radio, or some other media, these also can be tested, and if there is not a specialized firm available, your advertising agency should be able to construct a research design that should do the job.

This gets us to a key point. During the planning for the testing of the advertising, you must work closely with your advertising agency. Each agency has its own philosophy, preferences for techniques, suppliers with whom they feel comfortable, and so forth. Since they are your partners in the communications process, you must make sure that they will be comfortable with the output of your research. Therefore, you should be working closely with the Research Director and with the account and creative people who are preparing the advertising. Within the philosophy of the agency, you should be able to get a kind of playback that will allow you to judge whether the advertising is doing the job. This is your responsibility, and no one else's.

THE OUTPUT OF ADVERTISING TESTING

What you receive as output of the advertising test can differ by service. Generally, you should look to receive the following:

1 *Recall of the Advertisement.* What this means is, does the respondent remember your ad? Does it have any stopping power, or does it merely remain unnoticed in its environment. Every service will have a great deal of normative data for this, and you should be at least average for your category or advertisements of your type.

2 *Recall.* Recall really measures a respondent's memory of what you were saying. In your case, you are looking for recall of the end benefits and recall of the supporting attributes. In other words, you are looking for recall of the Positioning Blueprint (or some part of the Positioning Statement). IDEALLY, THE SUPPORTING ATTRIBUTES SHOULD BE IN MUCH THE SAME PROPORTION AS THEY WERE IN THE BLUEPRINT.

3 *Attitude Change.* The next thing you should look at is some type of attitude change measure. This may be called brand preference, or desire to try. Did you change anybody's mind about wanting to buy your product against some other? What percentage of the people did you switch? Many marketers place high emphasis on this kind of measurement. They feel this way because obviously some kind of attitude change (positive) has to preceed behavior. So, it follows then that if

you find that a certain percentage of people who did not previously purchase your product now say they will, it seems to follow that you are actually predicting future sales. Personally, I have some serious questions about this measurement. The question is: will people do what they say they are going to do? However, a lot of people are interested in this measurement, and you should make sure that the service you are using will provide it for you (along with some kind of normative standard).

4 *Image Profile.* A number of the services will provide you with what I call an image profile. This will be some kind of projective technique that will allow the respondents to show their feelings about your product (or, since this is a brand new product and they have never used it, their feeling toward what you communicate about your product). If the research indicated that you communicated the positioning, this kind of measurement may be of less importance. It can, however, show you if there is something about your advertising that might merit looking into. For example, is your advertisement and product described as "harsh" or "hard sell?" Is it described in terms that would make it seem that the product is "right for me," or does it seem that the respondent feels it more appropriate for someone else? If you are communicating what you want to communicate, you probably are in good shape. However, advertising is so important that you must cover all the bases, and if you can get some additional feelings about the way you are communicating to people, you may be able to get some insight into ways of making your advertising more effective.

NAMING THE NEW PRODUCT

Naming the new product can involve several different kinds of decisions. Basically, however, it usually boils down to two. First, should the product carry a brand name that we already own? And second, if we are going to create a new name for it, what should the criteria for the name be?

The answer to the first becomes obvious if you dwell on two areas. First, what would be the strongest possible position for the new product (would it be best for it to carry a well-known brand name, even if this brand may not be exactly appropriate; or, would it be best and strongest for it to have its own brand)? Secondly, will giving an old brand name to a new product have a positive effect on the old brand, or a negative effect (or perhaps none at all)? In other words, what is the optimum name for the new brand and what trade-offs are involved? Clearly, this is an area that requires good judgment. A few marketers test these kinds of decision, but they are not all that easy to test. If the answer isn't obvious, it probably doesn't matter much either way. However, you have to address yourself to these questions.

Let me suggest the following as key criteria (the list can be expanded, but we will not do it here):

1 *Does it communicate some key portion of the positioning?* By this we mean, does it communicate the end benefit or does it communicate some key supporting attribute (that may even be unique to your product). My preference is for names that communicate the end benefit. However, you can easily understand how the communication of a key supporting attribute can actually communicate the end benefit. For example, if you were to market a special diaper washing powder whose key end benefit is that it leaves the diaper very soft, a name that communicates the end benefit might be "Young Softee;" a name that denotes the key supporting attribute, but which really connotes the end benefit might be "Lanolin Wash." How you do this is, again, a matter of business judgment. But let me emphasize a point—a name is not good unless it communicates something key about the product. Being unique is usually not enough.

2 *Not easily better-able and unique.* The name you select should be as good a statement of a positioning, or of a special benefit for a product like yours, as it is possible to make. You'll have to assume that competition may choose to follow you into the market or market segment that you are entering. You have to assume, also, that the competition will look for a strong name. You should close off many of their best options by selecting a legally protectable name, and if there is more than one name, you may want to register several and save them for future use (and therefore, deny them to your competitors). Also, the name you select must have some uniqueness about it. It must be catchy and, if possible, be a little fun to say and hear. Names that are too prosaic, no matter how well they communicate the key elements, are really not doing a full job.

3 *No negative connotations.* Obviously, the name should not have any negative meanings to any segment of the population in which you are going to market your product, whether they are your target consumer group, or not.

4 *Protectable.* It is key that you be able to protect your name legally. This should be checked with your corporate legal people before you are too far along on your naming process.

There may be other criteria; for example, how well does it fit into other brand names owned by the corporation, and how flexible is it for future use?

We now have covered the key criteria for naming a new product. When you have set your criteria, discussing your problems with a professional naming firm and, also, with your advertising agency will help you refine your thinking about it. You may well chose to go outside for help. A name is a very important part of the communications package, and it is a good place to spend extra time and money to insure that what you have is as close to the optimum as possible.

This chapter will not dwell on creating packaging or point-of-sale material—the other two key communications devices to your consumer. But it is useful to note at this point that although the chapter deals primarily with advertising (the key communication device for most new products), the criteria for excellence for the packaging and point-of-sale material are the same as that for advertising—does it communicate the key aspects of the positioning statement?

CASE: THE MIDDLE SOUTH MILLING COMPANY— CREATING THE COMMUNICATIONS PACKAGE FOR THE NEW BEVERAGE

When you and Jerome decided to continue with the project, you placed a call to Mel James, one of the two brothers who owns James & James. James & James, Middle South's agency for about 10 years, is in Chicago and is a full-service, medium-sized agency.

James & James was owned by Mel and Rick James—the "James Boys," as they like to style themselves. James & James was an agency that had a reputation for creative strength, and was seen as about average in its marketing and media abilities. Therefore, you and Jerome agreed that you would take special care to insure that the creativity was on strategy, but that you would not put undue constraints upon James & James' creative process—knowing that you would require the strongest possible effort from them.

You agreed with Rick James that the next step would be for you to prepare a Positioning Statement and a competitive presentation. In addition to this, you prepared a fact book (competitive advertising expenditures and copy, sales of other brands and categories of drinks, etc.). This was done with the help of James & James Information Center.

When this is finished, you prepared and presented the following:

Positioning Statement

The benefit of this product is that it is a drink that all members of the family will enjoy, especially children, and which contains only healthy, nutritious ingredients.

Supporting Attributes:
   70%–good fruity taste because it is made from dried fresh fruit and fruit sugar.
   20%–no harmful ingredients, and so forth.
   10%–contains body-building protein.

You went on to state that, in your competitive presentation, you expected about 80% of the business to come from powdered drink users, and about 20% to come from canned-frozen users. In addition, you reviewed the demographics and psychographics of the target and other research data.

Further, for the name (James & James was going to do the naming and the packaging), you set the following objectives:

1 The name must reinforce the end benefit, either directly, or by incorporating into the name the single key supporting attribute.
2 The name must be unique and legally protectable.
3 The name must be the best exposition of positioning possible.
4 The name must contain no negative connotations.
5 Names that can be integrated into the creative effort will be seen as having a plus.

For the packaging, you said that the end benefits and supporting attributes for the advertising would hold for the packaging objectives, but they should be expanded to contain more of the data from the Product Blueprint and Positioning Blueprint. You agreed with James & James that the next step would be for them to prepare a creative strategy statement that you and Jerome could review and, once approved, would serve as the basis for the creative effort.

After several sessions, James & James produced the following creative strategy statement that you and Jerome accepted:

Creative Strategy—PROFRUIT

1 We will communicate the end benefit by showing children drinking the product with obvious gusto.
2 We will communicate the health-nutrition aspects of the positioning by attempting to communicate the supporting attributes in the weight portion of this Positioning Statement:
   a 70%–fruity taste, dried fruit, fruit sugar.
   b 20%–no harmful ingredients, chemicals/natural ingredients.
   c 10%–contains protein.
3 We will primarily show children using the product but, in most usage situations, adults will also be seen holding a glass of the product to make it seem an all-family drink.
4 Through the tone of the advertising, we will create the image of a healthy drink, but not a health food.

As a first step, names were generated: the output of this work was a list of 235 names. By being rigorous in your application of the naming objectives, you managed to reduce the list to 56 names. After discussing the matter with Jerome and getting his preferences, and culling those that had some type of legal problem, you reduced the list to the following four leading candidates:

1 PROFRUIT
2 NATURALLY FRUITY
3 FROOT JOOCE
4 COOL 'N HEALTHY

The question now was which of these names was the best; further, to decide this, what kinds of consumer research to use, or whether to make the decision on judgment. The agency indicated that not one of the names was inexorably tied to a specified execution, so that criterion seemed less important.

In a final meeting that included you, Red, Jerome and the agency, it was decided to utilize NATURALLY FRUITY. It seemed to be most on target. Further, no other name was seen worthy of protection, and the matter proceeded to the creation of the advertising.

After four weeks, James & James showed you seven executions of the strategy in the TV format (the preliminary opinion of the Media Department was that the most cost-effective way of reaching the target audience would be through TV, and therefore, all executions were prepared using the format of this medium). All the material was in a rough form and the meeting was cast in an experimental and exploratory light. From the meeting, it became apparent that three of the seven executions were really not on strategy. Of the other four, all were deemed to be on strategy, and there was a wide range of executions. However, given the cost of testing advertising, you knew that you would have to reduce the number to two, or at most, three.

The problem was complicated by the fact that one of the executions seemed to be the best of the bunch. It was selecting the second execution to test that was the problem. Each of the remaining three had strong proponents who could make a convincing case for their favorite. To solve this problem, it was agreed that Focus Groups would be held among members of the target audience living in a nearby city. All four executions were redrawn so that they would be easier for nonadvertising people to understand. It was emphasized by the Research Director that each group would be educated to the product concept and positioning before any prospective advertising was shown. This would ensure, as much as possible in this type of research technique, that the respondents would understand the product for which they were seeing the advertising. On the basis of the Focus Groups, two executions were selected and were refined slightly to improve their communication ability. One of these was called "Ingredients" (Figure 8-2); and the second was called "Children Playing" (Figure 8-3). It was interesting to note, you felt, that the one that you and the advertising agency had preferred, "Children Playing," was seen as average by the women in the focus groups, and that they didn't seem to have any particular response, positive or negative to it. "Ingredients," which was one of the three that you and the marketing and advertising team had thought a candidate for the second slot, had received very solid responses from the women in the group.

The next step, obviously, was to test these commercials in more finished form. On the basis of the recommendation of the Research Director of James & James, it was decided to use a laboratory technique. The commercials would be put into a semifinished form referred to as animatics—the technique of drawing cartoon-type cells and putting them on film so that they appear to be a commercial. However, in this case, it was decided that still photographs would be used instead of drawings, because, for a food product, it seemed useful to get this kind of realism. The agency proceeded to make test shots and produced its own commercials.

In the test James & James was careful to make sure that the kind of research questions that produced the demographic, psychographic, desire to try, and positioning blueprint data were used so that comparability could be drawn.

As was often your experience in these matters, the research results did not provide a clean decision. Using the trial intent measures that you had used previously, "Ingredients" was slightly better, but not significantly (in a statistical sense) so. However, the similarities ended there. There appeared to be key differences between the commercials. The important ones were as follows:

KEY RESEARCH RESULTS SHOWING DIFFERENCES

	"Children Playing"	"Ingredients"	Creative Strategy[b]
End Benefit Communication			
Thirst-quenching, particularly for children	70%	30%	
Good for all members of family	30%	70%	
Supporting Attributes			
Fruit taste/dried fresh fruit/fruit sugar	60%	50%	70%
No harmful ingredients/natural	35%	20%	20%
Body-building protein	5%	30%	10%
Buying Interest[a] (Norm=10)	+11	+13	

[a]From the research service, not your "trial intent" questions.
[b]The objective from the creative objectives and strategy.

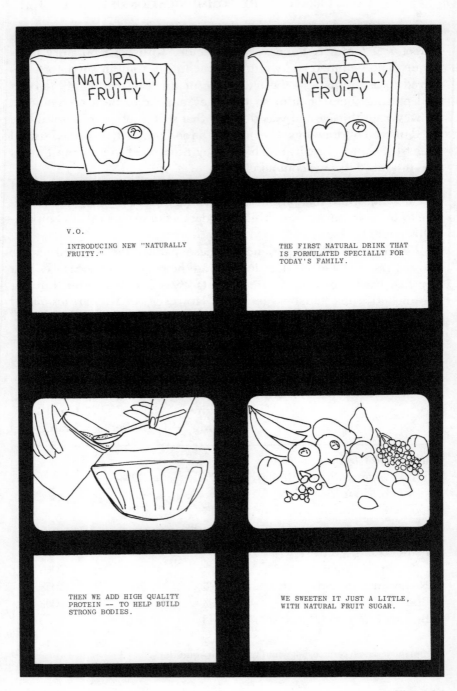

Figure 8-2

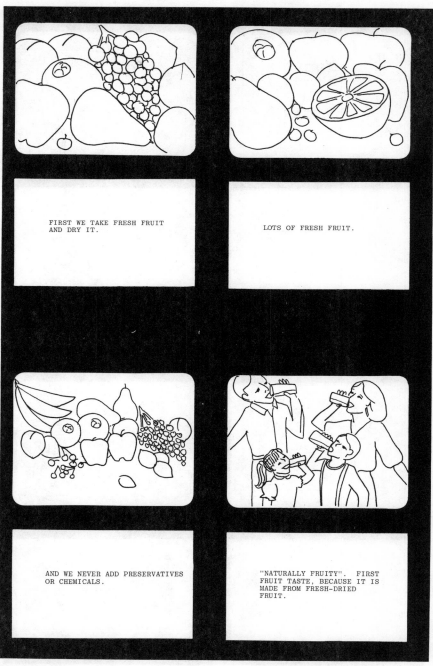

FIRST WE TAKE FRESH FRUIT
AND DRY IT.

LOTS OF FRESH FRUIT.

AND WE NEVER ADD PRESERVATIVES
OR CHEMICALS.

"NATURALLY FRUITY". FIRST
FRUIT TASTE, BECAUSE IT IS
MADE FROM FRESH-DRIED
FRUIT.

"Ingredients"

165

Figure 8-3

166

"Children Playing"

"Children Playing" was obviously superior in communicating the direct end benefit. "Ingredients" was seen more as an all-family drink. With respect to the supporting attributes, "Children Playing" definitely leaned too strongly in the "natural/no harmful ingredient" direction. It understated, also, the protein story a bit.

"Ingredients" was viewed more as a health food (even though in the Focus Groups it did not seem that way). It overstated the protein story, and understated the fruit story. As you and Jerome and the advertising agency management team discussed this, you drew the conclusions that "Children Playing" probably constituted the superior commercial. However, it was decided that, in the final production, the fruit story would be strengthened as much as possible in preference to the "natural/no harmful ingredients" story. It was generally agreed that these kinds of differences were generally too subtle to be adjusted much and that the commercial would be produced, with the minor changes, much as it was. It was also concluded that "Ingredients," in its execution, had somehow moved off strategy. The positioning changed into an all-family health drink, as opposed to nutritious thirst-quencher for children.

The question remained, however, if one were to believe the buying intent scores, then was this the stronger positioning? By the research company's measure, "Ingredients" did better. Looking back at the results of the buying intent on questions that you had carried from the previous research, it was obvious that "Ingredients" again scored higher—albeit not significant statistically. There was no good way of judging whether the frequency of use of one positioning would be the same as the other, although both you and Jerome agreed that the positioning, as you had started it, probably had the higher usage implicit in it. This positioning was communicated by "Children Playing." Thus, even though the trial might be slightly higher for the positioning suggested by "Ingredients," the resulting sales might not be.

The question remained as to what should be done. Should both commercials be produced and then tested in a test-market simulation model? Or, should the matter be resolved by judgment or another piece of research. Further, if the test market simulator were to be used, you really would be testing two different commercials in it. Would it be the best use of this kind of research tool? Or, would it be better to test price differences or marketing pressure differences? The question was resolved in a meeting with you and Jerome and Red. It was decided to proceed with the project using the "Children Playing" and the positioning as it had been agreed to and refined along the way. As Jerome stated, "The evidence is so far that we are doing the right thing. We are meeting our objectives, and there is no real evidence that the slight differences in test results of the commercials shows that we are off our target. In fact, it strengthens my point of view rather than weakening it."

You agreed with this conclusion although you had reached it from a somewhat different point of view (feeling that, in reality, "Ingredients" with a different positioning, would probably not have the same volume potential). "Red" Jackson gave Jerome his proxy and indicated his desire to move on with the project so that the introduction into the markets could be made in time for the following summer.

Just after the meeting, you received word from one of your brokers on the West Coast that a health food company that had previously marketed all of its products through health food stores, was talking to the trade about introducing a powdered fruit drink that, according to the broker, had milk solids in it. This raised some very sticky questions. For example, just how accurate was the broker's information? What claims could and would this company make for this product when and if it marketed it? Thirdly, would this alert other powdered beverage manufacturers to this market segment and start them moving earlier than you had hoped?

You and Jerome sat down to discuss the situation. First of all, you decided that you would attempt to verify the data. However, since the product had not been sold, it was still hearsay. Second, both you and Jerome agreed that speed and flexibility in the marketing process can be important marketing tools. There was no immediate danger from the company in question. Both you and Jerome felt that the marketing muscle of Middle South Milling would be sufficient to take on a competitor of this type in the marketplace. There was always a chance, though, that the other company's formula could be quickly copied by a larger competitor, or even that the health food company could be acquired. This would change the name of the marketing game very quickly. Of course, all these were just possibilities. None of the data was confirmed and there was no need for an immediate decision. But the rumor did have implications. For example, in the pricing policy, would it be better to have a penetration pricing policy than a skimming strategy? Further, in allocating marketing funds, would it be better to over-spend—take a longer payout? That way, you might logically hope to capture a larger share of the market before competition arrived. Other questions also suggested themselves. Should more than one firm occupy the niche in the market, is Middle South's R&D sufficiently sophisticated to keep abreast of product improvements? Also, if Middle South only marketed in 30 states, would facing a competitor who marketed in all 50 states with some assumed production economies-of-scale put it in a difficult competitive position?

As you and Jerome discussed this, it became apparent that nothing essential had changed in the equation. The need for moving quickly, albeit it precisely, had increased, however. Therefore, you decided to proceed and Jerome began to explore, with the Vice President of Manufacturing, co-packing arrangements.

9 Pricing New Products

Of all the decisions leading up to the introduction of a new product, setting the price is usually the most difficult and causes the most impact—although it often seems an obvious decision. Pricing affects demand, investment levels, and ultimately profits. It is difficult because often we have only the vaguest idea of the demand for the product, let alone demand at various price levels. Further, researching price is, at best, a controversial area (will people really buy a product at a specified price when they say they will?). However, it may seem to be an easy decision because the price is often set by marking-up (full or partial) costs. But cost-plus pricing rarely results in the best price for the product. The matter of pricing is further complicated by the fact that many firms have pricing policies, and your decision must fall within these constraints. Perhaps it would be best to start there.

PRICING OBJECTIVES AND POLICY

In broad terms, pricing objectives and policy deal with the survival of the firm. This requires that top management be involved and direct their marketing managers to set tough, clear, and quantifiable objectives and policies. But new product pricing does not take place in a vacuum. It must recognize market conditions and support corporate marketing goals and objectives. These corporate goals and objectives normally deal with future sales levels, market share, diversification, new products, profit and return on investment, and so forth. The new products manager must adjust his behavior to meet the corporation's goals. An example of a clear, understandable marketing goal is "We will double our sales revenue in five years." There may be a number of strategies for achieving this goal, but every manager knows what has to

171

be done. However, for the new product developer, this may be inconsistent with other aspects of the introductory program (e.g., this might militate against a skimming strategy).

Conflicts between policy and objectives must be reconciled by senior management to develop a total corporate effort. For example, doubling sales may require larger marketing expenditures, which can only be done by accepting a reduction in return on investment or by a skimming price on a new product, thereby incurring the risk that a competitor may be enticed into the market. Once the conflicts are reconciled, the new product developer can establish objectives in support of the total corporate strategy or plan.

The most common question regarding the pricing of a new product is what effect this decision will have on its potential contribution to the company's profits. This contribution may come from the product itself, or from stimulation of another line product. For example, a new product may lose money but through strong brand loyalty stimulate future sales of profitable products.

The pricing of a new product should support the company in optimizing its profits over time on all its products. Management must define the optimum in terms of production capacity, financial capability, personnel, costs, market share, investor expectations, and other factors by developing tough, realistic, and meaningful goals and objectives.

What marketing management really needs to know about a new product's price is the minimum price necessary in order to proceed at all, and the best price to achieve the total package of goals and objectives. Effective pricing focuses on this best price. It requires judgment and an in-depth knowledge of the product and market as well as the company's own capabilities and objectives.

COST-PLUS PRICING

Although cost is not a good direct determinant of price, companies must price their products at least to recover operating costs over time, let alone make a profit. Fairly uniform cost-price ratios develop in many industries and markets. The leading firms operate at about the same level of overall cost efficiency while competition brings product prices within a narrow range. These cost-price relationships differ by

industry and by type of product. For example, food products are characterized by a higher ratio of variable cost to price than paper or cosmetic products.

Cost-plus pricing is fairly common because the concept is easy to
grasp and apply. Firms within an industry often compare their own
operating ratios and results with competitors and make adjustments if
necessary to products, prices, and costs.

Determining price based on costs can also relate price to the firm's
profit or return on investment objectives. For example, if a company's
before-tax profit target for the coming year is 15%, then estimated costs
must be marked-up by an average of 17.6%. The following formula
illustrates this:

$$\frac{\text{profit}}{\text{sales-profit (cost)}} = \text{markup} \qquad \frac{15}{100-15 \ (85)} = .176$$

Cost-plus pricing also has appeal because it is a logical way to
determine the minimum acceptable price. This is of special significance in new product pricing in making go or no-go decisions. The
decisions are made against profit criteria. The minimum acceptable
profit plus the cost will equal the minimum acceptable price.[1]

One question that always arises is: "what cost should be used?" A
pricing decision affects the future, and therefore estimated future costs
should be used. But, should these costs be incremental costs only or
include fixed costs? Incremental costs will give the new product the
total increase in profit from its introduction. Incremental costs plus
fixed costs (full cost) will assign lower profit to the new product and
somewhat higher profit to the other products already in the line.

In theory, incremental cost is correct, but in practice a number of
problems arise. If a new company is formed to produce and sell a
single new product, the distinction between incremental and full costs

[1]*Note.* The formula for a markup percentage corresponding to a rate of return on
investment objective is as follows:

$$\frac{\text{investment} \times \text{desired rate}}{\text{estimated costs}} = \text{markup}$$

is small. In most settings, however, new products join an established product line. As new products are introduced, old products are phased out in a continuous cycle of growth and development. Management is generally committed to stay with a new product through its life cycle. In the case of a commercial airliner this might be fifteen, twenty or more years. For a fad product, it might be less than a year. The cycle for most new consumer products probably falls within a 2 to 10 year range.

All products require some fixed cost support to exist at all. Although a case might then be made that a new product should have less fixed cost allocated to it than an older product, it is difficult to determine how much less. There are many uncertainties surrounding new products. The rule-of-thumb is to load a full share of fixed costs to new products and then average them over their life cycle. The approach is consistent with the going concern concept. Allocating full costs results in a somewhat higher minimum acceptable price for a new product than pure economic theory would dictate, but there is a margin of safety as well which is difficult to quantify. In cases where the obtainable market price and computed minimum acceptable price are close, management must use its judgment in deciding whether to proceed.

Many companies use a cost-plus approach to pricing existing products. Prices obtained from applying standard markup factors to costs are compared with the competitions' prices. Adjustments are then made to the computed prices to reflect actual market conditions and marketing strategy.

Cost-plus pricing does two things: (a) it develops a price (not necessarily the market price) based on cost recognition and stimulates interest in cost efficiencies, and (b) it ties price to a desired financial objective such as return on sales or investment. Although market demand and competitive conditions control price and volume, management has a say also. It does not have to sell a product at a loss. In many cases, however, a product can be priced within a range of established prices, all of which enable the seller to make a profit.

DEMAND PRICING

Demand pricing focuses on the product and the market, and it carries with it a number of questions. The first question to be answered in demand pricing is whether the product will sell at any price, as discussed in Chapter 7, where the concept of the demand curve was discussed.

The next question is how much price flexibility do you have with respect to competition. New products are often introduced in a market that either already has similar products in it, or very close substitutes. There is either a prevailing price or one or more ranges of prices. For example, pet food has three major product categories—canned, semi-moist, and dry. There are price ranges within each category that seem to depend upon factors like product content (all beef) and positioning. Dry food has about one-third of the market and has been the major choice of economy-minded buyers. Recently the price range was approximately $1.40–$1.55 for a five-pound bag. However, a segment of dry food buyers apparently desired other qualities besides economy. This gave birth to the semi-moist products introduced a few years ago, with a price about 20–30% above the crunchy dry. This new premium priced segment charged a premium over the dry segment, yet delivered a new desired product and positioning.

Mineral water is another example. This market has a relatively wide price range (approximately $.01–$.04 per fluid ounce) and a new category has developed. In fact, Perrier has been quite successful in establishing its water as a drink by itself rather than just a mixer. Perrier's price is substantially above the domestic mineral waters. New brands are entering this new segment of the soft drink market, and, among other decisions, must look at price. Usually the effective range is between the price of domestic brand waters and Perrier's price. Price ranges are typical in many markets, but as shown with dog food, they do not necessarily set the limits for a new product that satisfies buyer needs.

Some products have no price range. They are sold at a price. These products are highly similar (little or no distinctiveness) with many buyers and sellers. Many such as wheat, oats, copper, and the like are traded on commodity exchanges. Another example is nuts and bolts sold to large industrial users. The price of nuts and bolts sold to the home market, however, can vary depending upon packaging and place of sale.

Thus, intelligent demand pricing requires some understanding of the distinctiveness of the products. With similar products, price is very sensitive. With consumer products, there is less price sensitivity since a number of other factors enter into the decision to buy. There are real and perceived product differences as well as judgments about such things as quality, service, styling, and availability. Advertising tends to focus on the distinctiveness and has an immediate as well as a cumulative effect. Salesmanship can also be important.

But *distinctiveness is not the only factor affecting your pricing flexibility. The maturity of the category is also important.* A new category, such as the mineral water category (some brands have been around for years, but in most respects it is a new category) offers a great deal of flexibility. A mature category, such as gasoline, shows little price differentiation, and it would be difficult for a new product to be priced much different from the market.

This brings us to the strategic question of skimming versus penetration pricing, which we will cover in more detail later. If you have the only product in the market, you have an interesting choice. You can price the product high initially, and skim the cream off the top of the market (really the top segment) before you lower it to be attractive to other segments. Of course, this takes time. If you fear a quick entry by a competitor, you may prefer a penetration strategy. This involves setting a lower price, and thereby capturing a large piece of the market before your competitor(s) arrives.

Of course, if you are not the first in the market, then some thought must be given to competition's reaction to a new product's price. If a product is introduced at a lower than prevailing price, competition may not react at all (particularly if there are product differences) if the potential share of market loss is low. There is a reluctance to reduce price (and profit) on a large share of market to retain a small percentage of the share. If the new product is successful, competition may introduce a lower-price competing product instead.

On the other hand, if the product is basically similar and the lower price results in major inroads on market share, competition will lower price to compete. This is particularly true if the product is important to the competitor's product line. Entering an established (but not declining) market with a similar product and attempting to take a sizeable share through lower price is risky and often requires a heavy and long commitment of financial resources. Since the stakes and risks are high, the potential rewards must be substantial. The strategy can be successful, however, if there is a major, protected (secret formula or patent) breakthrough in production technology that substantially reduces costs or produces a demonstrable product difference. However, competition can often duplicate new technology in a short time if the incentives are great.

Obviously we have raised a number of questions about demand pricing. A key one is the matter of flexibility. Let's examine that one first.

LIFE CYCLES FOR PRODUCTS AND CATEGORIES

When you introduce a product, you have to recognize that it will have a life cycle. However, if you are entering a market (or category) that is already established, then you must recognize that your product, for all practical purposes, enters at the level of the market's maturity. Thus, if your product enters a mature market, to a very great degree, it acquires the same constraints that effect other products in this market. This is tempered, however, by your level of distinctiveness. We will get to that in a moment.

The life cycle of a category (or product) seems to proceed in fairly well defined steps. In each step, pricing has different levels of flexibility. The following is an excerpt that explains this as well as anything I have seen.[2]

The life of a product can be divided into four major stages: product introduction, market growth, market maturity, and sales decline. A product's marketing mix must change during these stages, because: (1) customers' attitudes and needs may change through the course of the product's life cycle; (2) entirely different target markets may be appealed to at different stages in the life cycle; and (3) the nature of competition moves toward pure competition or oligopoly.

In addition, the sales history of the product varies in each of its four stages, and more importantly, the profit picture changes. It is significant that the two do not necessarily move together. Profits may decline while sales rise.

In the introduction stage, a company needs promotion to pioneer the acceptance of the product, since it is not sought out by customers. Potential target customers must be told about the existence, advantages, and uses of the new product.

[2]McCarthy, E. Jerome. *Basic Marketing, A Managerial Approach*, 5th Ed., 1975, Richard D. Irwin Co., Homewood, Ill.

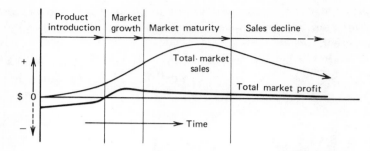

Figure 9-1   Life cycle of a typical product. Courtesy of Stockton & Ott, Inc.

Even though a firm has successfully carved out a new market for itself, the product may not be an immediate success. This introductory stage usually is characterized by losses, with much money spent for promotion and product and place development. Funds, in effect, are being invested with the expectation of future profits.

In the market growth stage, the innovator usually begins to make substantial profits. Competitors start coming into the market, and each tries to develop the best product design. There is much product variety. Some competitors copy the most successful products. Monopolistic competition with downsloping demand curves is characteristic of both the product introduction and market growth stages.

During this stage, the sales of the industry are rising fairly rapidly as more and more customers enter the market. This second stage may last from several days to several years, depending on whether the product is hula hoops, credit card service, or color television sets. This is the time of peak profitability—*and also the beginning of the decline of profits.*

By market maturity stage, many competitors have entered the market unless oligopoly conditions prevail. In either case, competition becomes more aggressive, with declining profits. Industry profits decline throughout the market maturity stage because promotion costs climb, and some *competitors begin to cut prices to attract business.* Even in oligopoly situations, there is a long-term downward pressure on prices. Prices actually may be cut even as total industry volume is rising. Promotion becomes important during the market maturity stage. Products differ only slightly (if at all), because most of the companies have discovered the most effective appeals to the market. There is a tendency to copy competing features. And in the industrial goods sector, buyers tend to encourage the development of oligopoly conditions when they buy by specifications and want to have several sources of supply. In the United States, the markets for most automobiles, boats, many household appliances, most groceries, television sets, and tobacco products are in the market maturity stage. This period may continue many years until a basically new product idea comes along to completely change the market. Gasoline-powered automobiles, for example, replaced horse-drawn carriages, and eventually may be replaced by some other method of transportation, such as electric autos and high-speed mass transit.

In the fourth and final stage of the life cycle, new products replace the old. Price competition from dying products may become more vigorous, but products with strong customer franchises may make profits almost till the end. These firms will have down-sloping demand curves because they have successfully differentiated their products.

As the new products go through the introductory stage, the old ones may retain some sales by appealing to the most loyal target customers, perhaps older people or those who found unique satisfactions.

Our earlier discussion of consumer behavior showed that some customers accept new ideas more readily than others. The former would 'discover' the new product; more conservative buyers might switch later, smoothing the sales decline.

The total length of the cycle may vary from 90 days, as in the case of hula hoops, to possibly 90 years for automobiles. In general, however, product life cycles seem to be shortening.

In the highly competitive grocery products industry, they may be down to 12–18 months for really new concepts. Simple variations of such a grocery product may have even shorter life cycles. Competitors may copy flavor or packaging changes in a matter of weeks or months.

Even copying of products is not uncommon, and this speeds up the cycle. Westinghouse found a company copying its new hair dryer *and* instruction book almost exactly. And patents may not be much protection. The product's life may be over before a case would get through the courts.

Later, in the same book, Professor McCarthy goes on to relate product life cycles with the market they propose to enter.

To fully understand the *why* of a product life cycle, we should carefully define the market area we are considering. The way we define a market is quite relevant to the way we see product life cycles, and who we have as competitors. If a market is defined very generally, then there may be many competitors and the market may appear to be in market maturity. On the other hand, if we focus on a narrow area and a particular way of satisfying specific needs, then we might see much shorter product life cycles as improved products come along to replace the old.

However, to think clearly about this situation, you need to introduce the matter of distinctiveness. After all, even in a mature market, if your new product has some differences, you will probably have some pricing flexibility. But it is important to realize that this flexibility is a function of the maturity of the market. Figure 9-2 depicts this situation.

In the first stages (IA and IB), the innovator has considerable pricing flexibility. Distinctiveness may matter little. In this stage the early followers also have pricing flexibility depending upon their own product benefits. They may follow the innovator's price or even exceed it if the product benefits are superior. The market is not price sensitive (within reason) because buyers are not completely familiar with the product and are highly interested in knowing what it can do for them. It is not necessary for an early follower to lower price to attract business.

The product innovator and early competitors often lose money during this introduction and acceptance stage. Promotion costs are high. Risk of acceptance is also high. But those whose products deliver will carve out a good share of the market.

Proceeding clockwise, which is the growth phase for products with some distinctiveness, market growth starts in Section IIB. Other competitors then enter the market as growth potential and profitability become more evident. There is still room for product variety or differentiation and pricing discretion, although the potential rewards based on market share may be somewhat narrower. Pricing at this stage has considerable flexibility.

As we proceed into the market maturity phase (Section IIIB) more definitive patterns develop. The market starts to stabilize. Buyers have assessed a number of products in terms of benefits and have started to fix their buying habits. New product pricing flexibility begins to narrow, and market share changes become less volatile. There is less price discretion because price ranges will be established in terms of product differences, and value established for this distinctiveness. The pricing objective at this stage is to secure enough of the remaining market based on the new product's distinctiveness to make a satisfactory profit. Pricing may be more defensive perhaps falling in the middle or lower part of the price range.

With market stability (Section IVB), market shares are well defined. Competitors are firmly entrenched and have solidified their position. Styling and new formulations perpetuate product distinctiveness but within more narrow limits, and prices show relatively little flexibility. Eventually, some products may begin to experience a decline in sales and profit. Each firm tries to maintain a satisfactory price-volume-

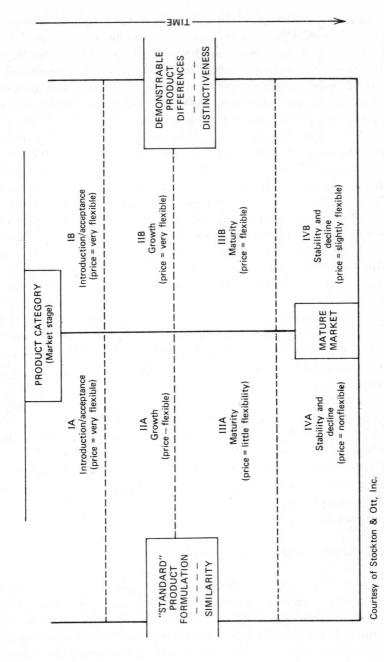

Courtesy of Stockton & Ott, Inc.

Figure 9-2. Pricing flexibility as a function of market maturity and product distinctiveness.

profit relationship, and some may reduce price to try to hold volume or tap new segments. Others will continue to try to rely on successful differentiation. Finally, some products will disappear entirely, although others may continue indefinitely. New products introduced in Section IVB are usually "me too" with little opportunity left (unless a way is found to increase frequency of use or for market segmentation). Often these are priced using a "contribution to overhead" pricing strategy. Of course, if a new product is introduced that has significant new benefits, the cycle starts over again in a new product category.

In dealing with new products where there is little distinctiveness, we can start at the top of the illustration and proceed *counter-clock-wise.* The major difference is that price tends to be more important through all stages of product category development, since buyers can more easily satisfy their needs with any one of a number of highly similar products available. By the time IIIA is reached, little price flexibility is left. By IVA, there is no point in selling for less than market price and attempts to sell at more than the market will result in no sales at all.

For most products, some distinctiveness can be found. It may be based on brand, availability, service, quality, use, or other factors. Of course, this distinctiveness must be important to the customer. Unique positionings can help, but most customers will not pay much above the going price for a special positioning.

In pricing a new product in a market in these later stages, there will be a prevailing price level with little flexibility. If there is some recognition of distinctiveness, (*your consumer research will have given you some clues whether your product has some distinctiveness*), there may be a relatively small price range. If there is no meaningful distinctiveness, then you either must price at a prevailing price or use a lower price as a competitive tool—which might invite retaliation, if your competition feels threatened.

Price Skimming and Penetration

The pricing choice, when introducing a completely new product is between a high initial price which skims the cream or a lower price aimed at securing as much of the market as possible (penetration). The more unusual you are, the more you have this option. The closer you are to other products (substitutes) the less flexibility you have. A policy

of high initial price and heavy promotion expense has proved successful for many new products. Referring to the discussion of Figure 9-2,
new products with demonstrable benefits are usually less price sensitive. This may lead to a skimming policy. A high initial price helps to
recover promotional and other start-up expenses and enables the firm
to reach profitability in a shorter time. On the other hand, the high
price attracts more competitors (sooner) so that your market share may
be lower over the life of the product category.

Penetration pricing tries to hit the major portion of the market as
soon as possible and reduce the effect of competition. Penetration pricing takes the longer term view and hopes for the larger share of the
market over the life of the product.

Returning to Figure 9-2, where there is significant product difference, price tends to be insensitive, and makes skimming attractive.
Also, since the life of new products has been growing shorter (12–36
months is not unusual), it becomes desirable to price high at the outset.
Development and promotion expenses have to be recovered. Given the
consumer, and the competitive environment today, it is difficult to
think of any new product whose life might extend beyond five years
with enough certainty to be willing to defer profit.

If we examine the left side of Figure 9-2, we find that price is more
sensitive, and the pricing options are fewer. The maximum price may
in effect be a penetration price. It may require a large volume and
market share to be profitable.

For effective penetration:

▶ The product must be relatively "standard" (within the context of
the specific market).

▶ It must have the potential to be quickly accepted in the "mass"
market.

▶ It must have a relatively long product life cycle.

Nylon is an example. But subsequent introductions of synthetics met
with considerable competition limiting market share and shortening
product life.

If there is a clear option available for skimming or penetration, a
decision can be made based on the respective cash flows to the firm
over the life of the product for each option. The option with the *highest*

184 PRICING NEW PRODUCTS

present value from discounting the future cash flows at the company's standard rate for new products plus a factor for additional risk (perhaps 3–5% extra for deferring profit and possibly being wrong), will be preferable in terms of profit contribution.

Discounting is based on the principle that $1 received sometime in the future is worth less than $1 received today, and we show how it is used for determining minimum price later in this chapter. The following example illustrates the use of present value (at a 25% discount rate) for comparing two alternative pricing strategies. This rate is not high and is based on a normal 20% earnings rate on investment for the company on total operations, and a 5% premium for the risk of a new product introduction.[3]

Net Cash (out flow)/in flow in Thousands of Dollars

Year	Skimming Price $2.50		Penetration Price $2.00	
	Cash Flow Amount	Present Value (25%)	Cash Flow Amount	Present Value (25%)
	(000)	(000)	(000)	(000)
1	(800)	(480)	(2000)	(1600)
2	700	448	800	512
3	2200	1126	2750	1408
4	2500	1025	3300	1353
5	2500	820	3300	1082
Total	$7100	$2939	$8150	$2755

This example shows that skimming is economically preferable at a 25% discount rate since the *present value* of the net cash flow ($2,939,000) is *higher* than penetration ($2,755,000).

Often an attempt is made to develop a price that has the benefits of both skimming and penetration. Hedging one's bets usually means a lower return. Effective pricing aims at the *best price* to accomplish tough objectives regarding volume and profit.

[3]Assuming you are entering an area where you have some expertise - this could be increased to 8–10% if you are entering a new area.

Price/Volume/Profit Objectives

The following table shows possible pricing strategies for a new entry as a function of market maturity:

Market Category at time of Introduction	Risk	Investment	Potential Rate of Return	Price Objective
Introduction (1A&1B) (first entry)	Highest	Highest	Highest	Highest
Acceptance (1A&1B)[4]	High	High	High/ Average	Highest/ High
Growth (IIA&IIB)	Medium	Medium	Average	High/ Average
Maturity (IIIA&IIIB)	Medium/ High	Medium/ Low	Low	Low/Below Range
Decline (IVA&IVB)	High/ Medium	Low	Low/ Marginal	Below Range

We can now examine pricing a new product in terms of potential volume and profit. The Dro-Mar Company has introduced a new product at a price of $2.30. Based on the product benefits and growing acceptance among consumers, the Beelow Company believes it can introduce its own competing product. Beelow's market study shows an annual market potential of seven to eight million units. It has capacity to manufacture between 1.8 and 2.2 million units annually without additional plant investment. Annual production can be increased to three million units in two or three years when the production of another product is planned to be phased out, but that decision does not need to be made at this time.

Beelow uses a standard profit return on investment for its total operation of 15%. An additional 5% is added for risk on new products. In order to produce and sell two million units per year, a $500,000 investment is needed for special machinery for introducing the product, and additional $500,000 for initial advertising and promotion.

[4] Still the introductory period, but not the first entry.

Beelow then determines its *minimum* acceptable price and volume to achieve a 20% rate of return (the minimum).

Figure 9-3 (cash flow profile) shows the minimum annual cash of $334,380 for five years (the expected life of the product) to yield a 20% return on the estimated investment of $1 million. For simplicity we have assumed volume is steady at 2 million units per year starting in the first year (annual cash flows for various rates of return for different numbers of years can be obtained from published tables). Using the required cash flow to produce a 20% rate of return, a pro-forma profit and loss statement is then constructed (in this case the same for each one of the five years). The annual cash flow of $334,380 represents $134,380 of net income plus $200,000 investment recovery per year. Working from the average annual income of $134,380 upward toward sales, $134,380 must be added for income taxes (assumed at 50% rate) and $200,000 for the amortization of the $1 million investment in five equal annual installments. Adding the income, income tax, the applied overhead of $400,000 and amortization, a gross margin target of $868,760 is obtained. The direct cost per unit to manufacture this product is $1.74 (obtained from the controller of company), and multiplying $1.74 by 2 million units results in total direct costs of $3,475,040. Beelow's direct cost per unit is constant over the 1.8 to 2.2 million unit capacity. The gross margin of $868,760 is then added to total direct costs of $3,475,040 to obtain the required sales amount of $4,343,800. Sales of $4,343,800 divided by volume of 2 million units gives a *minimum* sales price per unit of $2.17.

Beelow next examines the effect of volume changes on unit price (all to produce a minimum 20% rate of return) within its production capacity range. The following schedule shows the results:

Millions Units (1)	(1) × $1.74 Direct Cost (2)	Required Gross Margin (3)	Required Sales (2) + (3)	Minimum Unit Selling Price (2+3)÷(1)
1.8	$ 3,128,000	$868,760	$3,996,760	$2.22
2.0	$ 3,475,000	$868,760	$4,343,800	$2.17
2.2	$ 3,823,000	$868,760	$4,691,760	$2.13

The schedule shows a price range of $2.13 to $2.22 and relates about a 2% change in price to a 10% change in volume. Volume would have to

ASSUMPTIONS: $1 million initial investment—no value at end of 5 years
Product life—5 years
Volume objective—2 million units annually
Average direct cost per unit—$1.74
Even cash flow all years
Minimum rate of return:

Normal operations	15%
New product risk premium	5%
Total	20%

Pro-Forma Profit & Loss Statement

Years 1-5

Sales	$4,343,800	(÷2,000,000 = $2.17)
Direct Costs	3,475,040	(÷2,000,000 = $1.74)
Gross Margin	868,760	
Applied Overhead	400,000	
Investment Amortization	200,000	($1,000,000 ÷ 5)
Profit Before Tax	268,760	
Income Tax (50%)	134,380	
Average Profit	134,380	

Total Net Cash Flow-Profit

$671,900 ÷ (5 = $134,380)

Annual Cash Flow

Profit	$134,380
Amortization	200,000
Total	$334,380

Cash Flow Profile
Net Cash (Outflow) Inflow

Year		
0	$(1,000,000)[a]	Annual cash flows represent recovery of investment ($1,000,000) plus profit at 20% annual return.
1	334,380	
2	334,380	
3	334,380	
4	334,380	
5	334,380	

Discounted Rate of Return = 20%

[a] All in first year.

Figure 9-3 Cash flow rate of return analysis of price-profit.

be relatively sensitive to price for Beelow to increase volume through a lower price and still meet its internal profit objectives. Beelow's management believes its product benefits are at parity with Dro-Mar's product and that consumers are not price sensitive at this point in product category development. The market points toward obtaining the highest price in the range which is between $$2.13 (Beelow's minimum price at maximum volume) and $2.30 (Dro-Mar's price). If Beelow's product were demonstrably better than Dro-Mar's, a price above $2.30 would be appropriate. For a parity product, a price of $2.30 is indicated. With a price of $2.30 and a volume objective of 2 million units, Beelow has a potential annual rate of return of slightly more than 35%. This 35% is computed by using present value analytical techniques—cash flows each year from using a $2.30 price are discounted at various trial discount rates until the total discounted cash flow equals $1,000,000 (the original investment). A 35% rate of return is very attractive, but of course, it may be lowered by subsequent developments in the market. Future developments must be handled at the time they occur.

Beelow can now establish a clear, quantified marketing objective that supports the company's production and financial objectives. The marketing objective for the first year is: sell at least 2 million units at an average price of $2.30 per unit. If sales exceed 2 million at this price, bonuses would be in order.

Although we assumed equal annual volume of 2 million units to simplify the illustration, the more usual sales patterns for new products is for lower sales in the early years and higher sales in later years. In these cases the average minimum price can be found by testing various prices and obtaining different present values. When the present value of the annual cash flows equals the original investment, the price used to determine those annual cash flows is the minimum acceptable price.

For example, if Beelow's estimated first year volume was 1 million units (instead of 2 million) and volume for years two through five was 2,250,000 units per year, the average price would have to be higher than $2.17 to obtain the minimum 20% rate of return. If a price of $2.17 were assumed, the rate of return would be below 20% (the present value would be lower than the original investment of $1.0 million). If a price of $2.20 were assumed, the rate would be above 20% (the present value would be higher than the original investment). The following schedule illustrates:

Determining Minimum Price

Years	Estimated Units Sold	Annual Cash Flow @ $2.17	Annual Cash Flow @ $2.20	Annual Discount Factors @ 20%	Present Value @ 20% @ $2.17 Unit Price	Present Value @ 20% @ $2.20 Unit Price
1	1,000,000	$ 115,000	$ 130,000	.833	$ 95,795	$ 108,290
2	2,250,000	383,750	417,500	.694	266,323	289,745
3	2,250,000	383,750	417,500	.579	222,191	241,732
4	2,250,000	383,750	417,500	.482	184,968	201,235
5	2,250,000	383,750	417,500	.402	154,268	167,835
Total	10,000,000	$1,650,000	$1,800,000	—	$923,545	$1,008,837

Interpolation for minimum price at 20%:

$$\$2.17 + (\$2.20 - \$2.17) \times \frac{\$1,000,000 - \$923,545}{\$1,008,837 - \$923,545} = \frac{\$2.197}{(\$2.20)\,(\text{rounded})}$$

Inflation and New Product Pricing

It appears that inflation will be around for the foreseeable future. Questions often arise about its impact on new products. Consumer buying patterns may well change as discretionary income decreases in real terms.

As we have shown, however, pricing new products takes place within existing market conditions. Once the product is priced, a number of other forces take over. Inflation requires managers to take more frequent looks at price-cost relationships and adjust prices where possible to maintain profit targets.

Inflation has an impact on new product pricing in two areas: (1) the price of substitute products generally is higher, and (2) the profit standard for establishing the minimum price is higher. The cost of labor, management, materials, equipment, *and capital* all increase as a result of inflation. An 11% to 13% after tax average cost of capital today is not unusual for a large, prime credit-worthy company. This compares to 8% to 10% several years ago. For second tier, well managed companies, the rate may be 13% to 16%. For smaller, less-known companies, the rate may start at 15% and higher.

As the cost of capital rates increase, the minimum price for new products starts to increase more dramatically because of the larger compounding effect. If company standards have not been changed for a number of years to reflect inflation, a new look is needed at today's climate.

The large company with a lower capital cost can often price a new product at a level well above its minimum, but it may be very difficult for the smaller company to match it without adverse financial consequences. Thus, setting a lower price could be disastrous, even after allowing for the lower risk of being a follower.

TESTING PRICE

The market points the way to pricing new products. There is either a prevailing price or a range of prices. Where there is range, managers can judge which price best ensures meeting their volume objectives. As the market matures, however, there are still times when the new product marketer has a great deal of price flexibility; for example, when he first enters the marketplace; or when the market is still in its early growth stages—particularly when there are differences among products.

The price can be tested at various points in our system. One good point is when the actual product is being tested. Different research cells can be asked their desire to buy the item at different prices. For example, assume you are testing a new floor wax. Let's assume that we have priced it at $1.50, $1.89, and $1.90. The results might be:

Strong Intention to Buy

		Price
Cell 1	80%	$1.50
Cell 2	50%	1.80
Cell 3	45%	1.90

These results can only be interpreted in terms of the firm's own mix of price/volume effect on profit. For example, given a volume objective, a price of $1.90 would provide more profit than additional sales at $1.80

by a wide margin. The decision might, therefore, be made to price the product at $1.90 and focus on improving product acceptability. The results must be used with care since they represent intentions—not actual behavior. However, some research firms claim to have ways of adjusting the responses to reflect actual behavior more closely (they have compared intentions versus actions for previous projects). The objective here is to begin to understand what the demand curve for the product looks like.

Price can also be examined during test marketing. Actual sales can be measured at different prices in different markets. Although results are based on actual buying behavior and can be used with somewhat more confidence, they are not completely free of uncertainties. It is difficult to eliminate or control the many reasons other than price that lead to sales such as differences in income, regional or local buying habits, local promotion, differences in buyer expectations, and so forth. However, test marketing is expensive, and usually price is not one of the variables tested in test marketing.

On the other hand, test market simulation is often used for testing different prices. It is far quicker and less expensive than actual test marketing, although it is not without its disadvantages. We will discuss this further in the following chapter. Regardless of the technique you select, if there is some reason to believe that you have some flexibility in pricing, you should perform some type of price elasticity research to help you define what your options really are.

CASE: THE MIDDLE SOUTH MILLING COMPANY— MAKING THE PRICING DECISION FOR THE NEW POWDERED BEVERAGE PRODUCT

After deciding on the advertising approach, you and Jerome, as a matter of discipline, put the new product, NATURALLY FRUITY, through the Business Evaluation System. The result remained positive —but the process showed that one key variable yet remained to be defined, the retail selling price. You and Jerome had realized this, and although at one time there might have been a tendency to look at the demand curve for the product to find the optimum price (greatest profit) for the product, the situation had become much more complicated.

Obviously, this was a big opportunity for Middle South. The potential sales volume was large enough that not only would it be acceptable to Middle South but also it was reasonable to think that it would be attractive to any other food companies currently marketing a powdered beverage. In fact, the opportunity was sufficiently large that they might be examining it already. Even more to this point, rumors were spreading that a small health food company on the West Coast was already looking seriously into the area and might soon be introducing a product. As you and Jerome looked at the pricing question, there was much give and take about various points. It became obvious that you and Jerome saw some points quite differently, and that in the main the disputed points tended to center around the future of the market. It was obvious that what you needed was some kind of an agreement about what the future held. Therefore, it was agreed that you would jointly draw up a projection of the future situation. Once this was done, the other decision would fall into place relatively quickly, you felt.

The following emerged as an agreed-to forecast:

Statement of Future Situation

The powdered drink market will continue to be dominated by the consumption of children with almost all purchases being made by the head of the household (female). This market will continue to grow at about the current rate (between 10–20% per year) irrespective of the introduction of new products.

NATURALLY FRUITY is a unique product. It is based on technology that is not protectable and probably can be duplicated in one year by a sophisticated and determined competitor. It is possible that this development work is currently under way at one or more companies. It is reasonable to expect that, within one to one and a half years of our exposing NATURALLY FRUITY to the market, several competitors will enter the market with similar and potentially superior products. The West Coast health food company should not be considered as a serious competitor since it lacks the marketing and distribution muscle of Middle South in the markets in which we compete.

With this agreement, the pricing decision now became more structured. Obviously, from your last piece of product research you had some ideas of the demand for this product. You also suspected that from the growth rate the market was in the second or third stages of its life cycle. Your inclination was to think the second, rather than the third. Further, NATURALLY FRUITY had some very distinct and valuable differences. Thus, there was some flexibility available to you in your pricing decision. It could now become a marketing tool rather than a "given" as you had noticed so often in the past. In fact, the pricing question, given impending competition, boiled down to a penetration versus skimming question.

You went back and reviewed the marketing data. The average retail for a canister of powder that made eight quarts of beverage was $1.99. You intended to market your product in a six-quart canister and had used, as one price, $1.99 in your testing. Certainly this constituted a skimming price. The other price tested, $1.69, represented a penetration price, although the cost-per-quart was still a little higher than for the competitive products (28 ¢ versus 25 ¢). However, with your level of distinctiveness, or product differentiation, you felt this difference would be insignificant—that you could penetrate the market at this price. Thus, the decision began to form—attempt to penetrate the market at $1.69 or use the skimming policy at $1.99.

Quite obviously, a number of issues were involved here. First, there was the matter of profit. Which of these would return the best profit to Middle South? Then, there was the matter of risk. Certainly a skimming policy makes the market more attractive for a competitor, thereby possibly increasing the number of competitors and, further, causing them to hasten their efforts. At the same time, a skimming policy usually offered an earlier break-even point. This would be desirable in a situation such as this in which competition was seen as coming quickly. Less important, but also necessary to be considered, was the effect it would have on Middle South's general pricing policy. Heretofore, it had been pretty much at market. Middle South's advertising had attempted to create consumer differences by emphasing factors such as its Southern heritage, the fact that the product was made locally and, therefore, was fresh on the shelf, and so forth. In a sense, both the penetration and skimming strategy deviated from this policy. Another factor was the matter of the skimming price of $1.99. Given recent inflationary price trends, you suspected that this price could be pushed past the $1.99 level after about one year. The question in your mind was whether this constituted a psychological barrier that would create a problem for the consumer.

You discussed your thoughts and feelings with Jerome. It was agreed that you would prepare the financial data, operating under the following assumptions:

1 That the product should provide an after-tax profit during a "going year" of between 8–12%, with 10% the target.
2 That during the introductory period the product should be operating at the break-even point at the end of its 24th month and should have returned the initial investment by the end of the 36th.
3 That regardless of the pricing assumption as much money should be available for marketing use as possible.

That data was prepared. For a "going year", it was as follows:

Financial Planning—P&L's Going Year

Unit price at retail	$1.99	$1.69
Case (24) at retail	$47.76	$40.56
Case sales forecast	1,900,000	2,200,000
Retail dollars	$90,744,000	$89,232,000
Factory dollars[a]	$68,058,000	$66,924,000
Cost of goods	$25,992,000	$30,096,000
Direct profit	$42,066,000	$36,828,000
Indirect expenses (5%)	$ 3,402,900	$ 3,346,200
Marketing	$25,052,040	$20,097,000
EBIT	$13,611,600	$13,384,800
EAT	$ 6,805,800	$ 6,692,400
Three-years' available funds [b]	$126,198,000	$110,484,000

[a]Assuming 25% margin to trade.
[b]Direct profit for three years.

In looking over the data, you noticed some interesting aspects of your decision. Because of the nature of the demand of the product, factory sales at the higher price were very close to factory sales at the lower.

When you applied the 10% earnings after tax (EAT), this resulted in profit figures that were very close also. Also, even though there were slightly different investments involved, the return on investment (ROI) figures also were very similar. In fact, given the range of reliability of

ROI Calculation
Investment

	$1.99 Plan	$1.69 Plan
Inventory[a]	$ 4,332,000	$ 5,016,000
Accounts receivable[b]	5,671,500	5,577,000
Marketing[c]	2,087,670	1,674,750
Total	$12,091,170	12,267,750

ROI

$$\frac{6,805,800}{12,091,170} = 56.3\% \qquad \frac{6,692,400}{12,267,750} = 54.6\%$$

[a] Two-months' sales costed at cost-of-goods costing.
[b] One-month's sales.
[c] One average month's expenditures.

the forecasting procedure, you held the opinion that the alternatives were equally attractive from a financial standpoint.

There were some important differences. The higher retail price plan resulted in much more marketing funds being available. On a going year basis with full costing and full profit, the difference was about $5 million ($25,052,040 versus $20,097,000). On a marketing available funds basis in which, after direct and indirect costs were accounted for, the rest of the funds were available to marketing, there was a difference in that in one case you were talking about $33.5 million (the $1.69 price) and the other $38.7 million (the $1.99 price). At these levels, the magnitude of the available funds was significant. Although you personally felt you had to resist any spending plan based on no profit taking, or partial costing, still, if needed to beat back a competitive effort, funds would be available. But the real difference was a philosophical one. In one case, as you and Jerome agreed, you were talking about a high pressure system. This involved a higher price and a higher level of marketing funds. On the other hand, you had a low pressure system: lower price and a lower amount of marketing funds available, or, in other words, a skimming versus penetration question.

You and Jerome begin a dialogue that lasted with off and on meetings for three weeks. You both agreed that the closeness of the profit figures was somewhat artificial. After all, the incremental marketing funds could easily wind up in the profit column—making the higher price more attractive from an investment analysis standpoint. But you both agreed, also, that this was somewhat unrealistic because the higher price would make the market more attractive for competitors. Therefore the larger marketing funds would (a) be necessary for achieving the greatest penetration of the market because of competitive activity, and (b) be necessary to counter competitive activity after it had started. Therefore, although the similarity of the profit figures might be judgmental, there was some solid marketing basis for this.

Then there was the matter of the lower price strategy. The lower price, together with what appeared to be adequate marketing funds, probably would allow the greatest penetration of the market during the three-year introductory period. The lower price also probably posed a barrier to at least some of the firms that would consider entering this market. This, in the light of the future competitive activity forecast that you and Jerome had already agreed to, was attractive. But there was a potential fallacy here. Middle South would be using contract packers. Some of the potential competitors would have their own production facilities, and this could give them a cost of goods advantage (in addition, some of them were already buying some of the basic ingredients in large quantities and this also could affect their cost of goods positively). Further, if some of these competitors already had manufacturing facilities, what would prevent them from dealing with their products on a variable cost basis (and letting the other brands absorb the overhead). This would allow them to match Middle South's price and possibly have greater marketing funds. But you and Jerome agree that this was a corporate philosophy decision on their part and, regardless of your pricing decision, they might or might not perform this way.

Ultimately the decision seemed to boil down to two questions. Both evolved from your assumption that competition would be in the marketplace within two years. The first question was, given this assumption, what is the best way to obtain trial (assuming that we would develop an adequate repeat rate), extra advertising weight or a lower price? How much of a competitive barrier, really, was the lower price? Obviously, both of these were judgmental. If the question was only price, it might have lent itself to testing at two different levels with a market simulation device. But a critical difference between them was that one was a marketing strategy with heavier marketing expenditures

—something that you weren't sure a market simulation program would accurately reflect.

You discussed the matter of the difference in potential advertising budgets with the media director at James & James. He pointed out to you that, given your target, the incremental funds would be adding frequency, and not additional reach against your target audience. Further, he said that your frequency levels—even at the lower level—were quite respectable.

You and Jerome went back to the original two questions. Would the lower price present a barrier to firms that might consider entering the market? The answer you agreed to was "yes," but how effective a barrier would be difficult to say, and it would be safer to assume that it would only be somewhat effective. Second, which would give you the greater trial (and therefore penetration) of the market—a higher price with greater marketing pressure or a lower price and somewhat less marketing pressure? Here, you and Jerome leaned toward the answer that showed the lower price strategy would be superior because the marketing budget would still be quite healthy.

It was therefore decided that the lower price strategy would be the one that Middle South would follow. It was further agreed to review this decision at a later time and, if it was deemed still a worthwhile alternative, to test a higher price strategy in one portion of the country or in some test markets when and if NATURALLY FRUITY was put into the marketplace.

In sum, the pricing decision is complex because it involves corporate policy and profit, and marketing strategy. If you can, you should price your new product on the basis of demand information. This allows you the option of using pricing as a strategy.

If you are going to use pricing as part of your marketing strategy when entering a market, then you have the option of a penetration strategy or a skimming strategy.

Penetration involves setting the price relatively low to obtain the highest share of the market in the shortest possible time.

Skimming really is based on the idea that an inelastic demand curve exists for your product, that you can price it at a relatively high level initially, and then reduce it later to gain those buyers who did not buy at the higher price.

Of course, whether or not you can use pricing as part of your marketing strategy depends on a number of factors. Two important ones are (a) the life-cycle stage of the market and (b) a degree of distinctiveness or product difference.

The earlier in the market's life cycle and the more distinctive your product, the more options you have for making price a marketing variable.

10 The Last Step Before the Marketplace

You have now reached a point where, very often, a new product developer turns over his work to someone in the marketing department whose function it is to manage a brand on a day-to-day basis. At this point, it is assumed that you have a physical product that has tested well and that matches the Product Blueprint. You have advertising that has also tested well and matches the Positioning Blueprint. Further, you should have the kind of financial data (sales volume, profit potential, and the supporting data like cost of goods, indirect costs, marketing expenditures, etc.) that have allowed you to consider and accept this product as a viable investment alternative for the firm. Now you face a critical question. Do you need to test the marketing plan under some type of real marketing conditions before you introduce it to the entire market? Frankly, although I have some very strong preferences in the area, it's not an easy question to answer. Let me suggest a few thoughts that may help you decide in your particular instance.

1 If your product enters the marketplace and its competitors react quickly to the product (and indeed can duplicate it in a very short time), testing your product in the marketplace can be very risky (in that case, you may prefer a test market simulation, which I will discuss later).
2 Testing of any type is expensive. Test marketing will cost in the low six figures for a year. A test-market simulation would cost in the low five figures. In many instances your budget may not allow for this kind of expenditure.

199

3 Sometimes the risk associated with going directly into full distribution is small. For example, consider the level of risk involved if you are introducing a product with very little advertising money and very little new production investment (other than the variable costs). It may be that testing, in this case, is a luxury. Of course, the other point of view may be argued, namely that too many failures will soon make it difficult for you to convince the trade that any of your new products are worthwhile and that they should accept them into their distribution system.

These three factors give you a flavor of the decision process. In many industries, for example, in the fashion industry, very little testing is done (perhaps showing the potential new item to a few key buyers to get their opinions). In certain areas of industrial marketing, the same process holds. Obviously, in both these cases a few buyers can make critical decisions. Showing the new product to them and discussing it with them is a kind of test-marketing. In these instances further testing, if you are happy with the results to date, is not necessary. But most of the time, this isn't the case. A new product represents a meaningful investment for most companies. A new plant must be built; large promotion expenditures are indicated; an inventory investment must be made. In these circumstances you will need to get a tighter definition of the size and nature of the risk, and the quality of the investment opportunity your firm is facing.

WHAT SHOULD YOU BE TESTING

In test market simulations or actual test marketing, there are two areas that you should consider testing.

1 Certainly you will want to test the total package as you developed it. You are finally exposing the communications, and the total product to the actual consumer, determining how well they buy it (trial), and whether they will continue to buy it (repeat). In other words, you're seeing whether or not you have a potential business on your hands.

2 You may also want to test strategic alternatives. For example, you can test at different prices. Or, you can test two advertising weights. Or, you can test different kinds of trial devices (couponing, free samples, etc.).

Actually, there are other marketing variables that you can also test, but these seem to be the most common.

Should you decide to test market, you have two choices. The first option is what we call a test market simulation. In a test market simulation, a sample of people who closely match your consumer target are put through a sequence of events that look something like this:

1 They are exposed to the advertising for your product (usually in the context of some kind of programming and other advertising, so it's not too obvious).

2 The respondent then goes into a real or mock-up store in which your test product and other products that form the overall category are displayed. They may or may not have been given a coupon, sample money, or some other trial stimulation device.

3 Those who purchase your product are allowed to use it.

4 They then are given the chance to purchase this product again (often several times, although this depends partly on the usage cycle of your product).

5 At some point, they are interviewed about the product.

6 All this data is put into a mathematical model that has been developed to take data of this type and convert it into actual trial, repeat, and ultimately annual sales volume figures.

Firms that own and promote these models claim a high degree of correlation between their testing activities and those observed when the product is actually marketed. The result is that you are able to (ideally) closely forecast the actual performance of your prospective product in the marketplace, and, thus, be more precise in your thinking of it as an investment alternative for your company.

The opinion of professional new product developers is that many of these models do work very well and that they have a place in the new-product development process. A number of them have been active for quite a few years, and I must assume that, if they have lasted for this long, they really are providing a worthwhile service.

The other alternative you have is actual test marketing. Test marketing means selecting one or several geographical areas (anything less than two is fairly dangerous, since it is easy for one market to give you a false reading), and then having your product sold, advertised, serviced, and so forth in that market as if you were doing it on a full national basis.

Of the two systems, obviously, test marketing gives you more precise results. It also has some drawbacks, as we shall see later in this chapter, but some of the most sophisticated marketers in the United States continue to use test marketing. I must also add, however, that in many cases, they are using test marketing to refine strategies that are not testable by simulation in addition to judging the quality of the investment proposition.

Sometimes you will do both. You will go from test market simulation into test marketing, and then into full-scale marketing. My observations are that this usually is done when test market simulation is used to decide some strategic issues, and then actual test marketing is used to generate the necessary financial data. The bigger the risk, the more often both types of testing are employed. You do this to have further confirmation that you have a potential business, and to further reduce the risk level you are facing.

PREPARING THE MARKETING PLAN

Before you move into any kind of market testing, you need to develop the marketing plan. While developing the plan, you may discover some marketing strategy alternatives that you need to explore. You should reflect seriously on this topic because you are coming to the point where you can test some alternatives that you might want to look at seriously.

In writing the marketing plan, you need to do two things: (a) you need to present your management with the complete body of data that affects this product in the marketplace; (b) you need to prepare the specifics of your marketing objectives strategies and financial data. Sometimes the former is called a Fact Book and the latter the Marketing Plan. Other times they are combined into one document. My preference is to split them. Keep the Fact Book as an ongoing, constantly updated book and the Marketing Plan as an action document. This saves you from what ultimately will become an unwieldly document. It allows you better protection of the confidentiality of the Marketing Plan because you can release the Fact Book to disseminate information. Regardless of how you do it, the following data should be included in the "Facts" section:

1 *Competitive Data*
- ▶ Sales for all competing products, by dollars and units. Often, with a new product, this may cover several categories (as defined traditionally by your industry). They all must be included.
- ▶ Sales for these products by various kinds of breakouts that seem appropriate: for example; geographic, product size, flavors, type of end customer, season, and so forth.
- ▶ Pricing data (historical and current) should be included for all relevant brands that form the category that you will be entering.
- ▶ Where possible, the above data that incorporates sales for brands in the entire category should be given on some historical basis, and the trend should be made obvious.

2 *The Consumer*
- ▶ The demographics (and psychographics, if available) of the target consumer should be shown. This data should be broken out in such a way that you can identify heavy versus light users, users by different usage situations, etc.
- ▶ If the ultimate consumer and the purchaser are different, this must be made clear, and trends for the ultimate consumer group be made explicit (for example, children's products).
- ▶ Long term demographic trends, such as population growth, per capita income growth (if this is relevant to your type of product), source of supply trends, etc. should be included if they affect your business.

3 *Channels of Distribution*
- ▶ The Fact Book should give sufficient information about the channels of distribution so that the reader should be able to understand what the important issues are. This should include sales by type of channel (if more than one is to be used). This should also include such data as channel pricing policy, the mark-ups taken typically by various members of the channel, who the channel captain is (that member of the channel that seems to have the most power—for example, in the automobile business it is the manufacturer; in the fashion business, it is usually the retailer), and growth by type of retailer, if more than one is to be used.

4 *Competitive Promotion History*
- ▶ Advertising expenditures for each category in total and by individual brand, and by region of the country, if this data is available.
- ▶ The positioning (as you understand it from the advertising), and copy strategy for each of the relevant brands.
- ▶ An example of advertising (sample ads, copies of TV photo boards, radio scripts, etc.).
- ▶ Estimated competitive expenditures, per sales dollar, for each of your major competitors.
- ▶ The brand awareness for each of your competitors, if you have it.
- ▶ Examples of promotional tools used by your competitors.

5 *Your Research History*
- ▶ This area should include the concept refinement work and the conclusions you drew from it.
- ▶ The results of any advertising copy testing (including an example of the advertising tested).
- ▶ The results of product testing that you performed.
- ▶ The results of any type of name testing, and packaging testing that you might have done.
- ▶ Any testing of competitive advertising copy that was not included in one of the above sections.

These may not cover all the areas relevant to your industry. Your industry may have certain kinds of government data available to it, certain other kinds of laboratory testing such as quality assurance testing, and the like. If this data was not incorporated here, it should be made into a separate section. The Fact Book should provide you, or the readers, with access to all the data they will need to understand the business proposition.

THE MARKETING PLAN

The Marketing Plan for a new product introduction should contain the following kinds of data:

1 *Overall Business Goals.* This section should show how you see your product performing in the marketplace until its early maturity. Generally, this will mean at least three to five years, but it differs by industry. The objective of this is to allow you to present a scenario to your management so that they see how this product will fit into the marketplace and also understand your thoughts about how the marketplace will evolve. It should state how this product fits into your firm's long range plan. If you forecast that there will be product line extensions as part of this family, this should be included. The C.E.O. must understand how this proposed business fits into the company's overall business goals.

2 *Financial Data and Justification.* This area must provide the Treasurer (and the Chief Officer) with the necessary data to view your proposal as a prospective investment for the firm. This means that you will have to provide profit and loss statements for the first year, and quite probably for future years if you see this product returning your initial investment after the first year. The data must be structured to use the financial tools that are common in your firm for analyzing investment alternatives. Often, this means return on investment. Other firms use return on assets, payback period, discounted cash flows, and the like. Also, this section must include the kind of investment you are expecting from the firm and the time period in which it must be made. This should include plant and equipment, advertising, inventories, and so forth. If there is any reason that this product should be judged by other than the standard financial criteria for the firm (for example, a situation where it will absorb much of the heavy fixed cost burden), then it must be made explicit in this section.

3 *Marketing Objective and Strategy.* This area may be limited to one year, or, if the investment is such that the payback takes more than a year, you may want to include objectives and strategies for future years. The kind of data this area should have is:

- ▶ Sales (in units and dollars).
- ▶ Distribution objectives (number of stores accepting the line, etc.).
- ▶ Spending strategies (if you intend to spend your investment dollars in some special way).
- ▶ Any other kinds of business objectives or strategies that were not included in the overall business goals section.

4 *Activities During Introductory Period.* The Marketing Plan must give a tight outline of all activity that you plan during the introductory period. If this introductory period is over one year (which it often is), then the Marketing Plan should include goals and activities for the first marketing year and show for the remainder of the introductory period how these activities will continue. Generally the activities are divided into three kinds: advertising, promotion, and market research. For each of these, you should include the following types of data:

▶ *Advertising*
  a. Creative objective and strategy.
  b. Media costs by month.
  c. A flow chart showing all media activities.
  d. Any media testing that is planned.

▶ *Promotion*
  a. Consumer promotion objectives and strategy.
  b. Trade promotion objectives and strategy.
  c. Examples of consumer promotions.
  d. Trade promotions and financial details relating to both.
  e. A promotion flow chart that also shows the advertising on it.
  f. Promotion expenditures by month.

▶ *Market Research*
  a. Dates and details of surveys to acquire information such as awareness, trial, repeat, attitude and product use.
  b. Plans for measuring retail movement.
  c. Plans for testing of current creative or new creative material.
  d. Plans for double-checking that the consumer or trade is not misusing any kind of promotion vehicle.

Once management has approved your plan (particularly about agreeing that it appears to be a reasonable alternative as an investment) you are now ready to move into the last area of testing. At this point, these activities become basically a translation of the plan.

TEST MARKET SIMULATION

Test market simulation is presenting, to a sample group of consumers, your advertising, packaging, point-of-sale material, price and store location strategy within the context of some type of simulated store conditions. (It may be a mocked-up store, or it may be a panel of actual stores.) The purpose, obviously, is to see how the consumer reacts to your product and the various elements of your marketing mix in as close to real life situation as is possible.

Test market simulation has some big advantages over test marketing. First of all, there is the cost. Forgetting for the moment the production costs of advertising and manufacturing a small quantity of the product (with actual packaging), test market simulation can have a research cost of under $35,000. Compared with test marketing, even for a relatively short test market using smaller cities, this is somewhere between 5–10% of test marketing costs. A further economy also results from the fact that often you can use rough advertising copy, which can save you the production costs associated with advertising. This you could not do easily in a real test market. Another advantage of test market simulation is time. Generally, you can obtain your answer in six to ten weeks. Test market timing takes six to twelve months. In marketing, as in everything else, time is money. Further, in categories that are extremely competitive, you want to beat your opponent to the marketplace with as much lead time as possible. In this case, the time efficiency of test market simulation can be very valuable.

The last advantage of test market simulation is the secrecy factor. For test market simulation, you can keep your plans reasonably well hidden. In real market test marketing, your product, advertising, promotions, and so forth are exposed for everyone to see. From your behavior in a test market, a smart competitor can ascertain the important facets of your marketing strategy. For categories with short life cycles, or where competition is very intense, or where it is difficult to obtain any kind of protection (technological, legal, etc.), your test marketing in an actual market can be a problem. Your competition can read your plans and beat you to the marketplace. Under these circumstances, test market simulation becomes very attractive.

But test marketing simulation has a couple of strong drawbacks. To begin with, the consumer exposure to your advertising and your product is artificial. Although the degree of artificiality changes with the type of simulation system you use and the model theoretically compensates for this, the artificiality still remains. This means that the tightness of the reading that you get from the results is less than you would obtain in test markets. Another big drawback of simulation is the complete lack of trade data. How the trade will react to your product and your promotion plans, where in their stores they would like to put it, and all other variables in dealing with the trade are not obtained with test market simulation. Perhaps these things are not important to you, but if they are, then test market simulation will not really test all the marketing variables. The last disadvantage of test market simulation is that most of the work on formalized models has emphasized products that are sold through the grocery and drug channels. This means that you are talking mainly about food products, health and toiletry products, and proprietary drugs. The input data for these models are based on these kinds of products. Therefore, if your proposed product does not fit into this grouping, it is possible that the available models are not appropriate simulators for your market. The problem is that the normative data used for internal controls in the model, and for comparison of predicted and actual market results, will not be appropriate. You will have to generate it yourself. That can be a long procedure.

Don't believe that I am against test market simulation. Actually, in many instances I am for it, and as test marketing itself becomes more expensive while test market simulation becomes more sophisticated, I suspect we'll be doing more and more of it. It's just that under some circumstances it can be very risky, and under the best circumstances it still has risk associated with it. You have to understand these risks to use it correctly.

REAL MARKET TEST MARKETING

Real market testing usually involves going to a group of cities or a panel of your customers and attempting to sell your product under conditions that, as closely as possible, simulate what you would do if you were selling in your total marketing area. To keep the record straight, the usual objective of test marketing is to make sure that the kind of sales and profit projections that are required to justify putting a new product into full distribution (as an investment for the firm) are sufficiently tight, and that everyone feels comfortable with them. Of course, testing marketing has other implications: we can test different pricing strategies, media weight strategies, and so forth. Sometimes, test marketing is done just for these purposes alone. In new product development, however, the requirement of the hard financial data almost always is the paramount objective of test marketing.

How Do You Choose A Test Market?

Choosing a test market varies from industry to industry. Industrial marketers can select one group of consumers (a panel). They can sell only to these people and, by adjusting their media strategy, advertise only to these people. In a sense, they are translating their marketing plan which is directed to a specific group of industries, or buyers within an industry. Generally, consumer marketers think in terms of cities (some of them limit themselves to panels of stores in a few cities). Most often, though, two to four cities are isolated and the product is distributed and promoted in these markets.

Regardless of how it's done, there are some characteristics that your test area(s) should have. First, the buyers must be representative of the whole. Normally, this is limited to demographics. This means that the people in the test cities, in terms of age, income, buying power, and the like, should be representative of the marketing area in which you ultimately want to distribute your product. Sales Management Magazine is one good place to obtain demographic data.

Another characteristic is that the use of products you are considering marketing should be about average in the test market. It is always a temptation to select markets with higher than normal use characteristics, making the justification that these people will view your product more intensely and, therefore, give you a quicker or more thorough reading. This is almost always a mistake. The only time I recommend using markets with extremely high usage patterns is when you are interested only in finding out whether people will buy your product and whether they will repeat, and not in making any financial projections from it.

A third characteristic is the competitive situation. The market you select should not have a competitive level much different from the national average, although this is somewhat difficult to judge and control.

A fourth characteristic is the media coverage. The market you select should have similar kinds of media and, more importantly, the media should cover the market thoroughly with little spill-over (something we will discuss a bit later). Generally, this is not as big a problem as it may seem, and there are ways to adjust for any minor differences. It is, however, a very important criterion unless you intend to use no media whatsoever or, conversely, intend to use only direct media such as direct mail.

The last criteria is the measurement of sales data. We will get into this as the chapter unfolds, but suffice it to say here that it will be necessary to get accurate readings on your sales in the market and to know that these sales are, indeed, coming from the area in which you are advertising, and not from outside (a prerequisite for financial calculations).

Selecting the Cities

If you are going to test market in various cities, the next decision is which cities to select. Actually, there is a question to be answered just before that, and that is, "Do I want to use a whole city with its complete distribution system, or will I want to use some portion of it with a panel of stores constructed to reflect a representative sample of the city?"

A number of firms have store panels set up in cities, and they audit (measure) consumer sales in these panels on a regular basis. This can be an attractive way to test because it allows you to gain distribution quickly through their auspices (and keep tight control of the sales situation). Thus, this can be a way to test market a product without some of the problems of gaining distribution and controlling sales. You should look into it before you decide on a regular test market in which you would have to obtain distribution and measure the sales on your own. Some names of companies involved in this research are: Audits & Surveys; Burgoyne; Market Facts; and A.C. Nielsen. If you are interested in chatting with these people, your Marketing Research Director, or the research people at your advertising agency will be knowledgeable about them and can put you in touch with the right firms.

Whether you use a store panel system or your own distribution system, you must select the right cities, and in thinking about this selection process, you should keep in mind the criteria discussed above. Further, to keep your costs in line, you should select cities that are less than 1% of the U.S. population. The following is a list of cities that have a high usage rate as test markets. The list was constructed by a New York advertising agency (Dancer, Fitzgerald, Sample).

1. Albany-Schenectady-Troy, NY
2. Albuquerque, N.M.
3. Amarillo, TX
4. Austin, TX
5. Cedar Rapids, IA
6. Chattanooga, TN
7. Cleveland
8. Colorado Springs, CO
9. Columbia-Jefferson City, MO
10. Corpus Christi, TX
11. Davenport-Rock Island-Moline, IA-IL
12. Denver
13. Des Moines, IA
14. Duluth, MN
15. El Paso
16. Fargo, ND
17. Grand Rapids, MI
18. Greenville-New Bern, NC
19. Greenville-Spartanburg, SC
20. Indianapolis
21. Jackson, MS
22. Jacksonville, FL
23. Kansas City, MO
24. Knoxville, TN
25. Lexington, KY
26. Louisville
27. Lubbock, TX
28. Memphis, TN
29. Milwaukee
30. Mobile-Pensacola, AL-FL
31. Nashville
32. New Orleans
33. Norfolk, VA
34. Oklahoma City
35. Orlando, FL
36. Paducah, KY
37. Peoria, IL
38. Portland, OR
39. Richmond, VA
40. Rochester, NY
41. Rockford, IL
42. St. Louis
43. San Antonio
44. Savannah, GA
45. South Bend, IN
46. Springfield-Decatur-Champaign, IL
47. Tampa
48. Tucson
49. Tulsa, OK
50. Wichita, KS

This list should act as a starting point for you. Frankly, I would not use several of the cities on the list (unless a panel were constructed in them —the problem being, mostly, distribution difficulties). Regardless, from this list you should be able to select two to four geographically dispersed cities that will form a test market cell for you.

TRANSLATING YOUR PLAN AND CONTROLLING YOUR RESULTS— THIS MATTER OF PROJECTABILITY

The whole purpose of running a test market is to be able to project from it to the whole world and to make inferences about your future in that world. In other words, everything you do in test market must be projectable to the whole world. This means, you must minimize certain kinds of problems as you run the test market, and you must avoid certain kinds of mistakes. First, let's look at the problems.

The first one is media spill-out. When you translate the national media plan into a test market, the translation must be done on an impressions basis. It should not be done on a dollar basis, as is sometimes the case, for media costs differ by market, and there are almost always penalties involved in test market translations. Further, you should be certain that the media impressions falling into the area from which you will measure the sales are the correct amount. Some of your media impressions will fall outside the test area. This is called media spillout. It is regrettable, perhaps, and it is certainly wasteful. However, it is a fact of test marketing, and you should accept it. MAKE SURE THAT THE IMPRESSIONS FALLING IN THE TO-BE-MEASURED AREAS ARE A DIRECT TRANSLATION OF THE NATIONAL MEDIA PLAN.

Another thing you must handle is media spill-in. When you put together your national media plan, you often will think in terms of share of spending. In other words, you might project that you will spend about 10% of the total media dollars in this category. Then assuming similar media efficiencies and planning, you might well estimate that you will be receiving about 10% of the impressions. So far so good. However, in your test markets, there may be unusual media activity on the part of your competitors. First, look for unusually heavy media activity after you have introduced your product. They may be trying to stop you right in the test market. However, the opposite situation is often the case. You might have selected test markets that, for your competitors' media efforts, will only get the national media program, and that would not be on any supplementary media lists for these competitive brands. Thus, your share of media might be disproportionately high. For example, I once test marketed a product in Boise, Idaho. I found that the competitive media pressure in that market was twice what I would have projected for the national average. It is difficult to make adjustments in this area because you do not want to lower your spending to the correct share of spending percentage (this may affect trial and, ultimately, your pay-out because you would be reaching fewer people). Of course, you do not want to buy media for your competitors to bring them up to the correct weight. Thus, often no compensation is possible. The point is, however, that you should be aware that this can be a problem and you should view the test market results on that basis.

Next you must handle sales measurement. If you are using a panel within a city that is put together by a research firm, this usually is a small problem. However, if you are going to sell through your regular sales channel into the cities you have selected and obtain distribution through the regular retailers, your measurement of sales could present a problem. Most cities have large retailers. These retailers will take items into their central distribution system and distribute it to all of their stores. Often, these stores fall outside your media area in which you are going to measure your sales. Generally, these retailers can't or won't stop distributing your product to these outside stores. Obviously, you need some way to measure the sales that come from the stores only within the area in which you are running the test. This can be difficult. However, if you are alerted to the problem, it can be solved. The problem often is exacerbated by the fact that the stores outside the advertising area may have your product in stock and the sales may be very disappointing without any marketing effort behind the product. From the retailer's standpoint, the sales of the product may be grouped into one single figure. If the outside sales are disappointing (we assume those in the test area will be acceptable), then this figure may fall below the cut-off point for handling an item like yours, and your product could be removed from distribution. Of course, you can run extra media in the outside area, and not bother to measure sales, to make sure that the product is selling. Unfortunately, it is rare that this problem can be handled smoothly. However, keep in mind that this is a problem and that you will run into it in most markets. Sales spill-out is an area that you will have to be careful about because it strikes at the very heart of what you are trying to do—make a financially projectable test.

This brings us to the mistakes that are made, quite often, in test marketing a product. I will cover each one briefly. You should have no trouble getting expert help if you want to delve into these more thoroughly.

The first mistake is over attention. This can take a number of forms: extra visits by the brand manager to tell the sales force and the trade that this is a special and important situation, and extra effort by the field sales force to make sure the product is in stock and has the correct display, and so forth. Ideally, the brand manager should see himself as a behavioral scientist whose job it is to run a very tightly controlled experiment, an experiment in which all variables are kept at the same level as they would be nationally. Unfortunately, many brand managers become ego-involved in the project, and they work very hard to make it a success (by their definition). Over attention that creates hot house conditions is the biggest problem generally faced in test marketing.

The second problem, conversely, is under attention. Here the brand manager often assumes that the test is being run correctly by the sales force, the market research department and the advertising agency, and the like. Although this happens less often than over attention, it too, is a mistake. Again, the brand manager should see himself as a behavioral scientist who is conducting a tightly-controlled experiment. The marketing manager of the firm must be careful to impose the correct structure and discipline on all test marketing activities.

The third mistake is the failure to conduct marketing research during the test market. While you are test marketing, it is necessary to understand what is happening—measuring sales in not enough. You need to be talking to your consumer in some regular and disciplined way to obtain trial, repeat, awareness of advertising, attitudes toward the product, and other such data. Any worthwhile test marketing plan has as an integral part of the plan a sequence of market research steps that allow you at the end of the test marketing period to not only verify the sales results, but also to understand the market dynamics that took place during the sales.

The fourth mistake made is unrealistic in-store conditions. This is a variation of the over-attention mistake, but bears special mention. Any good field sales force can, for a limited time in certain geographical areas, accomplish what may seem to be the impossible. They can have as many facings as you want, unusual displays, no out-of stocks, eye-level displays—whatever. Unfortunately, to show their enthusiasm (and because senior marketing management often is checking the stores and displays in the test markets), the sales force often performs extraordinarily well in a test market—so well that they cannot repeat the performance when the product goes national. There is only one way to avoid that. Senior marketing management and the brand management must discuss this with the sales people before the test market starts. Reasonable and nationally attainable objectives should be set and agreed to. These should be executed on an extremely disciplined basis in a test market. No variations should be allowed unless they represent a change in the national marketing plan. The brand manager must be responsible for policing this area, and it should be made apparent to him by the senior marketing management that this is very important.

The last mistake that I would like to talk about is the area of competitive activity. Earlier, we mentioned the level of competitive media spending. Here, we are talking on a much broader front. Very often test markets are selected in which competitive activity is abnormal. More often, competitive activity becomes abnormal once you start test marketing. It is difficult, granted, to adjust for differences in competitive activity in a test market to reflect what seems to be happening nationally. Often, no direct adjustment is made during the test marketing. However, you must recognize, when you are reading the results of the test marketing, what abnormal competitive activity went on. You should be able to answer questions like the following:

1 Was our "share of media" about average (compared to if we were a national brand)?
2 Was there any difference in competitive copy between what was run nationally and what appeared in our test markets?
3 Was there any competitive activity in the test markets, such as couponing, special displays, etc. that was not observed nationally?

You may ask yourself what is the net of all this? In my opinion, it is simply that if the amount of investment is high and if you feel the amount of risk is unduly high, then test marketing probably is required —assuming that the matters of expense, confidentiality, or speed do not enter into the equation as overriding considerations. If this is not the case, then test market simulation may be adequate and, with its advantages, may be the better solution. The decision is yours. Just keep in mind that the question really is, "Is this a solid investment opportunity for my firm at this point, or do I want to buy more information and shift the risk to a lower level?"

CASE: THE MIDDLE SOUTH MILLING COMPANY—TESTING THE BUSINESS PROPOSITION

After the decision to pursue a penetration pricing strategy was made, the next question arose: "What, if any marketing steps are desirable before we begin full-scale marketing?" Putting this another way, "Would it be desirable to test market this product, use a test market simulation, or go directly into national distribution?"

You and Jerome began to discuss this question with the agency account management group. Over a period of time, the decision seemed to revolve around several questions:

1 If we test marketed this product in a live test market, and read it through the high consumption period (the warmer months), then would we give too much advance warning to our competitors since those who choose to react quickly could have a competitive product ready for the next warm-month cycle?

2 Is this a sufficiently big financial gamble for Middle South that we need to be more confident about the financial figures? Or, are we confident enough that we would be willing to go into a full-scale marketing program with what we know today?

3 Are there any strategic marketing questions that deserve some kind of advance testing? And, further, just how badly do we need to do this kind of testing?

As Jerome said, "If we go national with this without any further testing, the fat will really be in the fire." You agreed and said that it had been your opinion that some kind of testing would be necessary—testing that would allow a tight final financial plan to be constructed. The question of confidentiality was a particularly nagging one, however, and Jerome fully agreed with you. Middle South really couldn't stand a competitive onslaught from a heavily financed, aggressive competitor while the product was still being introduced. That was the reason for selecting the penetration pricing strategy. To test market the product was to invite this kind of competitive activity. In fact, test marketing the product would amount to doing part of the market research for one or several potential competitors.

But the problem was that anything less than test marketing would yield less perfect financial data. The size of the potential investment was one that would be significant for Middle South (Jerome had already contacted bankers because the $12.0 million average investment was beyond the means of Middle South's current financial position. The bankers agreed to seriously consider advancing this money on a short-term basis—maximum 36 months—only under relatively tight conditions, including some kind of preliminary test marketing activity).

The dilemma had to be resolved quickly because time was running short. As you put it to Jerome, "There is time for a test market simulation and then full-scale marketing during the summer months, or there is time for a test market simulation and then test marketing during the summer months, or there is time to prepare for only test marketing in the coming summer months. But there is not time to market the product full scale in the coming summer months after having tested the product in a test market simulator and a regular test market. The question is, what do we do? And we must do something quickly."

It was agreed that you, Jerome and Red would have dinner the next week. The objective was to complete the thinking and take a position on the issues at hand. As you began to think about the dinner conference, you realized that there really were no encompassing marketing strategies that you wanted to test in the marketplace, at least not in lieu of test marketing the product for financial reasons. You also realized that this was a significantly large financial gamble for Middle South, but that it was a gamble that looked like it was worth taking. The question really was how to take this gamble in an intelligent manner. You knew that Jerome saw it in this light also. You knew, too, that it would be up to you to make the proposal to Jerome and Red, because test marketing products was something you had the most experience in. At the dinner you explained your position. Basically, you voted for a test market simulation with a thorough analysis of the results. If the results showed the investment proposition was as expected or close to it (within 20% of the figure you were currently working with), then you suggested that a full scale rollout would be the appropriate next step. However, if it was more than 20% below your current projections, you felt test marketing, to get a tighter feel of the market, might be appropriate.

Red Jackson agreed with you fully. However, Jerome felt uncomfortable about a test market simulation with only one strategic marketing alternative being tested. He felt that Middle South did not have sufficient background to proceed into a marketing situation of this magnitude without an idea of some of the strategic alternatives. One that was particularly interesting to him was a heavy-up advertising test.

The question became one of the cost of information. Each test market simulation would cost about $25,000 in research. In addition, of course, there were the costs of manufacturing test runs of products and the cost of production of advertising (although both of these would be done in any case and were technically not part of the test marketing expenditure). Thus, the question became was it worth another $25,000 to test a heavier advertising expenditure level? Also, was there any other way of obtaining this kind of data?

After a good deal of discussion, it was decided to use the test market simulation device for the current marketing plan. If the results were attractive (within 20% of the firm's projections or above), then Middle South would use this data to obtain sufficient funds from its bankers and roll the product into its full marketing area in time for the summer selling season. If the results were unattractive (less than 20% of the annual forecast), than Middle South would reevaluate the entire program, and either test market or drop the project altogether. Red Jackson stated that he was loathe to drop the project unless it was a complete disaster in the test market simulation. He noted the signals had been positive so far and didn't feel comfortable with a "mathematical device" that he hadn't experienced before. It was further agreed that speed was essential on this project. All three at the dinner felt that any kind of success in the marketplace, whether it be with the traditional test market or full scale marketing, probably would invite competition within the next summer season. Jerome agreed that an incremental $25,000 for a test market simulation seemed like a lot of money to spend in addition to that being allocated, and it was agreed that, should the product be moved into full distribution, several markets would be isolated and used to test a heavy-up advertising campaign. Finally, Red Jackson said that, if the product was successful and near the level currently projected, he would like to return to the company on a special basis the following year with the objective of setting up a distribution that covered as many of the other 50 states as possible. This would be the product's second year in distribution. Middle South should have a sales story by then. All agreed that this was a good idea, but Jerome noted that his father might be in the position of setting up a distribution system in new areas with a product that just might be receiving extremely heavy competitive pressures from similar products during its first year in the new market. This would be without the goodwill that Middle South had built up, since it would not have been in that area previously. Red agreed that it might be tough, but felt it was a workable proposition with the right product, and the right kind of personal selling.

The next day, you held a meeting with the marketing department and members of the management of the advertising agency. It was agreed that the test market simulation would begin within the next 30 days, and that the research would emphasize the measurement of the repeat rate because several people still felt that the cost effectiveness of some of the competitive products might make NATURALLY FRUITY more of an occasional use item. Further, it was agreed that Purchasing and Manufacturing would begin making plans for a full-scale production schedule that could be started in time to sell and achieve distribution in the coming hot months.

The results of the test market simulation showed that the potential factory volume was $58,300,000. This was about 13% less than had been forecast. Further, trial was slightly higher than anticipated. The repeat was slightly disappointing because the number of repeaters was correct, but the frequency of use was less than expected. Qualitative data from the test market simulation experience showed that some women still would use some of the less-expensive products, and use NATURALLY FRUITY as a sometime substitute for these products. No negatives of any importance were found, although a slightly above forecast number of adults found the product a bit too sweet for frequent use. On the basis of these results, the decision was made to begin production of quantity sufficient to market the product in the full marketing area of Middle South during the coming hot months. In addition, it was agreed that the second generation (an improved product) of NATURALLY FRUITY should be examined as quickly as possible to gain an edge in what undoubtedly would be a very competitive area the following year. Further, it was decided that other products using the same consumer appeal of NATURALLY FRUITY would be explored with the idea that a product line might present more problems for competitors than a single item and also might allow some economies of scale for Middle South.

At this point we will leave the Middle South case. It helped to illustrate the process of systematic new product development. Middle South, of course, was quantitative and very disciplined. However, it also used marketing judgment—something that never can be taken away from new product development.

In sum, this chapter dealt with the final testing that you would do before marketing a product on a full scale basis. Generally, this is called test marketing. It may take the form of testing the product in the actual marketplace, or with consumers in some kind of simulated marketplace, called test market simulation. Regardless of whether you do one or the other, or both, the objective of the process is the same—the tightening of the financial data or, in other words, increasing the degree of certainty about the investment decision. It is useful to remember, however, that a test marketing program, although it may seem to be a marketing operation (and, indeed, it may be testing marketing strategy alternatives), is heavily a financial operation. This is the last chance to hone the financial data before the investment is made.

11 The Repositioning of a Mature Product

The repositioning of a mature product bears a great deal of resemblance to the development of a brand new product. In both cases you are developing a concept to fit a specific market. In the case of a new product, the market may be new to your company. In the case of a repositioned product, you may be selecting a new segment of a market that you are already in, or you may be attempting to say new and different things about your product to your current market segment, in the hope that it will see your product in a new way.

Unlike new product development, however, repositioning often involves no changing of the basic design or new formulation of the product. For this reason the theme of a large portion of repositioning work is the construction of the correct positioning blueprint (for the new positioning), and then the testing of the communication (advertising) of this new positioning with the consumer. Where there are questions about changing the formulation, of course, a Product Blueprint must be prepared.

As you must have surmised already, the tools of repositioning are similar to those of new product development. But they are used most often in somewhat different ways because the objective is to best reposition the current product, not the best new product concept, the objective of most new product work.

This chaper will attempt to illustrate the process of repositioning a mature brand. To demonstrate this a case format was selected because no new tools need to be introduced. We will use the material from the preceding chapters to reposition a mature brand. The case follows:

CASE: THE SKINCARESS BAR SOAP COMPANY

The Skincaress Soap Company had been in business for 97 years when Brian Chelstowski purchased it in 1959. Skincaress had been started by Hardwell Barker, who formulated a number of products as part of his pharmacy which he ran in New York City. When Mr. Barker retired, the company was taken over by a cousin and remained in the family until Mr. Chelstowski purchased it. By this time, Skincaress marketed only a bar of soap (in fact, in 1938, the company had changed its name to reflect just that). Basically it was a small bar-soap company.

Skincaress was sold on the Eastern Seaboard. Over 90% of its sales were between Boston and Washington, D.C. About 65% of the sales of this area were through drug stores and 35% through food stores. Generally, the stores that carried Skincaress were small, and in somewhat upscale neighborhoods. There was no distribution in mass merchandise outlets. With the help of a sales manager and a network of brokers and drug wholesalers, Mr. Chelstowski did most of the selling himself.

Selling came natural to Mr. Chelstowski. When he graduated from college, he took a job as a salesman for a large soap company. Over the 12 years he was with the company, he received a number of promotions, and eventually was brought into the home office to coordinate all marketing efforts between the Marketing Department and the sales force.

About a year and a half after taking this job, one of Mr. Chelstowski's children became very ill. While the child was recovering, Mr. Chelstowski took stock of his life. He realized that it was reasonable to expect that he would become National Sales Manager for the company. He realized, also, that this would continue to keep him on the road for large periods of time. This was a particularly unattractive feature of his work and he made the decision to look around for a small company that he could purchase and run by himself.

In about a year, he had managed to locate the Skincaress Company. The last descendant of the Barker family who had been involved in the company had passed away, and the next generation had no interest in the company. Skincaress was being run by a bank officer who had been appointed president pro tem by the bank which was handling the estate while they sought a purchaser for the company.

When Mr. Chelstowski bought the company, sales were at $3 million per year with an after-tax profit of 2%. Because the sales curve had been flat for many years, the bank was willing to sell the company for four times earnings ($240,000). Mr. Chelstowski put down 25%, and the bank carried a note for the remainder which was to be amortized out of earnings. In consummating the sale, the bank officer made the point to Mr. Chelstowski that he was making an extremely solid investment, and because it was a mature business, the bank was willing to take a lower multiple than it normally might have wanted. From Mr. Chelstowski's standpoint, he felt he was guaranteed a healthy return on his investment for life, plus a very handsome salary (the president of Skincaress had, historically, received a good salary. This, to some extent, depressed the earnings). For his part, Mr. Chelstowski felt that the brand still had a lot of life in it, and by opening new accounts and expanding distribution, he ultimately would be able to increase sales. Although he didn't know whether he would be able to improve the earnings after tax percentage, increasing sales should provide him with a greater profit. At the very least, Mr. Chelstowski felt that he was buying himself a good position for the rest of his life—including the life style that he felt he now preferred.

In 1978, a little more than 18 years after he purchased the company, he began to feel uneasy about the sales picture. Sales were still at $3 million, even though Mr. Chelstowski had succeeded in expanding distribution and opening new accounts. In fact, he could estimate fairly accurately that about a third of the current sales came from business he had developed during the last 15 years. What alarmed him was that he had not lost much of the original distribution. This meant that his sales were now $2 million where they once had been $3 million. Since there also had been one price increase in that period, Mr. Chelstowski knew that his sales were running at something less than two-thirds the original rate of those areas in which he had distribution when he had first bought the company. Clearly, something was going wrong.

DEFINING THE PROBLEM

Mr. Chelstowski began to mull over the situation and he realized that he was facing two questions: What is going wrong with our sales? And what, if anything, can be done about it? He realized that getting additional distribution was only a short-term solution to the sales problem and that something basic was the matter. In fact, he already could observe that additional distribution, as it moved further from the original Skincaress base of business, produced fewer sales dollars than it should have. And the little advertising that he could afford to open up new areas did not seem to be effective.

Mr. Chelstowski decided to attack the first question. As a means of solving the problem, he decided that he would interview people who had personal contact with the ultimate consumer (small drug store owners, etc.) and, without alarming them, attempt to find out from them what they thought the problem was. Given three months, Mr. Chelstowski knew that he would have a better idea on who was buying the product, and how they were using it. Also, he would have knowledge of what competitive activity had occurred in the last five years. In these questions, he felt, lay the basic problems facing his brand.

For three months, Mr. Chelstowski accompanied one sales person or another whenever he could. He counted that he talked to 137 small retailers. The results made the situation seem more clear. It was unanimous among the retailers that the purchaser of Skincaress was an older woman—always over 50, in many cases over 60. They usually used the Skincaress bar as part of their regular beauty regimen, and by almost unanimous agreement from the druggists, were very loyal to the product. Further, there seemed to be no specific competitor that was taking business from Skincaress. As one druggist in Tuxedo Park, N.Y., put it: "There isn't any product just like Skincaress—if that's what you want." The problem as Mr. Chelstowski came to realize it, was not that competitors had taken his customers, or that they were using the product less often, or in different ways that had been done heretofore. The problem was that each year there were fewer customers using his product. While he was inclined to view the jibes of his colleagues about owning a very mature brand with considerable humor, Mr. Chelstowski recognized the seriousness of the problem—each year the Skincaress customer base became smaller. Getting additional distribution and moving into new areas would not solve the problem. Women in the consuming group in these areas didn't know of Skincaress—and had already established their own product preferences. Mr. Chelstowski thought they would be hard to switch and, even if they did switch it would be to little avail, since he could not count on them being long-term customers. The answer seemed to be to make Skincaress attractive to a younger group. But the questions were, "which younger group" and "what do they want from a bar soap"?

Mr. Chelstowski decided that the first step would be to speak with the president of the advertising agency that Skincaress had used since 1962. During this meeting, the president of the advertising agency, Mr. Kitson, expressed awareness and sympathy of Mr. Chelstowski's problem. He indicated that what was necessary was to reposition the brand in a market segment that showed a lot more long-term viability.

He further mentioned that his advertising agency would produce the advertising once the repositioning had been defined, but that the research and concept work for repositioning a product had best be left to a firm specializing in this field. Mr. Kitson knew of several, and gave Mr. Chelstowski their names with the suggestion that he contact them.

Mr. Chelstowski interviewed three firms, one in New York City, one in Philadelphia, and one in Chicago. All three firms seemed to understand Mr. Chelstowski's problem, and stated that they had experience in helping firms solve problems of this type. Each promised to submit a proposal.

When he looked over the three proposals, Mr. Chelstowski was struck by the fact that they had a general similarity to them, although the starting point differed by firm. The New York City firm wanted to do a market segmentation and definition research project as a first step; the Chicago firm wanted to do concept generation and refinement against a selected target as the initial effort; and the Philadelphia firm proposed qualitative attitude research leading to concept generation as its first step. In fact, it was only the first step that differentiated the proposals.

IDENTIFYING THE MARKET SEGMENTS

After some thought and a long discussion about this area with Mr. Kitson, Mr. Chelstowski decided to use a firm that proposed target definition as a first step. In April 1979, Mr. Chelstowski authorized the Institute for Product Research and Development (IPRD) to begin working on the market definition study.

On July 15th, IPRD presented the results of its work. It had identified seven segments of the bar soap market. The largest segment was the "all family" bar soap, used in a variety of ways in any house. The smallest segment was one composed of people, primarily females, with sensitive skin. At one time, this market segment might have been called the hypoallergenic segment, but since the hypo-allergenic claim was now made by many soap manufacturers (in addition to other claims), it probably was best to think of this as a "therapeutic" segment.

Only two segments really were of interest to Skincaress. The most interesting was the group that preferred to use a different soap for their face as part of a morning cleansing ritual. This group accounted for about 15% of bar soap buyers, (an estimated 13% of dollar volume) and was almost entirely made up of females with no other demographics of special significance except that the family income was slightly above the national average. The second group of potential interest to Skincaress also was primarily female. However, the demographics and usage situation were much different. These females were seen primarily as using a special soap during the years in which skin care problems first manifested themselves (the teenage years) and then, often remained with the brand until their early 20's. Starting with a specific brand in their early teens, they usually acquired new brand preferences by the time they were 25. They accounted for approximately 15% of dollar volume for the bar soap category.

Among the first group there was some awareness of Skincaress. It was seen as a soap that "has been around for a long time" and to a slight extent, as a "soap used by older women." Among the second group, for all intents and purposes, there was absolutely no awareness of Skincaress. From what he could see, Mr. Chelstowski felt there was greater competition in the teenage market segment. The segment that used the soap as part of a morning beauty regimen (the "beauty bar" market) seemed to have no market leader. Rather, the market was composed of (a) a number of brands that were sold through department stores at quite high prices; (b) several less expensive beauty brands sold through normal channels—with no observable important consumer difference and no great consumer following; and (c) a good deal of use from all family brands that the women found convenient to use for this purpose. On this basis, and because he felt that positioning Skincaress against the teenage consumers would not solve his long-term problem of establishing a steady group of consumers, Mr. Chelstowski decided to try to position Skincaress in the beauty bar market.

UNDERSTANDING CONSUMER ATTITUDES AND PERCEPTIONS

As the next step, IPRD set out to understand the consumer's needs and attitudes about beauty bars. This was done in a two-step research project. The first step was to be Focus Groups. The second was a large scale consumer study in which the data from the focus group was to be quantified.

From the market definition study, the demographics of the research sample (beauty bar consumer) were obtained. The key demographics was that the person was a female, somewhere between 25 and 55—no other demographic was selected (Mr. Chelstowski had decided to eliminate the "family income criterion"). Six Focus Groups, involving women who met this requirement, were conducted—two each in three cities. From these groups it became apparent that there were several end benefits that women hoped to derive from using a beauty bar soap. If this was not confusing enough, the supporting attributes for beauty bar positioning also seemed to cover a wide range. When IPRD finished analyzing the tapes of the groups, there was a list of over 90. They seemed to, from Mr. C's point of view, fit into four general categories:

Soft/Smoothness of Skin
Deep-Cleaning
Clear, Clean Result—no residue
Mild, no irritation

As his contact at IPRD explained it, these four might constitute all the end benefit categories which the 90-some attributes would support, or there might be more. However, he did feel that Mr. Chelstowski seemed to identify the four basic categories. What was important, however, was how the end benefits and attributes fitted together into an ideal positioning for a product. A key question arose from the conversation with IPRD: would the ideal positioning require some formulation change in Skincaress so that the product would fulfill the promise made in its positioning?

Mr. Chelstowski felt uncomfortable about reformulating Skincaress. Granted, the market was declining. However, it still represented a healthy business for his company. Any attempts at reformulation might turn off the present consumers. It was conceivable that, at worst, he would lose his current market and not gain the new market. Although this worst-possible-case was unlikely, it seemed to Mr. Chelstowski to be an unnecessary risk. On the basis of this feeling, several attributes that would have required a formulation change, were removed from the list. The supporting attributes that remained were those that could be met by the current formulation.

The next step in the research process was exposing the end benefit and supporting attributes to a larger sample of women (a sample of 400 women throughout the United States) to obtain a Positioning Blueprint for the repositioning of Skincaress. This research involved two steps: initially the attributes were clustered to obtain the best way of stating each kind of attribute; then the research concentrated on isolating the strongest end benefit, and the selection (and weighting) of the relevant positioning attributes. This weighing plus the end benefit would constitute the Positioning Blueprint.

The results of the research showed that the *key end benefit* was clean skin, free of any dirt or make-up residue, ready for fresh make-up. The supporting attributes were : deep, full-cleaning action because of tested old-fashioned formula—80% weight; gentle/pure ingredients —20% weight.

Mr. Chelstowski reasoned that this would constitute a relatively straight-forward communication. Further, he felt that his product, as currently formulated, would support the end benefit and had the necessary supporting attributes.

TESTING THE NEW POSITIONING

IPRD prepared the positioning statement from which the advertising agency could prepare their creative strategy and advertising executions. However, IPRD suggested a checkpoint before advertising was produced. IPRD suggested that a group of consumers who represented the new consumer target be given a sample of the Skincaress product and the concept statement that communicated the new positioning. They reasoned that it would be necessary for the women in the new target segment to see the product as actually fulfilling the promises that would be made. Making the judgment on the product's action on the basis of Skincaress' management perceptions about its product and its benefits, would be dangerous. Mr. Chelstowski agreed, and a project was initiated which would answer this question.

Initially, 500 women, drawn from a panel of a national consumer marketing research firm, received a copy from the new "Skincaress" positioning statement (written in the form of a consumer print ad) and two bars of Skincaress. The respondents were requested to read the concept and use the product and after 30 days fill out and return the questionnaire. In addition, IPRD indicated that they would telephone interview about 20% of the responding women 20 days after the return of the questionnaire. These respondents would have had the product for about 60 days, and would have had enough time to use up one bar and begin the second bar. By that point they should have had considerable experience with the product.

Two months after the start of the research, IPRD was able to present the results of the 30-day test. Their research director said that the data showed no large problem with the product, and therefore the results of the 30-day test probably would not differ dramatically from the results of the 60-day test, although the telephone interviewing had begun in any case.

The results, in brief, were as follow:

1 83% of the women accepted the concept and used the product (the remaining figures are for concept acceptors only).

2 Whether the product performed as they had been led to believe by the concept statement the results were: "better"—(40%); "yes"—(35%); "no"—(15%); "couldn't tell"—(10%).

3 When the trial and repeat figures were adjusted to reflect estimated behavior and known frequency of use, the potential volume was about quadruple the current volume at Skincaress. Factoring this to reflect the current marketing area of Skincaress showed that Skincaress' current volume could double or increase perhaps as much as 2-1/2 times, if adequate trial could be generated.

4 There were no strong negatives associated with the product, although some women asked a question about the product—specifically, had it been around for so long that it might not be as efficacious as the newer brands?

The product test indicated that the basic product had no strong problems. The next step was to create and test advertising that would communicate the new positioning.

PREPARING THE ADVERTISING

Mr. Chelstowski, his contact at IPRD, and the agency's creative director met a week later in Mr. Kitson's office. IPRD reviewed the results of the product test, and presented to the agency a positioning statement that was based on data generated so far. Working together, the group produced a creative strategy based on the positioning statement. It was agreed that the next step would be for the ad agency to prepare advertising for testing.

Because of the media budget, it was decided to use print advertising (magazines with adaptations for newspaper). The nature of the target might have made television slightly more cost-effective, but the size of the Skincaress budget did not allow for this medium to be used with any degree of effectiveness. The advertisting agency created seven different campaign themes. Four of these appeared to be on strategy and could be summarized by their headlines:

1 OLD FASHIONED SECRET FOR THE NEW FASHIONED WOMAN
2 THE FORMULATION THAT HAS ALWAYS WORKED FOR ACTIVE WOMEN
3 PURE INGREDIENTS = PURE BEAUTY
4 HOW TO HAVE THE CLEAN SKIN THAT WILL MAKE YOU LOOK AS BEAUTIFUL AS YOU CAN

Mr. Chelstowski discussed the four themes in detail with Mr. Kitson and the creative director. Mr. Chelstowski had some preferences among the four. They were not the same as Mr. Kitson's and those of the creative director. Mr. Chelstowski also noted that there were differences in the way the ads were laid out around the four campaigns. He also realized, however, that the lay-out was part of the communication, and that although he liked a headline from one and a lay-out from another, mixing them might be possible, but that this represented moving outside his area of expertise. The question was which would be most effective in communicating the positioning-creative strategy.

TESTING THE ADVERTISING

The issue was to be resolved, as had been agreed to previously, by a copy test. The objective of this copy test would be to select the most effective communication of the positioning. How many alternatives to test was determined by discussing the cost with Mr. Kitson. Testing four variations was about half again as expensive as testing two, and Mr. Chelstowski saw this as good value for the money. He asked the agency if it would be possible to work in league with IPRD, since he wanted the agency's input in the testing process; on the other hand, he felt that this group would represent a needed outside point of view. Mr. Kitson quickly agreed to this and said that this was often the case in testing advertising.

The campaigns were finished with photography and set type. The result looked exactly like advertisements, and IPRD prepared to research them as they would any magazine ad. It was decided that two-thirds of the sample for each ad would be in the Skincaress marketing area, and one-third spread evenly outside it. Even though no geographical differences had been noted before, it was felt that this would allow viewing the data more than one way and would also provide an adequate number of people from the Skincaress marketing area if some differences were observed.

The results of the copy test were as follows:

1 One campaign ("The formulation that has always worked for active women") clearly stated the positioning of the product best.
2 A second campaign ("How to have the clean skin that will make you look as beautiful as you can") did reasonably well, but did not match the performance of "The formulation. . .active women."

The other two campaigns were less effective, and resulted in positioning that did not match the target positioning.

When the research was broken out for women under 55 versus women over 55, it was observed that a third campaign was the most effective among the older group in terms of interest in trying the product: "Old fashioned secret for the new fashioned woman." However, the positioning blueprint that it produced for the product still did not match that of the target blueprint. For women over 55, "A formulation that has always worked for active women" still produced a blueprint closer to that of the target blueprint. Obviously, one campaign had a little more appeal to them, but the other produced the required communication. With women under 55, "The formulation that has always worked for active women" produced the highest desire to try in addition to the correct product blueprint. The data was further broken out on several bases, but nothing significant was observed except the heavy users had a slightly higher preference for "Pure ingredients = pure beauty" from a standpoint of a desire to try. This was not quite statistically significant; however, purity of the ingredients did seem of interest to heavy users, and it was decided that any campaign would contain a strong statement in the body copy to this effect.

MARKET TESTING THE NEW STRATEGY

On the basis of the research results, Mr. Chelstowski authorized the agency to prepare a campaign based on the winning strategy. This campaign would be tested in two markets at a national expenditure rate of $500,000. The campaign's effectiveness would be measured not only by sales data, but also by telephone surveys to the target audience. These would measure awareness of the advertising, trial of the product, attitudes toward the product, repeat rate, and so forth. This campaign was to start in the spring, and the test would last one year. At the end of the test, Mr. Chelstowski felt that he should be able to produce a payout plan based on the test results that would tell him whether it would pay to advertise the product at that expenditure level. He also felt that even if the advertising did not pay out and that he could not expand the campaign at that expenditure level, he would continue to hold this new positioning for Skincaress and to use it in revised packaging and point-of-sale material. As distribution expanded, he would maintain this positioning in the new areas and avoid all references to the original positioning of Skincaress, even though the trade, in many of these areas, would know Skincaress from its old positioning.

As we have discussed, brands tend to mature over time, and so do the categories in which they exist. Sometimes this category/brand maturation is coincidental; other times the category matures slowly while brands come and go (often because of technological change). Thus, given this product life cycle, a marketer occasionally finds himself in the position of having to reposition a brand. Often this repositioning involves only changing the things you communicate about the product; however, sometimes the physical product must be reformulated or redesigned. In either case, the system demonstrated in this book can be applied successfully. The output of the system; volume estimates, blueprints, and so forth are applicable in either of these instances. The discipline is the same.

12 Applying the System to Industrial Products

Often consumer product marketers view industrial product marketing as an entirely different field, and vice versa. Important differences are drawn, and some of them do seem to make sense: for example, industrial marketers usually have fewer customers; pricing is more often a cost-plus (rather than demand) calculation, and new product development is more often technology-led (as against concept led) in industrial marketing.

But these differences are more of degree than of kind if, indeed, they exist at all. New product development in industrial marketing can be as disciplined a process as in consumer products, but the slight differences between these two areas often seem larger because the steps of the new product development process may take place in a slightly different sequence. Regardless, the discipline is there just the same.

The following is a short case study in which key elements of the system we have just discussed are applied in developing a new industrial product in a company that is relatively small in size and resources. In this instance, a product development discovery preceeded the concept, and the process became more one of positioning than pure concept development. But the result is the same—a product, a positioning, a price, and a financial projection.

THE TUFFTEX COMPANY

Tufftex was formed twenty-two years ago to manufacture carpeting for the industrial market. James Talley, founder, contributed the capital and the company began operations in a small town near Macon, Georgia. Its first customer was a truck manufacturer in Detroit. Over the years the company grew. In 1978, approximately 80% of its current business was to truck and automobile manufacturers. Sales for that year totaled $25 million. James retired five years ago, and his son, Harold, became President of the company.

The carpeting industry traditionally has been highly competitive. There are several major companies that advertise nationally and enjoy about 70% of the retail market. Further, there is a large number of smaller manufacturers who produce for local and regional markets, or for industrial customers. Tufftex, while located in the Southeast, sold little carpeting to any type of customer in that region.

Harold, when he assumed the Presidency of Tufftex, began a program to broaden its sales base. The program had been moderately successful, and from almost total reliance on the automotive industry, the company now sold about 20% of its production to industrial plants and institutions. At a meeting of the Executive Committee last year, Harold had stated that the company's goal was to establish additional new markets for its product so that reliance on automotive would not exceed 50% by the year 1984.

As a first step Harold formed a small group consisting of himself, the sales manager, and the manager of manufacturing to develop a program to ensure the corporate goal would be met. It was decided that this group would best work informally and would obtain information from finance and R&D as needed.

For his next step Harold reviewed the "assets" of the company and, for this project, stated them as follows:

DISTRIBUTION. There is little distribution muscle. Most sales are direct to the automotive industry. A new product to new markets would require new distribution with a considerable increase in sales effort and expense.

PATENTS. None; nor is it likely that they will be a factor.

TECHNOLOGY. Tufftex has a small but good R&D Department consisting of five employees. The company's focus has been on medium quality carpeting following standard manufacturing techniques.

PRODUCT. Tufftex has a reputation for producing a durable carpet that meets tight specifications.

MACHINERY. Various types of tufting machines are available and are underutilized. The machines can do shag or scroll work, generally useful only for carpeting manufacturing.

PLANT. Adequate size for foreseeable needs for the next five years. No expansion contemplated.

PERSONNEL. Adequate supply of both skilled and unskilled. Turnover has been low. However, if there is a major departure from existing manufacturing techniques, the work force would have to be trained.

FINANCIAL. The company is adequately financed. Tufftex has been profitable but not overly so. A local bank supplies working capital loans when needed. No financing is contemplated or needed.

RELATIVE COMPETITIVE STRENGTH. The company is small, and should avoid head-on competition with the large companies; rather, it should use its flexibility as a competitive tool—and further should attempt to serve market segments rather than markets.

After reviewing the capabilities of Tufftex, Harold decided that the company's focus must recognize that a *major* technical breakthrough from Tufftex's R&D group was unlikely. Personnel and financial constraints would also limit the company's ability to depart from existing techniques or to substantially increase production in the short run.

Harold, therefore, concluded that the best course for Tufftex was to develop a product, or products, that would increase the use of carpeting in specific market segments, and, at the same time, attempt to strengthen distribution in the Southeast, where it might have a slight cost advantage because of shipping costs, by attempting to *penetrate* this market with new (and existing) products. Further, he desired to continue the company's image as a producer of durable, medium quality carpeting. These, he hoped, would enable Tufftex to take advantage of the continuing growth of the Sun Belt.

After two meetings with the small new products group, Harold developed specific goals for Tufftex aimed at diversification in the marketplace and improvement in profitability. The broad, long-range goals were to reduce the risk of depending heavily on one market (automotive), increase efficiency by evening production over the year, and to improve profitability. These goals were then specified as follows:

Goals	Primary Responsibility
Increase volume from $25 million per year to $40 million by 1984 with nonautomotive sales of more than 50% at that time.	Sales
Increase return on investment from the current 8% to at least 13% by 1984.	President and Executive Staff
Increase production from 60% of capacity to 85% of capacity by 1984 without adding significant new machinery.	Manufacturing/Sales
Develop new products or new uses of products. Products are to be of established quality and provide good value for the dollar. At least five new products or uses are to be developed each year.	Sales/R&D

Based on these long-term goals, Harold then directed the managers to submit for his review their plans for 1980.

For example, the Sales Manager said that he would increase his calls on distributors in the Southeast, develop and train additional sales representatives, improve promotional materials, and submit a number of specific new product ideas. In addition, the Sales Manager's objective for the year was to increase total sales by 8% while reducing the automotive share from 80% to 75%. The actual amounts were agreed upon between Harold and the Sales Manager, based on market forecasts, as well as judgment.

The Manufacturing Manager had an objective of increasing production to meet the forecast increase in sales without an increase in fixed costs. Harold also suggested to Manufacturing that he hoped the average variable production costs per yard would decrease. The Manager, after lengthy calculations with the assistance of the controller, finally agreed that given the expected volume in 1980, average production cost per yard in that year could decrease by $.25. Harold felt this was attainable, and agreed to the objective.

Other objectives also were developed throughout the company for

1980 which supported the longer range corporate goals established by Harold. The total corporate effort was therefore coordinated around the primary goals to develop new products or uses for products and to improve profitability. In sum, it was agreed that there would be an expansion in sales and production without an increase in plant capacity or machinery. For new products or uses, sales would focus on identifying carpet user needs: R&D would focus on new processes and the current state of the art as it might be applied to different uses.

The R&D Effort

Although R&D at Tufftex was a small department, the engineers had considerable experience in working with nylon and other synthetics such as polyesters. Bill White, Manager, had been experimenting with combining a tighter yarn spacing with an improved backing or "tufloc" which held the fibers. Since carpet wear results largely from fibers pulling away from the backing, his objective was to achieve longer wear while maintaining an attractive nap.

One experiment produced an interesting result. Bill discovered that a certain combination of yarn spacing, primary backing, latex, and chemicals produced a very attractive carpeting with a 15% to 20% longer life. The carpet was smooth, thinner, but still had a feel of being thick or plush. The overall appearance was very attractive. It dyed well; colors appeared to be richer. Also, it was highly stain resistant and could be retreated every six months against stains (while still in use).

White discussed his discovery with Jim Smith, Manager of Manufacturing, and together with the controller, worked out rough estimates of manufacturing capabilities and cost before they brought this idea to the group. Actually, the carpeting could be produced with very little change in the existing process although chemical costs would be slightly higher. An initial full-cost estimate of $4.50 to $5.00 a yard was obtained. This cost estimate was within the range of existing carpeting costs and suggested that selling prices would also be within the current range of Tufftex carpeting. Since the carpeting would meet Tufftex reputation for durability and value for the dollar, Bill White sent samples and estimates to both the Sales Manager and Harold as a possible new product for consideration.

Refining the Concept

Harold, with the sales and manufacturing managers, examined several new product ideas and the consensus was that Bill White's new carpeting had the most immediate promise. The new carpeting met the company's criteria for cost, price, quality, and manufacturing. In addition, the longer-wearing feature was a product benefit that had sales potential in several attractive market segments.

At this point, the key questions were those of a marketing nature: for example,

- ► Would the carpeting appeal to any of our current consumers?
- ► Were there certain customers where the appeal would be greater?
- ► What can be said about the product that would be attractive to the customer?
- ► What benefit does the carpeting deliver to the customer?

In discussing these questions it became apparent that before these could be answered it would be necessary to define what was special about the product. Harold decided this could be done best, initially, by meeting with his informal group.

At the meeting of the new products group, the following attributes were listed for the new carpeting:

- ► Longer wearing
- ► Highly stain resistant
- ► Thinner but plush feel
- ► Smooth, rich nap
- ► Sharp, lively colors

Harold, even though he was relatively new to the carpeting business, felt he understood industrial buyers' views and attitudes. He believed the new carpeting had good general sales appeal, but his objective was to increase the *use* of carpeting in market segments that currently were not heavy carpet users as a means for broadening the Tufftex sales base. This would give Tufftex the edge on competition that Harold felt was necessary. He therefore asked the sales and production managers to think of possible new uses for this carpeting, and to meet again in two days to discuss further steps. Since Harold did not want the risk of producing carpeting for inventory (a problem associated with selling for home consumer use), he asked that ideas be generated for only new commercial and industrial uses.

At the next meeting of the group, Jack Hanley, the Sales Manager, took the lead with ideas. The session turned into a brainstorming session with the following possibilities appearing to be the best.

► Outdoor cafes
► Shopping malls
► Plant supervisory offices
► Office and plant reception areas
► Locker rooms (plants and schools)
► In-plant cafeterias

Harold and Hanley agreed that highly competitive carpeting was already available for the outdoor use. But since the new carpeting was highly durable but of medium quality, its use in plant offices for lower and middle managers might be possible. It was also agreed that carpeting for in-plant cafeterias might also be a viable market, since the product should be price competitive with existing floor vinyl-tile coverings, but would enhance the appearance of the room giving it more of a restaurant atmosphere) and also lower the noise level. It might also be possible to add a chemical to give a fresh, clean odor that could be renewed periodically. Harold saw that employee-relations benefits could be added to the positioning, and that it was possible that labor efficiency might increase as well. It was agreed that in-plant offices and cafeterias offered the best opportunity, and Harold asked Hanley to continue the development process by making a preliminary business analysis and researching the data.

Business Analysis and Research

Hanley used State Directories of Manufacturing Plants for the Southeast, and arrived at a total market of about 4000 plants. Not all the plants had cafeterias, and after eliminating the smaller companies he found that the market was closer to 2000 plants. Estimating that 10%

could be potential customers, and multiplying by an average of 3,500 square yards, the market potential was estimated at 700,000 to 800,000 square yards per year. This would represent about $5,000,000 in sales which met both the sales growth and the new market objectives. Manufacturing costs were confirmed at $5.00 per square yard, and the gross margin and contribution to overhead and profit were very attractive. Harold asked Hanley to divide the area into manageable sales territories and to develop a firm sales plan. It was agreed that the initial analysis showed the product, and this application (cafeterias), to be financially viable.

Harold agreed to budget $15,000 for marketing research. Hanley had initially talked with several plant managers and continued to believe that the sales potential was good. To get a better feel for the market, he asked a marketing research firm in Atlanta, Y&Y, to submit a proposal. The objective would be to test the product concept and learn what benefits and attributes would be most important to buyers.

Y&Y's proposal seemed to identify the right issues. They proposed to interview, in-plant, between 75 and 100 people who make the decision for carpeting offices and the cafeteria. In most small companies this person would probably be the President, but the purchaser would be identified before the interview. The research was scheduled to take three weeks and cost $13,500.

The research results confirm that the concept was viable. Forty percent of those interviewed showed a high interest in the cafeteria carpeting concept. They were shown samples and commented favorably on the texture and colors. They were asked to list in order of importance those product attributes necessary for cafeteria use. At the top of the list was "stain resistant" followed by "easily cleaned and maintained." "Color" and "appearance" were of average importance, while "plush feel" was rated as relatively unimportant.

Hanley knew that this information on what was important to the user would help him to position the product correctly and to prepare communication materials. He planned to develop brochures for the product that would communicate the customer benefit (more relaxed and productive employees at a lower flooring cost) and the key attributes. Hanley thought that a handsome brochure with pictures of employees enjoying a relaxed meal with plenty of hard sell supporting copy would do the job.

Further, Hanley and Jones considered a number of names for the carpeting that communicate either the key attributes or benefits. Since important attributes were stain resistance and longer life, the name selected was Permaguard.

The research thus confirmed there was a market for the new carpeting for cafeteria use. The most likely buyers were identified as companies with 500 to 2000 employees. The research firm found that there were 2000 such companies in the Tufftex marketing region. Using one-half of the "willingness to buy" responses, they confirmed that the estimated sales of 700,000 square yards was reasonable.

Preparing to Start the Marketing

Hanley broke the region into five sales areas for easier management. He estimated that he would need one full-time salesman to travel the area. In addition, he planned to establish three distributors and use five sales representatives. Initial travel, training, promotional materials, and a full-time employee were budgeted at $100,000 for the first year.

Harold stressed that production was to be run only against firm orders. There was to be no inventory stocking because he was concerned about competition from other carpeting as well as other types of floor coverings. Jack Hanley agreed, and indicated to Harold that manufacturing costs would have to be kept in line, because he knew that pricing would be very important. Industrial users are professionals and are prone to comparison shop for value.

The cost of manufacturing, including an allocation of fixed overhead, was reconfirmed at $5.00. Using a 20% profit margin, a price of $6.25 per yard was determined. After allowing for sales and administrative expenses, a pretax profit of $1.00 per square yard was projected. The after tax contribution (at a 50% tax rate) was computed at $350,000 for the first full year (700,000 square yards at $.50). Tufftex was ready to enter the market with its new product.

The reader should contrast this with the sequence of events in the Middle South Milling Company case. It should be noted that the disciplined process was the same in both cases: differences in things like size of firm, type of customer, initiation of product ideas, and so forth did not change the basic discipline of our systematic approach to new product development.

13 A Brief Reprise of Some Points Worth Repeating

Often after reading a book you try to recall what the key points were so that you can review them once more in your mind and, perhaps even test them in your thinking now that you have completed the entire book. The purpose of this chapter is to enable you to do this more easily.

The book made a number of points. Perhaps you have found some of them interesting and thought provoking. A few of the author's "favorites" are listed below. They have been listed with the thought that the reader should have a last chance to view the area of new product development from the author's viewpoint in a concentrated format. This offers an opportunity for you not only to compare your thoughts and impressions with those of the author, but also to use it as a little reminder check list.

NEW PRODUCT DEVELOPMENT

New product development is the preparation of business propositions that can be viewed as investment alternatives by your firm. To do this you must always keep in mind that what you are trying to do is generate a profit for your company. Therefore, whether you are talking about a new product concept, or monitoring test market activity, or any other stage you may be at, you must always remember that your firm will be making an investment on the basis of what you recommend and will be

243

expecting a return on its investment. Therefore, you must continually work at reducing the risk, and at every juncture you should review your work to date with the eye to seeing whether what you are developing still makes sense as a business proposition and, ultimately, as an investment alternative.

Setting the Stage for New Product Development

The stage for new product development must be set by the Chief Executive Officer. He must agree to the objectives and guidelines; he must lend his weight to the program so that it is viewed as important by other members of the firm who are not involved in the day-to-day activities of new product development. Further, he must monitor the new product activities periodically to make sure that the work is consistent with the overall corporate objectives. Lastly, it is his responsibility to make sure the function is properly organized and placed within the organization.

Setting the objectives and guidelines for the new product development is an extremely important step. These objectives and guidelines must stem from the long range corporate goals.

A key part of this process is reviewing the corporation's (growth-related) assets from the standpoint of new product development. This means looking at those strong assets (e.g., a brand name and image) that might be leveraged for new product development (or acquisitions). Other assets can be viewed as weak and of little value, but perhaps they can be strengthened from the process of new product development. By reviewing the assets and the long-range corporate goals, it is possible to put together a set of objectives and guidelines for the new product program that should last a number of years.

A Systematic Approach

It is important to have a system that you are following in your development of new products. This system need not be followed slavishly but should be a logical, step-by-step, risk-reducing process.

A key point is that the system should be accepted by the members of your firm as worthwhile and producing useful data. In fact, "selling" your system to the other members of your firm is an important function of your new product development work. You will need, often, help from a colleague in another department, and their appreciation of your work and the system is an important asset.

NEW PRODUCT CONCEPTS

In new product development, it is generally best to work with concepts in the early stages. This has many advantages, not the least of which is that it is usually far less expensive than dealing with actual products. In working with concepts, it is important to remember that the more concepts you have initially, the better the resulting concept(s) will be. There is a close relationship between quantity and quality in concept work and starting your new product development with many more than one or two good ideas almost always leads to optimum results in the end.

Concepts as Business Propositions

A key part of your system has to be a method for viewing new product concepts as potential business propositions (and thus investment alternatives). It is essential that you construct a system appropriate for your industry. This system should incorporate the best thinking of various members of your firm. If nothing else, the system will allow you to have a preagreed way of sorting concepts into priority groups. Thus you can easily isolate those concepts that all members of the team will want to develop.

Researching Concepts with Your Consumer

It is very important in concept research that from your research you know exactly what you must do to please your potential consumer (whether your consumer is a single person or an industrial corporation). This means that you should be able to obtain from the research the proper positioning for the product (the end benefit and facts people want to hear about the product), and how best to construct the product (the physical end benefit—if it is different—and the product attributes that support and are part of the product's physical performance). Once you have these, you can perform the necessary R&D. Also, you can prepare the advertising, knowing exactly what it is you want to communicate. It is also vital in concept research that you find some way of translating consumer interest in a concept to sales potential. This is critical because it is at this stage that you get your first inkling about the potential investment worthiness of the concept.

TESTING THE RESULTS OF YOUR WORK

Once you have formulated the product and prepared the advertising, it is necessary for you to test the results of your work.

In testing the product it is very important that you compare the results with those of the Product Blueprint that you started with. You should be delivering to the consumer the exact product they told you they want. Also, when testing the product, it is important to ascertain the interest in the concept among the potential product purchasers. It is vital to know how people feel about the physical product on the basis of whether they accepted the concept as desirable. Keep in mind, also, that product testing should be viewed as an improvement process, and not as merely a go/no-go decision process. Last, when testing the product, it is useful to obtain buying intent at more than one price level. This will give you a preliminary indication of the different volumes available to you at different pricing levels.

Getting the correct positioning for the product is extremely important. From your concept refinement work, you should have a Positioning Blueprint. The function of the advertising is to communicate the positioning. Ideally, when testing the advertising, the consumer should play back the proper end benefits and supporting communications attributes in the correct proportions.

It is important to note in testing advertising that it is not a good idea to test only one alternative. Testing one approach only becomes a kind of disaster check research, and what you are testing will usually be used ultimately unless it is showed to be absolutely unacceptable. It is much better to look at two or three alternatives that have been culled from a larger number, and to select the best of these.

It is important to remember that the package design and the naming are also related to the positioning, and must communicate it or selected facets of it. Although advertising is normally considered to be the primary communication device for a product, in reality the name and the package are often seen by more people than the advertising, and therefore it is important that these two items meet the same or similar objectives as the advertising.

PRICING A NEW PRODUCT

The pricing decision is an extremely important one because it has direct reflection upon the profitability of the product and also because the price represents a critical part in the purchase decision of the consumer and, therefore, must be set in an acceptable range.

Much pricing is done on a cost plus basis. Although this probably does not optimize the profits, it generally results in a competitive price that also results in the profit that the corporation requires. In many industries cost plus pricing is the normal method of pricing a product.

However, when it is possible, it is better to base the price on an understanding of the demand of the product. Pricing on the basis of demand allows you not only to produce the optimum profit but also to use pricing as part of your marketing strategy. Depending on the nature of the demand and your assessment of competitive activity, you might choose to price the product to maximize short-term profit or to obtain optimum market share and long-term market penetration. Of course, whether you have the option of skimming versus penetration, or indeed whether you have any flexibility at all in pricing, is usually a function of two things: (a) the maturity of the market, and (b) the amount of differentiation that you built into your product.

Pricing is a key marketing variable and often merits testing. Indeed, long before the pricing decision is made, some idea of the relative demand curve should have been obtained from earlier stages of consumer research.

TEST MARKETING

Most marketers agree that for many categories, some form of pre-full scale marketing test marketing is desirable. This may be accomplished by a test market simulation, or by actually selling the product to some segments of the total market (usually test market cities).

Test market simulation has several advantages. It is quick; less expensive, and maintains a confidentiality. But, it is not the same as actually selling the product under actual market condition. For this reason, many sophisticated marketers prefer actual test marketing, even with its disadvantages, and this author agrees. However, there does seem to be a trend toward greater use of test market simulation as a substitute for actual test marketing, and it may be that this will become more the case as models become more sophisitcated and accurate. Regardless, before the large investment necessary for full-scale marketing is made, it is usually necessary for you to use some kind of test marketing device to make sure that the financial data you have been using is still accurate and that the result will be the kind of return on your investment that you have planned for.

REPOSITIONING MATURE PRODUCTS

The new product developer often becomes involved in the repositioning of mature products. Sometimes this involves a reformulation or a redesign of a product. More often than not, it can be accomplished by changing the communications about the product. The tools that the new product developer uses for introducing new products are pretty much the ones used for repositioning mature products into a higher growth segment of the market.

Repositioning a mature brand carries with it some risk. Often, old and very loyal customers reject the new brand. The danger is that the newer customer is less loyal, or perhaps there are fewer of them than for the mature brand. Repositioning must be done with care and with an eye for losing as few of the old customers as possible while gaining new ones.

In sum, the development of new products, or the repositioning of a mature brand, is both a financial and a marketing operation. It is also an operation that involves a great number of people with quite different orientations and skills (scientists, social scientists, marketers, businessmen, etc.). For the program to be successful at all it requires clear-cut goals and a systematic, disciplined approach. It is hoped that the author has been able to suggest some useful thoughts on these subjects. The reader is wished success in his endeavors.

Bibliography

Charvat, Frank J., and Whitman, W. Tate, *Marketing Management—a Quantitative Approach,* Simmons-Boardman, New York, 1964.

Dean, Joel, *Managerial Economics,* Prentice-Hall, Englewood Cliffs, NJ, 1951.

de Bono, Edward, *Lateral Thinking,* Harper Colophon Books, New York, 1970.

Douglas, Gordon, Kemp, Philip, and Cash, Jeremy, *Systematic New Product Development,* Halsted Press, John Wiley & Sons, New York, 1978.

Gordon, William J. J., *Synectics,* Collier Books, New York, 1961.

King, Stephen, *Developing New Brands,* John Wiley & Sons, New York, 1973.

McCarthy, Jerome E., *Basic Marketing, a Managerial Approach,* 5th Edition, Richard D. Irwin Co., Homewood, IL, 1975.

Osborn, Alex F., *Applied Imagination,* Charles Scribner's Sons, New York, 1953.

Parnes, Sidney J. and Harding, Harold F., *A Source Book for Creative Thinking,* Charles Scribner's Sons, New York, 1962.

Prince, George M., "How to be a Better Meeting Chairman", *Harvard Business Review,* Jan.–Feb. 1968.

Prince, George M., *The Practice of Creativity,* Macmillan Publishing, New York, 1970.

Smith, Robert E., and Lusch, Robert F., "How Advertising Can Position a Brand", *Journal of Advertising Research,* Vol. **16,** No. 1, Feb., 1976.

Steiner, George A., *Strategic Planning,* The Free Press, New York, 1979.

Webster, Frederick E., Jr., *Industrial Marketing Strategy,* John Wiley & Sons, New York, 1979.

The Professionals Look at New Products, Edited by Brand, Gruber and Company, Bureau of Business Research, University of Michigan, 1969.

Index

251